A Commentary on Macaulay's History of England

A COMMENTARY ON MACAULAY'S HISTORY OF ENGLAND

SIR CHARLES FIRTH

Routledge
Taylor & Francis Group
LONDON AND NEW YORK

First published by Macmillan & Co. Ltd. in 1938
and now reprinted by their kind permission.

This edition published by Frank Cass & Co. Ltd.

First edition 1938
Second impression 1964

Published 2005 by Routledge
2 Park Square, Milton Park, Abingdon, Oxfordshire OX14 4RN
711 Third Avenue, New York, NY 10017

First issued in paperback 2014

Routledge is an imprint of the Taylor and Francis Group, an informa business

ISBN 13: 978-0-714-61475-5 (hbk)
ISBN 13: 978-0-415-76049-2 (pbk)

CONTENTS

INTRODUCTION

Prior to the great war Sir Charles Firth used to give from time to time a course of lectures on Macaulay's History of England. When he undertook the preparation of an illustrated edition of that work, published 1913-15 in six volumes by Messrs. Macmillan and Co., he began to revise his lectures in order to compile from them a commentary on the History. Unfortunately the task of revision was interrupted during the war and never resumed except to publish two articles, on Macaulay's Third Chapter [1] and Macaulay's Treatment of Scottish History,[2] which form chapters vi and viii of this book.

In a footnote to the latter article Sir Charles explained that it was

> part of a series of lectures delivered at Oxford on Macaulay's History of England. Their object was not merely to criticise the statements made by Macaulay and the point of view adopted by him, but also to show the extent to which his conclusions had been invalidated or confirmed by later writers who had devoted their attention to particular parts of his subject, or by the new documentary materials published during the last sixty years. It was hoped thereby to encourage students to investigate the history of the period with an open mind, and to try to weave the new evidence into the tissue of the national story. Accordingly the notes indicate some of the recent monographs and publications of documents, though they do not profess to give an exhaustive list of them.

[1] I am indebted to the editor of History for permission to reprint this article substantially as it appeared in History, xvii, October, 1932.

[2] Scottish Historical Review, xv, July, 1918.

When I came to examine these lectures with a view to their publication I found that, adopting the order of the present book, chapters i-viii and x required little more than a certain amount of condensation and the verification of references and quotations.[1] For chapters ix, on Irish history, and xi, on Macaulay's errors, there were only outlines and many quotations and references. All I have ventured to do with them has been to expand the notes where they were too brief into a consecutive narrative and to link up the quotations. Chapters xii-xiv, on James II, Mary II, and William III, needed revising in accordance with marginal directions.[2] They already contained a certain amount of my work, for in 1915 the original lectures on the three sovereigns above mentioned were entrusted to me in order that I might try my 'prentice hand on the task of preparing them for the press. I worked constantly under Firth's supervision, so that although in places I am responsible for the form of words used, the arrangement and subject matter are his. I am responsible for most of the translations from French and German documents and have deliberately made the rendering literal.

Generally speaking, no attempt has been made to bring the work completely up to date. The commentary really represents the state of knowledge, about 1914, of the Revolution of 1688. On the other hand, I have not hesitated to change a few statements which the passage of time has invalidated. There seems, for instance, to be no point in retaining in the text a statement that William III's

[1] The editions cited throughout are those used in verifying references and quotations.

[2] It is clear from some detached notes that Sir Charles contemplated additions to the chapters on James and on William III, in order to include a discussion of James in exile and to show how Macaulay's character of William would have gained had the History been finished to 1702.

letters to Bentinck remain unpublished, and then correcting it by a footnote to the effect that they have been published by N. Japikse.

The page references to Macaulay's History are to the aforesaid illustrated edition, but for the convenience of readers who may not have the edition, chapter numbers are supplied in parenthesis.

GODFREY DAVIES

HUNTINGTON LIBRARY
April 1937

CHAPTER I

THE GENESIS OF MACAULAY'S HISTORY

ENGLISH historians used to excel in the art of historical composition. Robertson, and Hume, and Gibbon earned European fame, not only as what were termed then 'philosophical historians' but on account of the skill with which they arranged and constructed their narratives of the past. The art seems almost lost in England now. Since Macaulay himself there has been only one great narrative historian, Froude, and he is in many ways inferior to Macaulay. Other recent historians, whatever learning and whatever literary merits they possessed, did not possess the art of telling a story: they were able at most to describe a scene or relate an episode, but the long, sustained, harmonious narrative, was above their powers or below their aims. And this art of telling a story is so essential a qualification for writing history, that it is desirable to enquire into the nature of the art and investigate the practice of its great exponents.

Regarded as a mere record of facts Macaulay's History is almost equally worthy of study. Written from sixty to seventy years ago it still holds its place. No English historian has ventured to retell in detail the story of the Revolution and the reigns of James II and William III. A sort of superstitious terror seems to prevent them from treading in the enchanted circle where Macaulay's magic works. His History is still *the* authority on the period. Yet at the same time it has shortcomings which diminish its value as an authority. Some of its defects are the inevitable result of time. Since its composition new documents have come to light which invalidate some of his conclusions and disprove some of his statements of fact. No history that is written can escape this fate. It will be a part of my business to point out what these new authorities are, and to show how they affect the present value of his narrative.

There are other defects which are not due to the insensible action of time, but were present in Macaulay's History from the beginning. There are some books and some sources of information, accessible when he wrote, which he omitted to consult, and these too want pointing out. There were some sides of the period, and some episodes in the story, which, for one reason or another, he omitted, so that his story was incomplete, and attention will be called to these. Finally there are some serious errors, caused not by defects of knowledge on the part of the writer, but by defects of character, or intellectual defects. The narrowness of view, the partiality, and the prejudice, which mar large portions of Macaulay's History, seriously diminish its permanent value as an account of a period of English history. These faults are most marked in his treatment of certain persons, and certain classes, and they have led to a number of controversies on which every critic of Macaulay has to pronounce judgement and every student of Macaulay has to form an opinion.

Yet even those contemporary critics who were most biassed against the party for whom Macaulay held a brief, and most hostile to Macaulay personally, admitted at once the greatness of the History as a literary achievement. Lockhart, the editor of the Quarterly, wrote to J. W.

Croker urging him to write an article upon it—and an unfavourable article too. 'If you could do it pure justice,' he said, 'nothing more is wanted to give the author sufficient pain.' At the same time he added that the History would always 'keep a high place among the specimens of English rhetoric', and confessed, 'I read the book with breathless interest, in spite of occasional indignations.'[1]

Professional historians, equally sensible of the defects of Macaulay's method and the errors his book contained, have been more emphatic and more generous in their recognition of his achievement. Take for instance Lord Acton—no one was more revolted by the injustice and the prejudice which marked certain portions of Macaulay's History, and yet no one admired it more. 'He remains to me,' Acton admitted to Mary Gladstone, 'one of the greatest of all writers and masters, although I think him utterly base, contemptible and odious for certain reasons.' Nobody could say after this that Acton was blind to Macaulay's defects, but to him the possession by Macaulay and the exhibition in his History of certain technical merits of surpassing greatness seemed to compensate, and more than compensate, for those defects. In another letter to the same correspondent, Acton said:

> When you sit down to read Macaulay, remember that the Essays are really flashy and superficial. He was not above par in literary criticism; his Indian articles will not hold water; and his two most famous reviews, on Bacon and Ranke, show his incompetence. The essays are only pleasant reading, and a key to half the prejudices of our age. It is the History (with one or two speeches) that is wonderful. He knew nothing respectably before the

[1] Croker Papers, ed. L. J. Jennings (1885), iii. 194-5. Lockhart to Croker, Jan. 12, 1849.

seventeenth century, he knew nothing of foreign history, of religion, philosophy, science, or art. His account of debates has been thrown into the shade by Ranke, his account of diplomatic affairs, by Klopp. He is, I am persuaded, grossly, basely unfair. Read him therefore to find out how it comes that the most unsympathetic of critics can think him very nearly the greatest of English writers.[1]

After this preamble, we will turn to consider the genesis of Macaulay's History, and to trace in his own letters the story of its conception and its production. The best introduction to Macaulay's History is perhaps the review he wrote, in 1835, of Sir James Mackintosh's history of the reign of James II.[2] There he states clearly and concisely the general views, about the place of the Revolution in English history, which he afterwards set forth in his five volumes. But it does not appear that he had as yet made up his mind to write upon it. The first indication of that resolution appears in a letter written three years later, and the scheme he originally formed was different from that which he finally carried out. The development of the scheme is clearly shown by the extracts from Macaulay's correspondence and diaries which Sir George Trevelyan has printed in his admirable life of his uncle.

It was in July 1838, whilst he was still in India, that Macaulay formed the plan of writing his History of England.

As soon as I return, I shall seriously commence my History. The first part, (which, I think, will take up five octavo volumes,) will extend from the Revolution to the commencement of Sir Robert Walpole's long administration; a period of three or four and thirty very eventful

[1] Letters of Lord Acton to Mary Gladstone (1904), pp. 326, 285.

[2] The best edition of Macaulay's Critical and Historical Essays is that by Professor F. C. Montague (3 vols.; 1903).

years. From the commencement of Walpole's administration to the commencement of the American war, events may be despatched more concisely. From the commencement of the American war it will again become necessary to be copious. These, at least, are my present notions. How far I shall bring the narrative down I have not determined. The death of George the Fourth would be the best halting-place. The History would then be an entire view of all the transactions which took place, between the Revolution which brought the Crown into harmony with the Parliament, and the Revolution which brought the Parliament into harmony with the nation. But there are great and obvious objections to contemporary history. To be sure, if I live to be seventy, the events of George the Fourth's reign will be to me then what the American war and the Coalition are to me now.[1]

Six months later, after further considering the matter, Macaulay came to the conclusion that he must prefix to his account of the Revolution not only a summary of the previous history of England, but a detailed narrative of the reign of James II.

I have thought a good deal during the last few days about my History. The great difficulty of a work of this kind is the beginning. How is it to be joined on to the preceding events? Where am I to commence it? I cannot plunge, slap dash, into the middle of events and characters. I cannot, on the other hand, write a history of the whole reign of James the Second as a preface to the history of William the Third; and, if I did, a history of Charles the Second would still be equally necessary, as a preface to that of the reign of James the Second. I sympathise with the poor man who began the war of Troy 'gemino ab ovo'. But, after much consideration, I think that I can manage, by the help of an introductory

[1] Letter to Napier, July 20, 1838. The Life and Letters of Lord Macaulay, by George Otto Trevelyan (2 vols.; 1876), ii. 13-14.

chapter or two, to glide imperceptibly into the full current of my narrative. I am more and more in love with the subject. I really think that posterity will not willingly let my book die.[1]

In February 1839, Macaulay returned to England, became Secretary at War, and was admitted to Lord Melbourne's cabinet in the following September. The History which he had begun on March 9, 1839, 'with a sketch of the early revolutions of England', had to be suspended. It was therefore with a sense of relief that he welcomed the general election of July 1841, although he lost office and income in consequence of it.

I own that I am quite delighted with our prospects. A strong opposition is the very thing that I wanted. I shall be heartily glad if it lasts till I can finish a History of England, from the Revolution to the accession of the House of Hanover. Then I shall be willing to go in again for a few years.[2]

At last, towards the close of 1841, he was able to concentrate on the work of his life.

I have at last begun my historical labours; I can hardly say with how much interest and delight. I really do not think that there is in our literature so great a void as that which I am trying to supply. English history, from 1688 to the French Revolution, is even to educated people almost a terra incognita. I will venture to say that it is quite an even chance whether even such a man as Empson, or Senior, can repeat accurately the names of the Prime Ministers of that time in order. The materials for an amusing narrative are immense. I shall not be satisfied unless I produce something which shall for a few days

[1] Ibid. p. 36.

[2] Letter to Ellis, July 12, 1841. Ibid. p. 93.

supersede the last fashionable novel on the tables of young ladies.[1]

It would be unfair to take too literally the words of a casual letter to a friend, but it looks a little as if Macaulay made knowledge of history to consist in remembering a list of names, and the aim of history the production of an entertaining story. One thinks of the remark of Anatole France defining history as 'une espèce de roman à l'usage des esprits avises et curieux'.

Macaulay's progress was slow. The ability to concentrate himself entirely upon his subject was the first thing he demanded: an interruption by other business was fatal, even if that other business was also historical or literary.

There are people who can carry on twenty works at a time. Southey would write the History of Brazil before breakfast, an ode after breakfast, then the History of the Peninsular War till dinner, and an article for the Quarterly Review in the evening. But I am of a different temper. I never write to please myself until my subject has for the time driven every other out of my head. When I turn from one work to another, a great deal of time is lost in the mere transition.[2]

Not only business or social distractions prevented him from the necessary concentration of thought, but the political news of the day diverted his attention, and sometimes so absorbed it that he could not fix his mind upon his task.

'Horrible news from India; massacre of Europeans at Delhi, and mutiny. I have no apprehensions for our Indian Empire; but this is a frightful event. Home; but had no heart to work. I will not try at present.' Again

[1] Letter to Napier, Nov. 5, 1841. Ibid. pp. 103-4.

[2] Letter to Napier, Jan. 18, 1843. Ibid. p. 126.

he says, and yet again: 'I cannot settle to work while the Delhi affair is undecided.'[1]

This being Macaulay's nature, the overthrow of Sir Robert Peel's government in June 1846, which brought him into office again, must have been a serious interruption. He became Paymaster General, and though his official duties were light and he did not often speak in Parliament, the loss of his seat at Edinburgh in July 1847 was an event for which the readers of the History ought to be thankful.

The first two volumes of the History were published in November 1848. They contained the introduction and the reign of James II. Thirteen thousand copies were sold in four months, and Macaulay was startled by his own success.

> Of such a run I had never dreamed. But I had thought that the book would have a permanent place in our literature; and I see no reason to alter that opinion. Yet I feel extremely anxious about the second part. Can it possibly come up to the first? Does the subject admit of such vivid description and such exciting narrative? Will not the judgment of the public be unduly severe? All this disturbs me. Yet the risk must be run; and whatever art and labour can do shall be done.[2]

It deserves noting that his success instead of making him content to do as well as he had done was an incentive to doing better. He was more careful, more laborious, more eager to produce something of lasting value, which might be a permanent part of English literature. One result was the formation in 1849 of a systematic plan of work for the reign of William III.

[1] Ibid. p. 434.

[2] Journal, Jan. 27, 1849. Ibid. p. 248.

I have now made up my mind to change my plan about my History. I will first set myself to know the whole subject; to get, by reading and travelling, a full acquaintance with William's reign. I reckon that it will take me eighteen months to do this. I must visit Holland, Belgium, Scotland, Ireland, France. The Dutch archives and French archives must be ransacked. I will see whether anything is to be got from other diplomatic collections. I must see Londonderry, the Boyne, Aghrim, Limerick, Kinsale, Namur again, Landen, Steinkirk. I must turn over hundreds, thousands, of pamphlets. Lambeth, the Bodleian and the other Oxford libraries, the Devonshire Papers, the British Museum, must be explored, and notes made: and then I shall go to work. When the materials are ready, and the History mapped out in my mind, I ought easily to write on an average two of my pages daily. In two years from the time I begin writing I shall have more than finished my second part. Then I reckon a year for polishing, retouching, and printing.[1]

A few notes from his diary show the progress of his plans, and his method of getting up the literature of the subject.

June 28. After breakfast to the Museum, and sate till three, reading and making extracts. I turned over three volumes of newspapers and tracts; Flying Posts, Postboys, and Postmen. I found some curious things which will be of direct service; but the chief advantage of these researches is that the mind is transported back a century and a half, and gets familiar with the ways of thinking, and with the habits, of a past generation.

June 29. To the British Museum, and read and extracted there till five. I find a growing pleasure in this employment. The reign of William the Third, so mysterious to me a few weeks ago, is beginning to take a clear form. I begin to see the men, and to understand all their difficulties and jealousies.[2]

[1] Journal, Feb. 8, 1849. Ibid. pp. 218-19.

[2] Journal, 1849. Ibid. p. 260.

When he had completed his reading for the moment, he proceeded to write an account of the particular episode he had been studying. His nephew describes minutely what Macaulay's method of composition was. The first step was to compose a rapid sketch of the episode.

As soon as he had got into his head all the information relating to any particular episode in his History, (such, for instance, as Argyll's expedition to Scotland, or the attainder of Sir John Fenwick, or the calling in of the clipped coinage,) he would sit down and write off the whole story at a headlong pace; sketching in the outlines under the genial and audacious impulse of a first conception; and securing in black and white each idea, and epithet, and turn of phrase, as it flowed straight from his busy brain to his rapid fingers. His manuscript, at this stage, to the eyes of any one but himself, appeared to consist of column after column of dashes and flourishes, in which a straight line, with a half-formed letter at each end, and another in the middle, did duty for a word.[1]

Then came a second and revised version written out at full length.

As soon as Macaulay had finished his rough draft he began to fill it in at the rate of six sides of foolscap every morning; written in so large a hand, and with such a multitude of erasures, that the whole six pages were, on an average, compressed into two pages of print.[2]

Sept. 22. Wrote my regular quantity—six foolscap pages of my scrawl, which will be about two pages in print. I hope to hold on at this pace through the greater part of the year. If I do this, I shall, by next September, have rough-hewn my third volume.[3]

This portion he called his 'task', and he was never quite easy unless he completed it daily. More he seldom

[1] Ibid. pp. 224-5. [2] Ibid. p. 225.

[3] Journal, 1849. Ibid. p. 267.

sought to accomplish; for he had learned by long experience that this was as much as he could do at his best; and except when at his best, he never would work at all. 'I had no heart to write,' he says in his journal of March 6, 1851. 'I am too self-indulgent in this matter, it may be: and yet I attribute much of the success which I have had to my habit of writing only when I am in the humour, and of stopping as soon as the thoughts and words cease to flow fast. There are therefore few lees in my wine. It is all the cream of the bottle.'[1]

I wrote the arrival of the news of the Boyne at Whitehall. I go on slowly, but, I think, pretty well. There are not many weeks in which I do not write enough to fill seven or eight printed pages. The rule of never going on when the vein does not flow readily would not do for all men, or for all kinds of work. But I, who am not tied to time, who do not write for money, and who aim at interesting and pleasing readers whom ordinary histories repel, can hardly do better. How can a man expect that others will be amused by reading what he finds it dull to compose?[2]

When the second and revised version was written out, there was still the final 'polishing and retouching to be done'. An 'immense labour', he rightly calls it. He made it immense because he was never satisfied unless every sentence was perfectly clear.

Worked some hours and got on tolerably. No doubt what I am writing will require much correction; but in the main, I think, it will do. How little the all-important art of making meaning pellucid is studied now! Hardly any popular writer, except myself, thinks of it. Many seem to aim at being obscure. Indeed, they may be right enough in one sense; for many readers give credit for profundity to whatever is obscure, and call all that is perspicuous shallow. But coraggio! and think of A.D. 2850.[3]

[1] Ibid. pp. 225-6. [2] Journal, Mar. 11, 1850. Ibid. pp. 275-6.
[3] Journal, Jan. 12, 1850. Ibid. p. 272.

Not only must every sentence be perfectly clear, but sentence and paragraph alike must run easily. There was to be no sense of effort anywhere visible—all, however laborious, was to seem unstudied and natural.

July 28.—My account of the Highlands is getting into tolerable shape. To-morrow I shall begin to transcribe again, and to polish. What trouble these few pages will have cost me! The great object is that, after all this trouble, they may read as if they had been spoken off, and may seem to flow as easily as table talk.[1]

Mere improvement of the style, however, was only one part of his care. The arrangement of his matter and the order of his topics were still more important. He did not hesitate to take a paragraph or a chapter to pieces and to rearrange it, in order to make the story develop itself more naturally and flow more easily.

After breakfast, I fell to work on the conspiracy of the Jacobites in 1690. This is a tough chapter. To make the narrative flow along as it ought, every part naturally springing from that which precedes; to carry the reader backward and forward across St. George's Channel without distracting his attention is not easy. Yet it may be done. I believe that this art of transition is as important, or nearly so, to history, as the art of narration.[2]

Feb. 6.—I worked hard at altering the arrangement of the first three chapters of the third volume. What labour it is to make a tolerable book, and how little readers know how much trouble the ordering of the parts has cost the writer! [3]

The result was the success which so much painstaking labour deserved, and an immediate and general success

[1] Journal, 1850. Ibid. p. 278.

[2] Journal, Apr. 15, 1850. Ibid. p. 276.

[3] Journal, 1854. Ibid. p. 377.

which no previous historian ever obtained in England. Take a couple of extracts as proofs, from the letters of the most critical and sober historical writer of Macaulay's time—a man very sceptical by nature and not liable to be carried away by popular enthusiasm or any other kind of enthusiasm, namely Sir G. C. Lewis. He says: 'Everybody is in raptures with Macaulay's "History". He gets 500l. for six years for his two volumes, and divides the profits after 6,000 copies. This number is *already* sold. It has had more success than any book since Lord Byron's poems and Walter Scott's novels.'[1] On volumes iii and iv, he comments: 'Macaulay's book has had a prodigious success. It is exceedingly interesting, and throws a flood of light upon the period; but it is too long, and it is overdone with details. All the part about Ireland is excellent. He is peculiarly strong upon ecclesiastical and controversial questions of all sorts.'[2]

Some authors write for fame and some for money. According to Pope, the greatest of all English writers wrote simply for money.

> Shakespear (whom you and ev'ry Play-house bill
> Style the divine, the matchless, what you will)
> For gain, not glory, wing'd his roving flight
> And grew Immortal in his own despight.

Macaulay, mainly seeking fame, found that he had won gain as well as glory, wealth as well as immortality. In 1856, on the publication of volumes iii and iv of his History, Longmans sold 26,500 copies of the work in ten weeks, and eleven weeks after publication the author received a cheque for £20,000 from his publisher. An

[1] Sir G. C. Lewis to Sir E. Head, Jan. 8, 1849. Letters of Sir George Cornewall Lewis (1870), p. 197.

[2] Ibid. p. 310.

American who visited him, George Ticknor, was dazzled by the opulence and luxury he saw. 'He lives in a beautiful villa with a rich, large, brilliant lawn behind it, keeps a carriage, and—as he told us—keeps four men-servants including his coachman, and lives altogether in elegant style for a man of letters.'[1]

However, the success of Macaulay's History was not due merely to the genius or the labour of the author. The prosperity of any book depends on the temper of the audience to which it is addressed. Macaulay's was happy in the moment of its appearance; it expressed ideas which just then were universally popular; it expressed them in such a way that it flattered the self-esteem of the English people. We are not as other nations, Macaulay seemed to say; compare their revolutions with ours. Our Revolution of 1688 was 'the least violent' and 'the most beneficent' of all revolutions. The panegyric upon it which closes Macaulay's account of the interregnum forms a kind of peroration to the first instalment of the History. It was written in November 1848.

> Now, if ever, we ought to be able to appreciate the whole importance of the stand which was made by our forefathers against the House of Stuart. All around us the world is convulsed by the agonies of great nations. Governments which lately seemed likely to stand during ages have been on a sudden shaken and overthrown. The proudest capitals of Western Europe have streamed with civil blood. . . . Meanwhile in our island the regular course of government has never been for a day interrupted. . . . And, if it be asked what has made us to differ from others, the answer is that we never lost what others are wildly and blindly seeking to regain. It is because we had a preserving revolution in the seventeenth century that we have

[1] Life, Letters, and Journals of George Ticknor (2 vols.; 1876), ii. 323.

not had a destroying revolution in the nineteenth. . . . For the authority of the law, for the security of property, for the peace of our streets, for the happiness of our homes, our gratitude is due, under Him who raises up and pulls down nations at His pleasure, to the Long Parliament, the Convention, and to William of Orange.

Ranke in his History of England points out the causes which account for the reception of Macaulay's History by Europe. He says that the Revolution of 1688 was important and interesting because the great contest of universal history, between absolute monarchy and monarchy limited by a parliamentary constitution, was brought to a decision here, and as the world in general has come to adopt the principle of a mixed constitution, the English had become almost a pattern for all nations.

'This general tendency is one cause of the immense success which Macaulay's History, appearing just at the right moment, had in Europe. Up to that time the Tory view, as represented by Hume, had not yet been driven from the field. Macaulay decided the victory of the Whig view.' [1]

[1] Ranke, History of England (1875), vi. 29.

CHAPTER II

MACAULAY'S CONCEPTION OF HISTORY

THE immediate popularity of Macaulay's History was partly due to its subject and partly due to the moment when it appeared. But there was a novelty about Macaulay's treatment of the subject which was a still greater factor in the success of his book. Something in the conception of history which it embodied and something in the way in which it was written, appealed to those whom other historians had failed to interest. From the first he proclaimed that he was an innovator and announced that he sought to reach the largest possible circle of readers. He has clearly explained for us both his aim and his method; we are not obliged to deduce them from the pages of his History. In his essays, his letters, and his journals, Macaulay sets forth his views about his art, gives us his estimates of other historians, and points out their merits and their defects. Evidently he had reflected on the theory of historical writing before he began to practise it, and all the time that he was composing he was endeavouring to realise an ideal which he had before his mind. His method of treatment, in so far as it differed from that adopted by other historians, was the result of a deliberate choice—he thought he saw more clearly than they did, what a historian ought to aim at achieving, and how that aim could be attained.

A passage in Macaulay's journal for 1849 proves this: 'There is merit, no doubt, in Hume, Robertson, Voltaire, and Gibbon. Yet it is not the thing. I have a conception of history more just, I am confident, than theirs. The execution is another matter. But I hope to improve.'[1] What was this juster conception of history?

It is certain that Macaulay did not underrate the difficulties of the historian's task. Some authors have not thought it difficult. 'It is natural to believe,' asserted Dr. Johnson in the Rambler, 'that no writer has a more easy task than the historian.' He explained to Boswell the reasons for this view.

> Great abilities are not requisite for an historian; for in historical composition, all the greatest powers of the human mind are quiescent. He has facts ready to his hand; so there is no exercise of invention. Imagination is not required in any high degree; only about as much as is used in the lower kinds of poetry. Some penetration, accuracy, and colouring will fit a man for the task, if he can give the application which is necessary.[2]

Macaulay's view, set forth in the Essay on History, published in 1828 in the Edinburgh Review, was exactly the opposite, though to a certain extent he agreed with Johnson.

> To write history respectably—that is, to abbreviate dispatches, and make extracts from speeches, to intersperse in due proportion epithets of praise and abhorrence, to draw up antithetical characters of great men, setting forth how many contradictory virtues and vices they united, and abounding in *withs* and *withouts*; all this is very easy. But to be a really great historian is perhaps the rarest of intellectual distinctions. We are acquainted with no history which approaches to our notion of what a history ought to be.[3]

[1] Journal, Dec. 7, 1849. Trevelyan, ii. 269.

[2] Boswell's Life of Johnson, ed. G. B. Hill (1887), i. 424-5.

[3] Edinburgh Review, May 1828, p. 331.

He goes on to explain that the sphere of history is a debateable land, partly ruled by reason and partly by imagination. A historian must possess a powerful imagination if he is to make his narrative sufficiently 'affecting and picturesque'. He must be a profound reasoner if he is to understand the relation of facts to each other and their relation to general principles. Leaving the general question, Macaulay at once plunges into a criticism of the Greek and Roman historians.

Herodotus he did not greatly admire—his book was 'an incomparable book' but hardly to be called a history. At most, he might be described as 'the earliest and the best' of the romantic historians, and belonged to the same class as Froissart.[1] Xenophon Macaulay despised, and for Plutarch he entertained 'a particular aversion'; the first was a dotard, and the second a pedant. As to the Latins, no historian was so indifferent to truth as Livy. 'He seems to have cared only about the picturesque effect of his book, and the honour of his country.'[2] Sallust was a partisan: his account of the conspiracy of Catiline had 'rather the air of a clever party pamphlet than that of a history'.[3]

This is a rough summary of Macaulay's verdicts: they must not be taken as representing his final estimates of the writers in question.[4]

The real value of the essay is that it shows that Macaulay

[1] Ibid. p. 332. [2] Ibid. p. 348. [3] Ibid. p. 349.

[4] Of Sallust for instance he expressed a more favourable judgement in his journal a few years later. 'I think Sallust inferior to both Livy and Tacitus in the talents of an historian. There is a lecturing, declaiming tone about him which would suit a teacher of rhetoric better than a statesman engaged in recording great events. Still, he is a good writer; and the view which he here gives of the state of parties at Rome, and the frightful demoralisation of the aristocracy, is full of interest.' June 10, 1835; May 6, 1837. Trevelyan, i. 468-9.

had carefully read the ancient historians, noted what seemed to him their merits and defects, and drawn from his examination of them very definite conclusions as to the way in which history should be written. He illustrates his conception of the art of writing history by a comparison with the analogous art of portrait painting. The portrait painter, he says, does not try to reproduce all the minutest details of the face of his sitter. So too the historian must not try to relate all the minutest details of the past. As a picture cannot be exactly like the original, so a history cannot exactly reproduce the facts.

> History cannot be perfectly and absolutely true . . . for to be perfectly and absolutely true, it ought to record *all* the slightest particulars of the slightest transactions—all the things done, and all the words uttered, during the time of which it treats. The omission of any circumstance, however insignificant, would be a defect. If history were written thus, the Bodleian library would not contain the occurrences of a week. What is told in the fullest and most accurate annals bears an infinitely small proportion to what is suppressed. . . . No picture, then, and no history, can present us with the whole truth : but those are the best pictures and the best histories which exhibit such parts of the truth as most nearly produce the effect of the whole.[1]

Macaulay's argument is that the business of the historian is to select the important and significant facts and details from the mass, and so to combine them that they produce a faithful representation of the portion of the past related.

He illustrates his view about the combination and arrangement of the facts by another comparison—this time with the art of landscape painting.

[1] Edinburgh Review, May 1828, p. 338.

History has its foreground and its background: and it is principally in the management of its perspective, that one artist differs from another. Some events must be represented on a large scale, others diminished; the great majority will be lost in the dimness of the horizon; and a general idea of their joint effect will be given by a few slight touches.

In this respect, no writer has ever equalled Thucydides. He was a perfect master of the art of gradual diminution. His history is sometimes as concise as a chronological chart; yet it is always perspicuous. . . . He never fails to contract and to expand it in the right place.[1]

Macaulay concludes by asserting that 'in the art of historical narration' Thucydides surpassed all his rivals. 'But narration, though an important part of the business of a historian, is not the whole. . . . The writer who does not explain the phenomena as well as state them, performs only one half of his office.' Thucydides failed as an interpreter of the facts; though he discussed practical questions very ably, and was undoubtedly a sagacious and reflecting man, some of his general observations were very superficial.[2]

On rereading Thucydides in later years Macaulay reiterated his conviction that Thucydides was the greatest of narrative historians. In 1836 he speaks of the intense interest which Thucydides inspired, and says that the Peloponnesian War made the Annals of Tacitus seem 'cold and poor' when he read them side by side. 'Indeed, what colouring is there which would not look tame when placed side by side with the magnificent light, and the terrible shade, of Thucydides? Tacitus was a great man; but he was not up to the Sicilian expedition.'[3]

In 1848, he had come to think that even in the art of

[1] Ibid. [2] Ibid. pp. 339-41.

[3] Letter to Ellis, July 25, 1836. Trevelyan, i. 449.

narration Thucydides did not always attain absolute perfection. 'I read the eighth book of Thucydides. On the whole he is the first of historians. What is good in him is better than anything that can be found elsewhere. But his dry parts are dreadfully dry; and his arrangement is bad. Mere chronological order is not the order for a complicated narrative.'[1]

Next to Thucydides, amongst the ancients, Macaulay placed Tacitus. 'Of the Latin historians, Tacitus was certainly the greatest.' But he thought that his style was inferior to that of Thucydides, and that he did not tell his story so well. 'His style indeed is not only faulty in itself, but is, in some respects, peculiarly unfit for historical composition. He carries his love of effect far beyond the limits of moderation. He tells a fine story finely: but he cannot tell a plain story plainly.'[2]

On the other hand, said Macaulay, there was one part of the historian's art in which Tacitus surpassed Thucydides—in which, indeed, he had no equal amongst ancient historians.

> In the delineation of character, Tacitus . . . has very few superiors among dramatists and novelists. By the delineation of character, we do not mean the practice of drawing up epigrammatic catalogues of good and bad qualities, and appending them to the names of eminent men. No writer, indeed, has done this more skilfully than Tacitus: but this is not his peculiar glory. All the persons who occupy a large space in his works have an individuality of character which seems to pervade all their words and actions. We know them as if we had lived with them. Claudius, Nero, Otho, both the Agrippinas, are masterpieces. But Tiberius is a still higher miracle of art. The

[1] Journal, Dec. 4, 1848. Ibid. ii. 245.

[2] Edinburgh Review, May 1828, p. 350.

historian undertook to make us intimately acquainted with a man singularly dark and inscrutable,—with a man whose real disposition long remained swathed up in intricate folds of factitious virtues, and over whose actions the hypocrisy of his youth, and the seclusion of his age, threw a singular mystery.[1]

Here, as in the case of his remarks on Thucydides, Macaulay's admiration for some particular quality in the author he estimates reveals his own ideals. The perfect historian must unite the narrative skill of Thucydides with the power of Tacitus to penetrate, to realise, and to depict persons. At the same time, there were certain qualities which the ancient historians did not possess, but the ideal historian should possess. In the latter part of the essay, Macaulay turned to consider the moderns. He felt that they surpassed their predecessors in two ways. They were far more strict in their adherence to truth than most of the Greek and Roman writers. They did not insert imaginary speeches, conversations, or descriptions. But their chief superiority lay in another direction. In the philosophy of history, the moderns had very far surpassed the ancients. The natural growth of knowledge accounted for something, but it would not altogether account for their 'immense superiority' in this respect. The cause was the constant progress of the human intellect due to the substitution of progressive for stationary societies, the breadth and variety of modern civilisation compared to the exclusiveness and narrowness of ancient civilisation, and other general causes. 'Hence it is, that, in generalisation, the writers of modern times have far surpassed those of antiquity. The historians of our own country are unequalled in depth and precision of reason; and even in the works

[1] Ibid. pp. 350-1.

of our mere compilers, we often meet with speculations beyond the reach of Thucydides or Tacitus.'[1]

On the other hand, modern historians had certain characteristic faults. Even the best of them were led astray by their desire to prove a theory or defend a system. 'They far excel their predecessors in the art of deducing general principles from facts. But unhappily they have fallen into the error of distorting facts to suit general principles.' 'This species of misrepresentation abounds in the most valuable works of modern historians'—in Hume's History of England or Gibbon's Decline and Fall or Mitford's History of Greece, for example.

> Hume is an accomplished advocate: without positively asserting much more than he can prove, he gives prominence to all the circumstances which support his case; he glides lightly over those which are unfavourable to it; his own witnesses are applauded and encouraged; the statements which seem to throw discredit on them are controverted; the contradictions into which they fall are explained away; a clear and connected abstract of their evidence is given. Everything that is offered on the other side is scrutinised with the utmost severity;—every suspicious circumstance is a ground for comment and invective; what cannot be denied is extenuated, or passed by without notice; concessions even are sometimes made—but this insidious candour only increases the effect of the vast mass of sophistry.[2]

Minor writers, such as Southey, Lingard, and Mitford, were advocates too.

> In the midst of these disputes, however, history proper, if we may use the term, is disappearing. The high, grave, impartial summing up of Thucydides is nowhere to be found.

[1] Ibid. pp. 353, 358-9. [2] Ibid. pp. 359-60.

While our historians are practising all the arts of controversy, they miserably neglect the art of narration, the art of interesting the affections, and presenting pictures to the imagination.[1]

The result was that while people read with avidity any tolerable biography that was issued they refused to read histories. 'Histories of great empires, written by men of eminent ability, lie unread on the shelves of ostentatious libraries.' A superstitious notion of the dignity of history led historians to omit the very things which interested readers most.

The writers of history seem to entertain an aristocratical contempt for the writers of memoirs. They think it beneath the dignity of men who describe the revolutions of nations, to dwell on the details which constitute the charm of biography. They have imposed on themselves a code of conventional decencies, as absurd as that which has been the bane of the French drama. The most characteristic and interesting circumstances are omitted or softened down, because, as we are told, they are too trivial for the majesty of history.[2]

Other conventions led them to neglect a whole series of facts of the highest importance. They looked only at the surface of affairs, and never thought of what was going on under the surface, and this vitiated their representation of events.

A history, in which every particular incident may be true, may on the whole be false. The circumstances which have most influence on the happiness of mankind, the changes of manners and morals, the transition of com-

[1] Ibid. p. 361.

[2] Ibid. pp. 361-2. Cf. the remarks on the dignity of history ('a vile phrase'), in Essays, ii. 256-9.

munities from poverty to wealth, from knowledge to ignorance, from ferocity to humanity—these are, for the most part, noiseless revolutions. Their progress is rarely indicated by what historians are pleased to call important events. They are not achieved by armies, or enacted by senates. They are sanctioned by no treaties, and recorded in no archives. They are carried on in every school, in every church, behind ten thousand counters, at ten thousand firesides. The upper current of society presents no certain criterion by which we can judge of the direction in which the under current flows. We read of defeats and victories. But we know that nations may be miserable amidst victories, and prosperous amidst defeats. We read of the fall of wise ministers, and of the rise of profligate favourites. But we must remember how small a proportion the good or evil effected by a single statesman can bear to the good or evil of a great social system.[1]

In short, modern writers of history were not merely partial but dull and superficial. They confined themselves to relating political events, and neglected social changes and social facts. They told only half the story, and they told that badly. History ought to be written in a more artistic and a more interesting way; the received conception of its province ought to be widened so as to include the life of the people as well as the fortunes of its rulers. Macaulay closes his essay by drawing the character of the ideal historian.

The perfect historian is he in whose work the character and spirit of an age is exhibited in miniature. He relates no fact, he attributes no expression to his characters, which is not authenticated by sufficient testimony. But by judicious selection, rejection, and arrangement, he gives to truth those attractions which have been usurped by fiction. In his narrative a due subordination is observed;

[1] Edinburgh Review, May 1828, pp. 362-3.

some transactions are prominent, others retire. But the scale on which he represents them is increased or diminished, not according to the dignity of the persons concerned in them, but according to the degree in which they elucidate the condition of society and the nature of man. He shows us the court, the camp, and the senate. But he shows us also the nation. He considers no anecdote, no peculiarity of manner, no familiar saying, as too insignificant for his notice, which is not too insignificant to illustrate the operation of laws, of religion, and of education, and to mark the progress of the human mind. Men will not merely be described, but will be made intimately known to us. The changes of manners will be indicated, not merely by a few general phrases, or a few extracts from statistical documents, but by appropriate images presented in every line.

If a man, such as we are supposing, should write the history of England, he would assuredly not omit the battles, the sieges, the negotiations, the seditions, the ministerial changes. But with these he would intersperse the details which are the charm of historical romances. At Lincoln Cathedral there is a beautiful painted window, which was made by an apprentice out of the pieces of glass which had been rejected by his master. It is so far superior to every other in the church, that, according to the tradition, the vanquished artist killed himself from mortification. Sir Walter Scott, in the same manner, has used those fragments of truth which historians have scornfully thrown behind them, in a manner which may well excite their envy. He has constructed out of their gleanings works which, even considered as histories, are scarcely less valuable than theirs. But a truly great historian would reclaim those materials which the novelist has appropriated. The history of the government, and the history of the people, would be exhibited in that mode in which alone they can be exhibited justly, in inseparable conjunction and intermixture. We should not then have to look for the wars and votes of the Puritans in Clarendon, and for their phraseology in Old Mortality; for one half of King James in Hume, and for the other half in the Fortunes of Nigel.[1]

Macaulay's words are quoted at length, perhaps at exorbitant length, because it is important to show exactly what he aimed at achieving, before we attempt to judge what he actually achieved. His History is the practical exemplification of the views set forth in his essay. He endeavoured to revive what seemed to him the lost art of historical narrative, to combine the qualities of Thucydides and Tacitus, telling his story as skilfully as the one and describing his personages as vividly as the other, but arranging his subjects as a whole rather better than Thucydides did, and avoiding in his style the over-elaboration and lack of simplicity which he blamed in Tacitus. But he took Scott for his model too. He endeavoured to make his History interesting by adding the characteristic details which historians usually omitted. He endeavoured to make the field of history include social as well as political life, and to give it some of the charm of historical romance by employing the materials the historical novelist employed and describing common people as well as kings and statesmen. He said at the beginning of his book:

I should very imperfectly execute the task which I have undertaken if I were merely to treat of battles and sieges, of the rise and fall of administrations, of intrigues in the palace, and debates in the Parliament. It will be my endeavour to relate the history of the people as well as the history of the government, to trace the progress of useful and ornamental arts, to describe the rise of religious sects and the changes of literary taste, to portray the manners of successive generations, and not to pass by with neglect

[1] Ibid. pp. 364-5.

even the revolutions which have taken place in dress, furniture, repasts, and public amusements. I shall cheerfully bear the reproach of having descended below the dignity of history, if I can succeed in placing before the English of the nineteenth century a true picture of the life of their ancestors.[1]

Nor was Macaulay's example without effect. A few years after his death, J. R. Green tried to do for the whole of English history what Macaulay tried to do for a particular period. 'I have preferred,' wrote Green in his preface,[2] 'to pass lightly and briefly over the details of foreign wars and diplomacies, the personal adventures of kings and nobles, the pomp of courts, or the intrigues of favourites, and to dwell at length on the incidents of that constitutional, intellectual, and social advance in which we read the history of the nation itself.' The difference is that Macaulay, while as determined as Green to write 'the history of the nation itself', was resolved also to write that of foreign wars and diplomacies, and the personal adventures which Green preferred to exclude. For he had none of Green's dislike and disdain for what is termed 'drum and trumpet history'. On the contrary, he rejoiced like the war horse in Job, when he sniffed a battle afar off, a thing very becoming in a former Secretary at War.

In conclusion, there is one characteristic of Macaulay's conception of history which must be pointed out. He treats history throughout as a part of literature—'a department of literature' is his precise phrase. In this he differs from most modern historians. Their tendency is to regard history as a branch of science rather than literature, and to enlarge upon the difficulty of finding out the truth,

[1] I, 2.

[2] A Short History of the English People (4 vols.; 1892).

whereas Macaulay enlarges upon the difficulty of stating it. The view generally taken by the professional historians of our own day is diametrically opposed to that of Macaulay. Take for instance the views set forth by Professor Bury in his inaugural lecture in 1903. According to him one of the great achievements of the nineteenth century was the transformation of the idea of history which is being gradually accomplished.[1] During the course of the nineteenth century mere erudition was supplemented by the introduction of the 'scientific method'. This movement, which began in Germany, 'gave historians the idea of a systematic and minute method of analysing their sources.' The aim of this analysis was to find out the exact truth about the past, and it led to a new conception of what history was. 'So long as history was regarded as an art', truth and accuracy were matters of minor importance compared to the artistic statement of facts or what were supposed to be facts. But history 'is not a branch of literature'.

> The facts of history, like the facts of geology or astronomy, can supply material for literary art; for manifest reasons they lend themselves to artistic representation far more readily than those of the natural sciences; but to clothe the story of human society in a literary dress is no more the part of an historian as an historian, than it is the part of an astronomer, as an astronomer, to present in an artistic shape the story of the stars.

The truth is, history is 'a science, no less and no more'.

This is a severe doctrine; it is not universally received, but it is so generally received by professional historians that it might almost be called the orthodox doctrine—'the pure milk of the word', so to speak; but it is a little too strong for my stomach. After all, when a man puts his pen

[1] An Inaugural Lecture (1903), pp. 7, 10-11, 12, 16-17, 42.

to paper and proceeds to print the result, he is attempting to convey his ideas to some other man. He presupposes the existence of a reader. It is therefore essential that he should arrange his ideas clearly, that he should state them so that they may be understood, and express them so that they may leave a lasting impression on the mind of the person to whom they are addressed. If he fails to achieve this, he has done only half of his work. Thus the historian's task is two-fold: he has first of all to find out the truth, which is a scientific process, and then to state the truth for the information of other people, which is a literary or artistic process. History is therefore in part a branch of science and in part a branch of literature. Professor Bury evades this conclusion by drawing a distinction; he narrows the meaning of the word 'historian' and restricts it to the man who performs the function of finding out the truth, using the term 'historiographer' to define the man who states the facts agreeably, and calling the function of statement 'historiography'.

Now, Macaulay goes to the opposite extreme: he forgets the scientific element in history and thinks only of the literary element. The defects of his History are mainly due to this one-sidedness, this underestimate of the importance of one part of the historian's task. Not that he neglected it altogether, but simply that he did not adequately realise its magnitude and its difficulty. His mind was too full of the other half of his task, the business of stating to the best advantage the facts he had collected by his investigations. The problem which occupied him most was how to reach the largest possible circle of readers.

He achieved this object: he reached at once a larger circle of readers than Hume or Robertson or Gibbon or any other English historian has done.

CHAPTER III

MACAULAY'S METHOD

MACAULAY'S choice of words, the formation of his sentences, and the construction of his paragraphs are subjects which have been adequately discussed in treatises on English composition and histories of English literature. There is an exhaustive treatise on the subject, with many detailed examples, in the late Professor Minto's Manual of English Prose Literature. Macaulay is one of three modern authors he treats with great minuteness, devoting over fifty pages to an examination of his writings. But the subject to be considered here is a larger one than Professor Minto's. It is not Macaulay's manner of writing the English language, but his manner of writing English history: the method by which he tells his story, connects the different parts of his narrative, explains the questions at issue, draws the characters of men, and describes incidents in the development of events or the scenes in which the events took place.

In some respects Macaulay's style is a model of what the style of a historian should be. Freeman in his book on the Methods of Historical Study expresses his admiration for it in words that many other historians would endorse.

'English historical literature can boast of at least three great writers, each of whom knew how to tell his tale, though they told it in ways as unlike each other as if the later in each case had striven to avoid the manner of the earlier.' These three were Gibbon, Thomas Arnold, and Macaulay. He adds:

I know that to run down Lord Macaulay is the fashion of the day. I have heard some speak against him who have a right to speak; I have heard many more who have none. I at least feel that I have none; I do not see how any man can have the right who has not gone through the same work through which Macaulay went, or at least through some no less thorough work of a kindred sort. I can see Macaulay's great and obvious faults as well as any man; I know as well as any man the cautions with which his brilliant pictures must be studied; but I cannot feel that I have any right to speak lightly of one to whom I owe so much in the matter of actual knowledge, and to whom I owe more than to any man as the master of historical narrative. Read a page of Macaulay; scan well his minute accuracy in every name and phrase and title; contrast his English undefiled with the slipshod jargon which from our newspapers has run over into our books; dwell on the style which finds a fitting phrase in our own tongue to set forth every thought, the style which never uses a single word out of its true and honest meaning; turn the pages of the book in which no man ever read a sentence a second time because he failed to catch its meaning the first time,[1] but in which all of us must have read many sentences a second or a twentieth time for the sheer pleasure of dwelling on the clearness, the combined fulness and terseness, on the just relation of every word to every other, on the happily chosen epithet, or the sharply pointed sarcasm.[2]

Other contemporaries, admitting Macaulay's power to tell a story, nevertheless condemned his style. 'It would be unfair,' wrote Mill, 'to measure the worth of any age

[1] Lord Morley remarks of Macaulay: 'He never wrote an obscure sentence in his life, and this may seem a small merit until we remember of how few writers we could say the same.' Critical Miscellanies, 2d Ser. (1877), p. 388.

[2] E. A. Freeman, Methods of Historical Study (1886), pp. 104-6.

by that of its popular objects of literary or artistic admiration. Otherwise one might say that the present age will be known and estimated by posterity as the age which thought Macaulay a great writer.'[1] Take again this record of a conversation between Herbert Spencer and Lecky: 'We talked much about style in writing . . . about the bad writing of Addison, about the especial atrocity of Macaulay, whose style "resembles low organisations, being a perpetual repetition of similar parts".'[2] A third critic, while pointing out with an unsparing hand the defects of Macaulay's style, dwells on its popularity and its influence. 'Where he set his stamp,' writes Lord Morley,[3] 'has been upon style; style in its widest sense, not merely on the grammar and mechanism of writing, but on what De Quincey described as its *organology*; style, that is to say, in its relation to ideas and feelings, its commerce with thought, and its reaction on what one may call the temper or the conscience of the intellect.' 'It is impossible to take up a newspaper or a review, for instance, without perceiving Macaulay's influence both in the style and the temper of modern journalism.'[4] His success in catching the ear of the public naturally produced a crop of imitators, some essayists, others historians. Arminius, the German critic of English life in Matthew Arnold's Friendship's Garland, defines Hepworth Dixon's style as 'middle-class Macaulayese'.

'I call it Macaulayese', says the pedant, 'because it has the same internal and external characteristics as Macaulay's style; the external characteristic being a hard metallic movement with nothing of the soft play of life, and

[1] Mill, Diary, Feb. 11, 1854; Letters of J. S. Mill, ii. 370.

[2] Memoir of W. E. H. Lecky, by his wife (1909), p. 113.

[3] Op. cit. p. 373. [4] Ibid. p. 377.

the internal characteristic being a perpetual semblance of hitting the right nail on the head without the reality. And I call it middle-class Macaulayese, because it has these faults without the compensation of great studies and of conversance with great affairs, by which Macaulay partly redeemed them.' [1]

Macaulay, who was a very honest critic of himself, recognised the defects of his own style, especially when he saw them reflected in the pages of other writers. He wrote in his journal,.about 1856 : 'I looked through . . . . 's two volumes. He is, I see, an imitator of me. But I am a very unsafe model. My manner is, I think, and the world thinks, on the whole a good one ; but it is very near to a very bad manner indeed, and those characteristics of my style which are most easily copied are the most questionable.' [2]

He felt that the language of history ought to preserve a certain dignity,[3] and he lived up to the standards he set. There may be a few passages which an austere critic would consider flippant, and there are instances in which he adopts for a moment a familiar and colloquial mode of speech. But his inclination is to use a swelling phrase when a plainer and more natural one would often be preferable. At times he exposes himself to the censure he bestows on Tacitus and 'stimulates till stimulants lose their force'. Exaggeration and excessive emphasis are his besetting sins, and he was either unconscious of those defects or deliberately closed his eyes to them. Over-emphasis often wearies the reader by the sense of strain and effort which it gives: in Macaulay's case the style seems to express the naturally exuberant vitality and

[1] Friendship's Garland (1871 ed.), p. 71.

[2] Trevelyan, ii. 452. [3] Ibid. p. 108.

energy of the writer, and carries the reader on from page to page. This was his object. The methods of Gibbon and Macaulay have often been contrasted. Gibbon labours to be emphatic by means of condensation and brevity, by the use of suggestive epithets, or short pregnant clauses. 'He conveys incidentally,' says one of his critics, 'by a passing adjective, information that Macaulay would have set forth in a special sentence.' Macaulay emphasises a point by expansion into a paragraph instead of condensation into a line or word. That they appealed to different audiences explains the difference in their methods. Gibbon wrote for men of letters who would appreciate his verbal felicities and his nice choice of words. Macaulay aimed at interesting everybody who could read. He assumed the tone of an orator addressing a great mixed audience, and the devices which he employed to excite and retain their attention were the devices of the orator rather than the writer—rhetorical in the strict sense of the word, rather than literary.

The style of Macaulay's History is the style of his speeches. Whatever subject he is treating in his History the orator is always appearing behind the historian, or rather the two are one: in reading we are continually reminded that his speeches never failed to fill the benches of the House of Commons with crowded listeners. Taine in his admirable study of Macaulay brings this out very clearly.[1] There is not an idea or a phrase in his writings, says Taine, in which the gifts and the instincts of the orator do not appear. Perhaps his incomparable lucidity was due to the habit of public speaking. A man who wants to convince a public assembly has to address himself to every member of it; to keep the attention of men who

[1] Histoire de la littérature anglaise, vol. v.

are tired, he has to make his meaning so clear that they have no trouble in understanding it. 'Il faut qu'ils comprennent trop pour comprendre assez.' [1]

One result of this attempt to make every point intelligible to the meanest or laziest understanding is that the speaker becomes prolix and verbose. Brougham, himself a sinner in that respect, complains of Macaulay's prolixity. He was annoyed because the editor of the Edinburgh Review allowed the new contributor more space than he was allotted himself. Macaulay's Sir William Temple, wrote Brougham to the editor, 'is an excellent paper, only he *does* take a terrible space to turn in. Good God! what an awful man he would have been in Nisi Prius! . . . He takes as long to delineate three characters of little importance as I have to sketch ten, the greatest in the whole world. I really wish you could give him a hint.' [2]

Another common sin with orators is repetition. A historian usually assumes in his readers a certain amount of interest in his subject; when he has explained a question once, or stated an argument once, he does not think it necessary to repeat the explanation or demonstration. Either the reader will remember it, or he can turn back to page 150 and refresh his memory. But the orator repeats his arguments, because he aims at carrying conviction to every one of his hearers; some may have imperfectly apprehended that particular argument, some may have forgotten it, but all must be made to understand it. A contemporary member of Parliament thus describes the practice of Charles James Fox.

[1] Ibid. p. 173.

[2] Selection from the Correspondence of Macvey Napier, ed. Macvey Napier (1879), p. 276.

The redundancy of Fox's oratory arose, partly, at least, from an opinion or principle which Fox had adopted. He assumed that one-third of his audience was always either absent, or at dinner, or asleep ; and he therefore usually made a short resumption or epitome of his arguments for the benefit of this part of the members. So that, after speaking at great length and sometime apparently summing up as if about to conclude, whenever he saw a considerable influx of attendance he began anew, regardless of any impatience manifested on the part of those whose attention was already exhausted by long exertion.[1]

Another result of the oratorical habit in Macaulay is a certain over-vehemence. The proper business of a historian is to relate what happened and explain why it happened: the business of the orator generally involves proving a case, and if he is very anxious to do so he is often inclined to be vehement and even violent. Macaulay sometimes falls into the error which he himself condemns in Fox's History of James II. 'Mr. Fox,' says Macaulay, 'winnowed and sifted his phraseology' with great care, but was not sufficiently

on his guard against those more serious improprieties of manner into which a great orator who undertakes to write history is in danger of falling. There is about the whole book a vehement, contentious, replying manner. Almost every argument is put in the form of an interrogation, an ejaculation, or a sarcasm. The writer seems to be addressing himself to some imaginary audience, to be tearing to pieces a defence of the Stuarts which has just been pronounced by an imaginary Tory.[2]

To avoid this fault, Macaulay adopted a device which gave him the opportunity of using his particular gifts

[1] N. W. Wraxall, History and Posthumous Memoirs, ed. H. B. Wheatley (5 vols. ; 1884), iii. 225-6.

[2] Essays, ii. 54-5.

without seeming to become an advocate instead of a historian. The device was what he termed the 'declamatory disquisition', namely, a summary of the arguments on one side or the other, or on both sides, cast into the form of a speech. He says in his journal: 'The declamatory disquisition which I have substituted for the orations of the ancient historians, seems to me likely to answer. It is a sort of composition which suits my style, and will probably take with the public.'[1]

There is a good instance in the first chapter of the History, when Macaulay describes the state of public feeling in 1642.

Neither party wanted strong arguments for the course which it was disposed to take. The reasonings of the most enlightened Royalists may be summed up thus:—It is true that great abuses have existed; but they have been redressed. It is true that precious rights have been invaded; but they have been vindicated and surrounded with new securities. The sittings of the Estates of the realm have been, in defiance of all precedent and of the spirit of the constitution, intermitted during eleven years; but it has now been provided that henceforth three years shall never elapse without a Parliament. The Star Chamber, the High Commission, the Council of York, oppressed and plundered us; but those hateful courts have now ceased to exist. The Lord Lieutenant aimed at establishing military despotism; but he has answered for his treason with his head. The Primate tainted our worship with Popish rites, and punished our scruples with Popish cruelty; but he is awaiting in the Tower the judgment of his peers. The Lord Keeper sanctioned a plan by which the property of every man in England was placed at the mercy of the Crown; but he has been disgraced, ruined, and compelled to take refuge in a foreign land. The ministers

[1] Journal, Dec. 10, 1850. Trevelyan, ii. 288.

of tyranny have expiated their crimes. The victims of tyranny have been compensated for their sufferings. It would therefore be most unwise to persevere further in that course which was justifiable and necessary when we first met, after a long interval, and found the whole administration one mass of abuses. It is time to take heed that we do not so pursue our victory over despotism as to run into anarchy. It was not in our power to overturn the bad institutions which lately afflicted our country, without shocks which have loosened the foundations of government. Now that those institutions have fallen we must hasten to prop the edifice which it was lately our duty to batter. Henceforth it will be our wisdom to look with jealousy on schemes of innovation, and to guard from encroachment all the prerogatives with which the law has, for the public good, armed the sovereign.[1]

There is a similar passage in chapter xiv, where Macaulay states the argument of the clergy for and against taking the oath of allegiance to William III,[2] and another at the beginning of chapter xxiii, where he sums up the controversy for and against a standing army.[3]

In these last examples, the views of the two parties on the point at issue are admirably condensed and stated, far better than could have been done by the ordinary method of quoting salient passages from speeches and pamphlets, and they are also far more briefly and effectively put. This result is due not only to Macaulay's rhetorical gifts, but also to the magnificent memory which enabled him to recollect the contents of all the pamphlets he had read, so that he had a sort of bird's-eye view of the whole controversy. His use of this device must be pronounced very successful: it answers the end of adding variety to his story, and it answers the end of reproducing the arguments

[1] I, 92. [2] IV, 1707-12. [3] VI, 2736-42.

of the two parties. In short, it serves both a literary and a historical purpose.

In these argumentative digressions on the questions at issue, Macaulay practises another device for enlisting the attention of his readers. The problem he had to solve, since he wished to secure the largest possible audience, was how to interest the mass of people who live entirely in the present and care nothing about the past for its own sake. What does interest such people is usually the politics of the day. Hence Macaulay never fails to refer to modern analogues to the seventeenth-century problems he is discussing. We get references to George III's scruples about the coronation oath,[1] Catholic Emancipation,[2] the Reform Bill,[3] and the disruption of the Scottish church.[4] Macaulay's political experiences enabled him to point his accounts of the parliamentary manners in the seventeenth century by allusions to the parliamentary manners of his own. Speaking, for instance, of a bill to disfranchise certain persons who had taken part in the oppressive acts of James II, he says:

> The Tories did not venture to divide. The rules of the House put it in the power of a minority to obstruct the progress of a bill; and this was assuredly one of the very rare occasions on which that power would have been with great propriety exerted. It does not appear however that the parliamentary tacticians of the seventeenth century were aware of the extent to which a small number of members can, without violating any form, retard the course of business.[5]

When he has to explain the fact that, in 1693, the Lords supported the bill for triennial Parliaments while the Com-

[1] III, 1412-13 (xi). [2] V, 2089-90 (xviii). [3] V, 2287-8 (xix).
[4] IV, 1938 (xvi). [5] IV, 1780 (xv).

mons hated it but dared not publicly oppose it, Macaulay makes a feeling reference to the troublesomeness and expense of a contested election in his own days.

> The near prospect of a dissolution could not be very agreeable to a member whose election was likely to be contested. He must go through all the miseries of a canvass, must shake hands with crowds of freeholders or freemen, must ask after their wives and children, must hire conveyances for outvoters, must open alehouses, must provide mountains of beef, must set rivers of ale running, and might perhaps, after all the drudgery and all the expense, after being lampooned, hustled, pelted, find himself at the bottom of the poll, see his antagonists chaired, and sink half ruined into obscurity.[1]

Still more interesting to the reader of to-day is Macaulay's discussion of the question, when the House of Lords can successfully resist the will of the House of Commons.[2]

These modern instances, directly or indirectly suggested, are so well employed that the reader does not feel that they are dragged in—they really elucidate the point at issue, and they make the reader feel that the questions these bygone statesmen were disputing about were much the same kind of problems as those which parties were fighting about in 1857. They give a singularly practical and concrete character to the History.

Besides this, there are examples and references drawn from every time to illustrate an argument or add interest to a fact mentioned. Sometimes they are quite modern. In describing the troops of William at the battle of the Boyne, Macaulay contrives to introduce an allusion to the Crimean War. Amongst William's troops, he says, there came 'from the neighbourhood of Lough Erne a regiment

[1] V, 2297 (xix). [2] VI, 2974-5 (xxv).

of dragoons which still glories in the name of Enniskillen, and which has proved on the shores of the Euxine that it has not degenerated since the day of the Boyne'.[1] In another place, describing the enthusiasm of Scotland for the Darien scheme, Macaulay argues that the hopes of commerce and wealth founded upon it had some element of reason in them. There was no reason that Scotland should not become fabulously wealthy through trade. 'Scotland was, indeed, not blessed with a mild climate or a fertile soil. But the richest spots that had ever existed on the face of the earth had been spots quite as little favoured by nature.' He proceeds to point out the natural and local disadvantage of Tyre, Venice, and Amsterdam and to enlarge at length on their wealth and greatness.[2]

Often he adorns a plain statement with a superfluity of historical parallels. Arguing that if the administration of James I had been able and splendid it would probably have been fatal to English liberty, he concludes by saying:

> Had James been, like Henry the Fourth, like Maurice of Nassau, or like Gustavus Adolphus, a valiant, active, and politic ruler, had he put himself at the head of the Protestants of Europe, had he gained great victories over Tilly and Spinola, had he adorned Westminster with the spoils of Bavarian monasteries and Flemish cathedrals, had he hung Austrian and Castilian banners in Saint Paul's, and had he found himself, after great achievements, at the head of fifty thousand troops, brave, well disciplined, and devotedly attached to his person, the English Parliament would soon have been nothing more than a name.[3]

This is rather overdone, but its purpose is obvious: Macaulay is not introducing these names out of the mere exuberance of his knowledge, but in order to clench his

[1] IV, 1875 (xvi). [2] VI, 2912 (xxiv). [3] I, 59 (i).

argument by a number of concrete examples, and so to convince those on whom the plain, simple statement of fact which he began with would have little effect.

The last passage illustrates another characteristic of Macaulay. He is fond of contrasting what actually happened with what might have happened or might have been expected to happen. He moralises thus on the fall of Richard Cromwell and the restoration of Charles II :

Had the Protector and the Parliament been suffered to proceed undisturbed, there can be little doubt that an order of things similar to that which was afterwards established under the House of Hanover would have been established under the House of Cromwell. But . . .

Had a prince, with a title as good as that of Charles, commanded an army as good as that of Cromwell, there would have been little hope indeed for the liberties of England. But happily . . .[1]

This is a way of making history more real by showing that what actually occurred might have happened otherwise—that events were not absolutely fated to take the particular turn that they did take. It is an expedient for making his readers think which Seeley continually employed. He says :

Historians are sometimes ridiculed by indulging in conjectures about what would have followed in history if some one event had fallen out differently. 'So gloriously unpractical! ' we exclaim. Now it is not for the sake of practice, but for the sake of theory, that such conjectures are hazarded, and I think historians should deal in them much more than they do. It is an illusion to suppose that great public events, because they are on a grander scale, have something more fatally necessary about them than ordinary private events ; and this illusion enslaves the judgment.

[1] I, 124, 136 (i, ii).

The contrast between what happened and what might have happened was with Seeley part of the systematic method of 'turning narrative into problems', which seemed to him the best way of understanding English history.

> So long as you think of history as a mere chronological narrative, so long you are in the old literary groove which leads to no trustworthy knowledge, but only to that pompous conventional romancing of which all serious men are tired. Break the drowsy spell of narrative; ask yourself questions; set yourself problems.[1]

Macaulay, whose object was not didactic, employs these contrasts purely as a rhetorical device. He suggests a problem now and then, but does not pause to examine seriously the might-have-beens of history. The questions upon which he prefers to expatiate are the practical questions which the statesmen of the seventeenth century had to solve. To discuss these, he is willing to interrupt for a moment the flow of his story, and he suspends it again and again to introduce the descriptions of persons or scenes in the time-honoured fashion of all narrative historians.

Macaulay's gallery of historical portraits is unusually comprehensive. It includes not only the great actors, but the minor personages who appear for a minute on the stage. He has been charged with unfairness to particular persons. Whether his conception of a man's character is right or wrong, the man's person is clearly and vividly depicted. He realises the actors in the drama as if they were present before his eyes, and he is determined that his readers shall see them too in flesh and blood. For instance, his hero, King William:

> His external appearance is almost as well known to us as to his own captains and counsellors. Sculptors, painters,

[1] J. R. Seeley, The Expansion of England (1900), pp. 189, 202-3.

and medallists exerted their utmost skill in the work of transmitting his features to posterity; and his features were such as no artist could fail to seize, and such as, once seen, could never be forgotten. His name at once calls up before us a slender and feeble frame, a lofty and ample forehead, a nose curved like the beak of an eagle, an eye rivalling that of an eagle in brightness and keenness, a thoughtful and somewhat sullen brow, a firm and somewhat peevish mouth, a cheek pale, thin, and deeply furrowed by sickness and by care.[1]

These brief portraits are usually introduced with remarkable skill. Take, for example, that of Sir Edward Seymour, the one man in the first session of James II's Parliament who dared to oppose the government and to complain of the corruption and intimidation practised by its agents to secure the election of the court candidates. The government had just proposed that the House should resolve themselves into a committee for the purpose of settling a revenue on the King. 'Then Seymour stood up. How he stood, looking like what he was, the chief of a dissolute and high spirited gentry, with the artificial ringlets clustering in fashionable profusion round his shoulders, and a mingled expression of voluptuousness and disdain in his eye and on his lip, the likenesses of him which still remain enable us to imagine.'[2] Then follows a summary of his speech, which loses nothing in point of force by Macaulay's rendering, and gains in interest from the vision of the man which Macaulay's description calls up.

The villains of the story are described with a touch of caricature. Macaulay's hatred of their characters seems to urge him to make them hideous and ridiculous. Take Ferguson the plotter. At the moment when he is described he was in hiding in Holland. English envoys at foreign

[1] I, 508 (iv). [2] II, 811 (vii).

courts had been warned to be on the watch for him, and the French government had offered a reward for his capture. 'Nor was it easy for him to escape notice,' writes Macaulay, 'for his broad Scotch accent, his tall and lean figure, his lantern jaws, the gleam of his sharp eyes which were always overhung by his wig, his cheeks inflamed by an eruption, his shoulders deformed by a stoop, and his gait distinguished from that of other men by a peculiar shuffle, made him remarkable wherever he appeared.' [1]

The portrait of Titus Oates is a companion to that of Ferguson. It describes the trial of Oates on the charge of perjury, which took place at the beginning of the reign of James II.

> On the day in which Titus was brought to the bar, Westminster Hall was crowded with spectators, among whom were many Roman Catholics, eager to see the misery and humiliation of their persecutor. A few years earlier his short neck, his legs uneven, the vulgar said, as those of a badger, his forehead low as that of a baboon, his purple cheeks, and his monstrous length of chin, had been familiar to all who frequented the courts of law. He had then been the idol of the nation. . . . Times had now changed; and many, who had formerly regarded him as the deliverer of his country, shuddered at the sight of those hideous features on which villany seemed to be written by the hand of God.[2]

These are by no means imaginary portraits. Each trait is based on some evidence, though it may be the evidence of satirists and caricaturists. Macaulay has distilled the essence of many contemporary accounts of the appearance of these men to provide colour for his picture, and has provided a little too much. He has exaggerated and over-coloured. In the later volumes of the History,

[1] II, 527 (v). [2] I, 477 (iv).

Macaulay's touch becomes lighter. The description of William Paterson and Fletcher of Saltoun, in the account of the genesis of the Darien scheme, is an excellent example. There is a piquant contrast between the two visionaries—the patriot and the projector—who for a moment became confederates and half ruined Scotland between them.

These eccentric men soon became intimate. Each of them had his monomania; and the two monomanias suited each other perfectly. Fletcher's whole soul was possessed by a sore, jealous, punctilious patriotism. His heart was ulcerated by the thought of the poverty, the feebleness, the political insignificance of Scotland, and of the indignities which she had suffered at the hand of her powerful and opulent neighbour. When he talked of her wrongs his dark meagre face took its sternest expression: his habitual frown grew blacker; and his eyes flashed more than their wonted fire. Paterson, on the other hand, firmly believed himself to have discovered the means of making any state which would follow his counsel great and prosperous in a time which, when compared with the life of an individual, could hardly be called long, and which, in the life of a nation, was but as a moment.[1]

The great projector was the idol of the whole nation. Men spoke to him with more profound respect than to the Lord High Commissioner. His antechamber was crowded with solicitors desirous to catch some drops of that golden shower of which he was supposed to be the dispenser. To be seen walking with him in the High Street, to be honoured by him with a private interview of a quarter of an hour, were enviable distinctions. He, after the fashion of all the false prophets who have deluded themselves and others, drew new faith in his own lie from the credulity of his disciples. His countenance, his voice, his gestures, indicated boundless self-importance. When he appeared in public he looked,—such is the language of one who pro-

[1] VI, 2908 (xxiv).

bably had often seen him,—like Atlas conscious that a world was on his shoulders. But the airs which he gave himself only heightened the respect and admiration which he inspired. His demeanour was regarded as a model. Scotchmen who wished to be thought wise looked as like Paterson as they could.[1]

Examples might be multiplied but these will suffice. The men pictured by Macaulay are not the grey shadows which figure in the pages of most historians, and therefore he succeeded in attracting readers whom they failed to interest.

The surroundings in which the events Macaulay narrated took place are described with equal vividness. He spared himself no labour in order to realise them, and he spares his readers no detail in order to make them see the scenes too. His first step, naturally, was to study the sites of battles or campaigns. Take as an example Sir George Trevelyan's account of the visit which Macaulay paid to Ireland in the summer of 1849.

The notes made during his fortnight's tour through the scenes of the Irish war are equal in bulk to a first-class article in the Edinburgh or Quarterly Reviews. He gives four closely-written folio pages to the Boyne, and six to Londonderry. It is interesting to compare the shape which each idea took as it arose in his mind with the shape in which he eventually gave it to the world. As he drove up the river from Drogheda he notices that 'the country looked like a flourishing part of England. Cornfields, gardens, woods, succeeded each other just as in Kent and Warwickshire.' And again: 'Handsome seats, fields of wheat and clover, noble trees:—it would be called a fine country even in Somersetshire.' In the sixteenth chapter of the History these hasty jottings have been transmuted into the sentences: 'Beneath lay a valley now so rich and so

[1] VI, 2910 (xxiv).

cheerful that an Englishman who gazes on it may imagine himself to be in one of the most highly favoured parts of his own highly favoured country. Fields of wheat, woodlands, meadows bright with daisies and clover, slope gently down to the edge of the Boyne.' [1]

Again, during the spring of 1852 Macaulay was writing an account of the plot to assassinate William III, which he relates in chapter xxi of the History. In his journal he notes: 'A cold 1st of May. After breakfast I went to Turnham Green, to look at the place. I found it after some search; the very spot beyond all doubt, and admirably suited for an assassination.' In the History he writes: 'The place was to be a narrow and winding lane leading from the landingplace on the north of the river to Turnham Green. The spot may still easily be found. The ground has since been drained by trenches. But in the seventeenth century it was a quagmire, through which the royal coach was with difficulty tugged at a foot's pace.' [2]

Many historians besides Macaulay have visited the sites of the great events they narrated. Carlyle examined the fields where Frederick the Great fought his battles; Mr. S. R. Gardiner was wont to follow on his bicycle the marches of Fairfax and Cromwell, and studied Drogheda as carefully as Macaulay did Londonderry. But the practice was not as common when Macaulay wrote his History as it is now. And further, Macaulay's peculiar gifts enabled him to put the results of his observations into a more picturesque form.

Perhaps the two best-known of these descriptive passages are those on the battlefield of Sedgemoor and the site of the Massacre of Glencoe.

[1] Trevelyan, ii. 219-20; cf. History, IV, 1870 (xvi).

[2] Trevelyan, ii. 302; History, V, 2594 (xxi).

Before the battle of Sedgemoor, Monmouth's army was encamped at Bridgewater, while the King's army lay on the plain some three miles away. Monmouth's attempts to reconnoitre the position of the opposing forces furnished an opportunity of which Macaulay skilfully avails himself.

> The steeple of the parish church of Bridgewater is said to be the loftiest in Somersetshire, and commands a wide view over the surrounding country. Monmouth, accompanied by some of his officers, went up to the top of the square tower from which the spire ascends, and observed through a telescope the position of the enemy. Beneath him lay a flat expanse, now rich with cornfields and apple trees, but then, as its name imports, for the most part a dreary morass.[1]

He goes on to describe in detail the natural features of the ground between the two armies, and then indicates the relative positions of the different villages in which the King's forces were quartered, and the character of the regiments who occupied them. At the end of the description he glides naturally into the story of the night march and the battle.

Another celebrated passage is the description of Glencoe. Taine quotes it at length as an example of Macaulay's skill.[2] After describing the conditions of the Highlands in 1691 and the difficulty which William's government experienced in its attempt to quiet the rebellious clans, Macaulay tells us that one of the smallest chiefs, Mac Ian of Glencoe, proved more intractable than great chiefs such as Lochiel and Glengarry. His country was more inaccessible.

> Mac Ian dwelt in the mouth of a ravine situated not far from the southern shore of Lochleven, an arm of the sea

[1] II, 592 (v). [2] Taine, v. 214.

which deeply indents the western coast of Scotland, and separated Argyleshire from Invernessshire. Near his house were two or three small hamlets inhabited by his tribe. The whole population which he governed was not supposed to exceed two hundred souls. In the neighbourhood of the little cluster of villages was some copsewood and some pasture land : but a little further up the defile no sign of population or of fruitfulness was to be seen. In the Gaelic tongue, Glencoe signifies the Glen of Weeping : and in truth that pass is the most dreary and melancholy of all the Scottish passes, the very Valley of the Shadow of Death. Mists and storms brood over it through the greater part of the finest summer ; and even on those rare days when the sun is bright, and when there is no cloud in the sky, the impression made by the landscape is sad and awful. The path lies along a stream which issues from the most sullen and gloomy of mountain pools. Huge precipices of naked stone frown on both sides. Even in July the streaks of snow may often be discerned in the rifts near the summits. All down the sides of the crags heaps of ruin mark the headlong paths of the torrents. Mile after mile the traveller looks in vain for the smoke of one hut, or for one human form wrapped in a plaid, and listens in vain for the bark of a shepherd's dog, or the bleat of a lamb. Mile after mile the only sound that indicates life is the faint cry of a bird of prey from some storm beaten pinnacle of rock. The progress of civilisation, which has turned so many wastes into fields yellow with harvests or gay with apple blossoms, has only made Glencoe more desolate. All the science and industry of a peaceful age can extract nothing valuable from that wilderness : but, in an age of violence and rapine, the wilderness itself was valued on account of the shelter which it afforded to the plunderer and his plunder. Nothing could be more natural than that the clan to which this rugged desert belonged should have been noted for predatory habits. For, among the Highlanders generally, to rob was thought at least as honourable an employment as to cultivate the soil ; and, of all the Highlanders, the Macdonalds of Glencoe had the least productive soil, and the most convenient and secure den of robbers.[1]

No one will dispute the vividness of this description, but several critics have denied its truth.[2] Macaulay, they say, in his account of the massacre, colours or mis-states certain material facts in order to exculpate William III at the expense of his instruments. And they argue that Macaulay heightens and exaggerates the barrenness and wildness of Glencoe in order to prove that its inhabitants must have been thieves. They quote an eighteenth-century writer who describes the valley as warm and fertile, full of singing birds and roes : ' it was always accounted (for its narrow bounds) a place of great plenty and security.'[3] Mr. Andrew Lang is particularly indignant.

It is intensely interesting and quite inexact. 'In the Gaelic tongue, Glencoe signifies the Glen of Weeping.' It signifies nothing of the sort. It is ' the very valley of the Shadow of Death '. It ought to be, but it is nothing of the kind. ' Mist and storms brood over it through the greater part of the finest summer! ' As a fact, the stream (the Coe) is usually almost as clear as a chalk stream. Through months of sunny days you see the sluggish salmon sheltering under the rocks at a depth of ten or twelve feet. The water is so transparent that you can watch their white lips lazily nibble at a worm if you descend to bait fishing. The stream ' issues from the most sullen and gloomy mountain pools '. In fact, it passes through a shallow reed-fringed lochan, full of tiny yellow trout ; it is more like ' casual water ' on the links after a wet day than a ' sullen and gloomy mountain pool '.[4]

[1] V, 2146-7 (xviii).

[2] John Paget, New Examen, in Paradoxes and Puzzles (1874), pp. 38-42.

[3] Mrs. Grant of Laggan, writing in 1773.

[4] Morning Post, Aug. 3, 1906.

Another description of Glencoe, by a third author, may be found in the pages of Stevenson's Kidnapped.[1] It was the 'prodigious valley, strewn with rocks', in which David Balfour and Alan Breck were tortured by heat and thirst while they hid from the soldiers for an endless summer's day. The fact is that landscapes, like the characters of men, take their colouring from the eye of the observer as much as from sun or cloud or changing seasons. Macaulay had something to prove. As Taine says, 'La description quoique fort belle, est écrite en style démonstratif. L'antithèse de la fin l'explique; l'auteur la fait pour montrer que les gens de Glencoe étaient les plus grands brigands du pays.'

[1] Chap. xx.

CHAPTER IV

MACAULAY'S USE OF AUTHORITIES

ONE characteristic of Macaulay's History is the air of certainty which pervades it. The facts it contains and the deductions from the facts are all set forth as positive and indisputable truths about which no doubt can exist. This was in keeping with Macaulay's character. He was not given to doubts about anything past or present. Lord Melbourne is reputed to have said that he wished he could be 'as cocksure about anything as Macaulay is about everything'. This is a dangerous temper for a historian, since it is difficult to be sure that a writer has before him the whole of the material for determining what took place two hundred and fifty years ago, and it is not always easy to ascertain the precise degree of credit to be attached to the evidence of any particular witness. Many of the greater facts are certain enough: many of the minor facts are much more uncertain: most of the details must always remain obscure. Sometimes the historian must be content with a relative not an absolute certainty. He is bound to indicate to his readers, if he is frank, that some of his statements are only probable, and some of his conclusions only provisional.

Macaulay neither recognises this truth himself, nor allows his readers to perceive it. A very acute critic, Walter Bagehot, points out this defect in the History, though he exaggerates the difficulty of ascertaining the facts.

You rarely come across anything which is not decided; and when you do come across it, you seem to wonder that the positiveness, which has accomplished so much, should have been unwilling to decide everything. This is hardly the style for history. The data of historical narratives, especially of modern histories, are a heap of confusion. No one can tell where they lie, or where they do not lie; what is in them, or what is not in them. . . . History is a vestige of vestiges; few facts leave any trace of themselves, any witness of their occurrence; of fewer still is that witness preserved . . . It is not possible that these data can be very fertile in certainties. Few people would make anything of them: a memoir here, a MS. there—two letters in a magazine—an assertion by a person whose veracity is denied,—these are the sort of evidence out of which a flowing narrative is to be educed; and of course it ought not to be too flowing. 'If you please, sir, tell me what you do *not* know,' was the inquiry of a humble pupil addressed to a great man of science. It would have been a relief to the readers of Macaulay if he had shown a little the outside of uncertainties, which there must be—the gradations of doubt, which there ought to be—the singular accumulation of difficulties, which must beset the extraction of a very easy narrative from the very confused materials.[1]

If Macaulay had expressed these doubts and shown these uncertainties, his book would not have been such a success with the general reader. The public likes to be told that the volume it is taking the trouble to read is all true, does not want to have the labour of distinguishing between hypotheses and facts, and is not in the least interested in the process by which the historian arrives at the truth. It demands a picture or a story. For students of history, however, the question how Macaulay got at his facts, and what right he had to be so certain about them, should be as interesting as the picture or the story. There-

[1] Walter Bagehot, Literary Studies (2 vols.; 1879), ii. 256.

fore, it is well to examine the authorities Macaulay used and consider how he employed them.

One can say this with perfect truth for Macaulay: he had a right to express himself with more certainty than previous historians because his narrative rested on a greater mass of evidence, a broader and more solid basis, and because he had taken more trouble than his predecessors to get at the truth. To say that he had before him when he wrote his account of James II twice as much evidence as Hume had, would be understating the case; and besides, the evidence Macaulay had before him was not only much greater in quantity but much better in quality, much more trustworthy. Part of it was entirely new evidence, and had not been accessible to previous historians. Of this new evidence some was brought to light by the researches of Macaulay himself, but he had the great advantage of finding much of the required new evidence assembled ready to his hand by the labours of other people.

The standard historian of the reign of James II, when Macaulay wrote, was Hume, whose narrative was a subtle apology for the Stuarts, and stopped short at the Revolution of 1688. Since his time, two historians had attempted to turn the tables by telling the story of the misrule of James from a Whig point of view, and by justifying the Revolution which overthrew him. One was Charles James Fox, whose history of the reign of James II, published posthumously in 1808 by Lord Holland, was a mere fragment ending with the execution of Monmouth in July 1685. The other was Sir James Mackintosh, whose History of the Revolution in England in 1688 appeared in 1834. That, too, was a fragment published a couple of years after the death of its author. Mackintosh had only carried the story down to June 1688 (the date of the birth of the Prince of Wales). His editor, Mr. Wallace, continued it to the accession of William III.

Fox's book had little historical value, but luckily Lord Holland printed in the appendix to his uncle's work the despatches written by Barillon, the French ambassador in England, during the year 1685. Fox had these letters copied from the originals in the Archives of the French Foreign Office, and had also obtained copies of other letters written by Barillon later in the reign of James II, and some by Bonrepaux, another diplomatist, sent by Louis XIV to England on a special mission. Quoting one of the latter, Macaulay says:

> It was transcribed for Mr. Fox from the French archives, during the peace of Amiens, and, with the other materials brought together by that great man, was entrusted to me by the kindness of the late Lady Holland, and of the present Lord Holland. I ought to add that, even in the midst of the troubles which have lately agitated Paris, I found no difficulty in obtaining, from the liberality of the functionaries there, extracts supplying some chasms in Mr. Fox's collection.[1]

To Mackintosh, Macaulay's obligations were much greater than to Fox. In the first place, Mackintosh's unfinished history was far better than that of Fox: it was, in fact, a really valuable and instructive bit of work, accurate, full of new information, and well written. It deserves a good deal of the praise which Macaulay gives to it in his essay on Mackintosh. Croker, in the hostile review which he wrote of Macaulay's History in the Quarterly, said that Macaulay copied Mackintosh, and endeavoured to conceal his obligations. That it not true

[1] I, 289 (iii). Extracts from French ambassadors' despatches were also available in F. A. J. Mazure's Histoire de la révolution de 1688 (3 vols.; 1825).

—on very many points the conclusions of the two agree, but the debt of the later to the earlier writer is much less than the reviewer asserts. Macaulay's debt to Mackintosh was of a different kind. Sir James had made a large collection of transcripts and extracts for the purposes of his history. These were freely placed at Macaulay's disposal. He says in a footnote:

> I take this opportunity of expressing my warm gratitude to the family of my dear and honoured friend Sir James Mackintosh for confiding to me the materials collected by him at a time when he meditated a work similar to that which I have undertaken. I have never seen, and I do not believe that there anywhere exists, within the same compass, so noble a collection of extracts from public and private archives. The judgment with which Sir James, in great masses of the rudest ore of history, selected what was valuable, and rejected what was worthless, can be fully appreciated only by one who has toiled after him in the same mine.[1]

Though this is a warm and generous acknowledgment, it does not state with sufficient precision the extent of Macaulay's obligations. Any reader who examines Macaulay's footnotes at all carefully can see what immense help the transcripts in the Mackintosh collection were to him. The whole collection has now found a resting-place in the British Museum.[2] It consists of forty volumes of papers, all dealing with the history of the period between 1688 and 1702. It is valuable not merely for its bulk, but for the systematic care with which the documents were selected. It contains a collection of newsletters for the years 1682 to 1688, twelve volumes of letters copied from the archives of the French Foreign Office, the letters of Cardinal Adda to Rome from 1685 to 1689, those of the

[1] I, 381-2 (iii). [2] Add. MSS. 34487-526.

Dutch and Spanish ambassadors in England for the same period, selections from the correspondence of the English ambassador in Paris between 1680 and 1688, and copies of the letters of William III to his confidants Bentinck and Heinsius. It was almost a complete collection of the materials necessary for writing the history of James II's reign, so far as they were supplied by the foreign archives accessible at that time, but the materials it afforded for the reign of William III were much smaller in quantity and by no means so complete. Thanks to this collection Macaulay, so far as the reign of James II is concerned, was spared much of the labour which ordinary historians have to do. He was not obliged to pay the long visits to foreign libraries and record offices which Froude and Gardiner had to undertake, and this saved time, toil, and money. He did supplement the material Mackintosh had collected for the reign of James II, but only slightly. For the reign of William III Mackintosh's materials were not sufficient: Macaulay had to research in foreign archives on his own account, and his narrative of that period naturally took a longer time to write. It cannot be too often repeated that the most original part of his History is the part relating to the reign of William III. The reign of James II was much better known: the reign of William III was comparatively untrodden ground, and at the same time it was much more difficult. England became the head of a great coalition and played a leading instead of a subordinate part in European politics. Thus the field Macaulay had to deal with grew wider, and the sources he had to consult in writing the history of William's policy grew more numerous. Owing to what may be termed the international position of William, and the fact that England, after being the stage on which European parties fought out their differences, became the head of one of those parties, diplomatic correspondence of every kind, for these particular years, is a source of much greater value than usual. It is well therefore to state roughly what the archives of different countries yielded.

Take France first. Barillon was ambassador from France throughout the whole reign of James II. As we have seen, Macaulay had in the Fox and Mackintosh collections copies of most of his letters and supplemented them by getting transcripts of others from the French Foreign Office. The despatches of Bonrepaux, an envoy employed in special missions in 1686 and 1688, he obtained in the same way. Then came the Revolution and the war with France. Diplomatic relations between England and France ceased, but since Louis recognised James II as the only lawful sovereign of England he sent an ambassador with James to Ireland, and the result was a series of letters which are of the greatest value to historians of the period.

The Count of Avaux was one of the ablest of the many able diplomatists in the service of Louis XIV. Macaulay devotes to him one of the full-length portraits in which he delights.[1] The Négociations d'Avaux, published in 1754, is full of information on the history of the struggle between the Prince of Orange and his great antagonist, and relates to the years 1679 to 1688, when Avaux was French ambassador at The Hague. Macaulay makes copious use of them, and states that the sagacity of Avaux detected all the plans of William, and in vain recommended a policy which would probably have frustrated them.[2] Avaux accompanied James to Ireland, and his letters hence during 1689 and 1690 are among Macaulay's chief sources for Irish history, especially for military events.[3] Some addi-

[1] III, 1462-4 (xii). [2] III, 1462. [3] See below, p. 216.

tional letters of Avaux were copied, for Macaulay's use, from the originals in the French Foreign Office, and he had also the letters of a certain Desgrigny who was employed in the commissariat,[1] though he missed those of Lauzun.

Of as great, if not of greater, value were the Dutch despatches. During the reign of James II events in England were of such importance to Dutch statesmen that accurate information on the subject was absolutely essential to them. They therefore sent their best diplomatists to England, not merely to negotiate but to observe and report. Macaulay, after referring to the despatches of Van Citters (the ambassador in England at the time of Charles II's death), adds the following note:

> As this is the first occasion on which I cite the correspondence of the Dutch ministers at the English court, I ought here to mention that a series of their despatches, from the accession of James the Second to his flight, forms one of the most valuable parts of the Mackintosh collection. The subsequent despatches, down to the settlement of the government in February 1689, I procured from the Hague. The Dutch archives have been far too little explored. They abound with information interesting in the highest degree to every Englishman. They are admirably arranged; and they are in the charge of gentlemen whose courtesy, liberality, and zeal for the interests of literature, cannot be too highly praised.[2]

In the period subsequent to 1693, Macaulay used, besides Dutch diplomatic correspondence, the letters of a French refugee, living in London, named L'Hermitage, who was employed by the Dutch government to supply it with intelligence of English affairs.

[1] IV, 1834 (xv). [2] I, 434 (iv).

His letters abound with curious and valuable information which is nowhere else to be found. His accounts of parliamentary proceedings are of peculiar value, and seem to have been so considered by his employers. . . . Copies of the despatches of L'Hermitage, and, indeed, of the despatches of all the ministers and agents employed by the States General in England from the time of Elizabeth downward, now are, or will soon be, in the library of the British Museum. For this valuable addition to the great national storehouse of knowledge, the country is chiefly indebted to Lord Palmerston.[1]

Of still greater significance from its intimate and confidential character is the correspondence between William III and Anthony Heinsius, who held the office of Pensionary of Holland. It covers the whole period from 1689 to 1702.

The original correspondence of William and Heinsius is in Dutch. A French translation of all William's letters, and an English translation of a few of Heinsius's letters, are among the Mackintosh MSS. The Baron Sirtema de Grovestins, who has had access to the originals, frequently quotes passages in his 'Histoire des luttes et rivalités entre les puissances maritimes et la France'. There is very little difference in substance, though much in phraseology, between his version and that which I have used.[2]

Spain, like Holland, was deeply interested in the foreign and domestic policy of James II, because it needed the support of England in its struggle against France. And since, by the formation of the Grand Alliance, it became the ally of William III in the war with Louis XIV, the question of

[1] V, 2368 (xx).

[2] III, 1373-4 (xi). Now published in the Third Series of the Archives ou correspondance inédite de la Maison d'Orange-Nassau, ed. F. J. L. Krämer (3 vols.; 1907-9).

the relations between William and his Parliament, and the progress of William's arms in Ireland, were not less important to it than to the Dutch. Consequently the despatches of the Spanish ambassador throughout the period from 1685 to 1702 supply information of value about domestic affairs as well as foreign relations. Pedro Ronquillo was the Spanish ambassador in England during James II's reign. A volume of the Mackintosh collection contained transcripts of a number of his despatches, and Macaulay obtained copies of others. At the opening of chapter iv of his History he quotes a letter of Ronquillo's to show that at the very beginning of James's reign the king was urged by Spain to keep on good terms with his people and Parliament. 'This despatch,' he adds, 'is in the archives of Simancas, which contain a great mass of papers relating to English affairs. Copies of the most interesting of those papers are in the possession of M. Guizot, and were by him lent to me. It is with peculiar pleasure that, at this time, I acknowledge this mark of the friendship of so great a man.'[1]

As to Italian diplomatic sources, Macaulay had copies of the letters of Count Adda (or Dada, as English contemporaries called him), the papal nuncio in England, but his footnotes contain no references to the letters of other Italian agents in England. The Relations of the Venetian ambassador who resided in England during the period were not printed till 1863. Ranke began his series of researches in the Venetian archives in 1830, but access to them was very difficult, and no Englishman was admitted to work there till 1850, when Rawdon Brown began his researches. The materials which they contained for the reigns of James II and William III were therefore not used

[1] I, 460 (iv).

by Macaulay.[1] Yet he seems to have attempted to obtain access to them in 1856. A letter from Abraham Hayward to Sir G. C. Lewis, dated September 21, 1856, says: 'I met Macaulay at Milan on his way to consult records at Venice.'[2] His visit to Venice is described in Trevelyan's Life,[3] but he does not seem to have worked in the archives. Armand Baschet, who was in Venice during these years, records that Macaulay 'vint en l'annee 1860 aux Archives de Venise, mais il ne fit que passer, il les regarda et s'en alla.'[4] Baschet is mistaken about the date.

There were in England during the reign of James II agents from Modena and Florence, of whose correspondence Macaulay knew nothing. Extracts from their letters were printed by the Marchesa Campana de Cavelli in 1871 in Les Derniers Stuarts à St. Germain en Laye. Moreover, the entire correspondence of the Florentine agent, Terriesi, has been transcribed and placed in the British Museum.[5] Two other states had representatives in England, during the reign of William III, whose correspondence Macaulay did not see. One was the Empire, which was represented by a number of ambassadors and agents whose despatches are quoted freely in Onno Klopp's History of the Fall of the House of Stuart. Owing to the close relations between England and Austria during the war of the Grand Alliance, these letters are a source of some importance for the history of William's foreign policy.

[1] There had been no ambassador from Venice since 1686. Sarotti, the Venetian secretary, left in May 1689, and Soranzo, the next Venetian ambassador, did not arrive till 1696.

[2] A Selection from the Correspondence of Abraham Hayward, ed. H. E. Carlisle (2 vols.; 1886), i. 294.

[3] ii. 406.

[4] Les Archives de Venise (1870), p. 101.

[5] Add. MSS. 25,358 et seq.

The other power referred to is Brandenburg. During the reign of William III the Elector of Brandenburg had in England an agent called Frederick Bonnet. His letters throw a great deal of light on the domestic politics of the period and are particularly valuable for their accounts of the proceedings in Parliament. Ranke, who esteemed them highly, prints a large number in the appendix to his sixth volume and uses them to supplement and correct Macaulay.

This general survey shows that Macaulay had at his disposal and employed a number of authorities not used by previous historians, and that he was therefore justified in asserting many facts with a certainty denied to his predecessors. On the other hand there were many diplomatic sources which he did not consult, because they were inaccessible or unknown to him, so that his successors have been able to correct him on a number of points, and a historian writing to-day has it in his power to attain a greater amount of certainty than Macaulay could. Macaulay's dogmatism implies a kind of blindness, a failure to recognise the inevitable progress of historical knowledge, a mistaken conviction that the whole of the necessary evidence was before him.

However, the business of the historian is not only to collect all the available materials but to make sure that he interprets the evidence rightly, for there is a great difference in the value of witnesses. The development of a more scientific method of treating historical evidence was one of the great achievements of the nineteenth century. Macaulay stands outside this historical movement. He does not weigh the value of the evidence he employs, with sufficient care, if he is judged by the standards of to-day. It is too much to say, as some people have done, that Macaulay is uncritical in his use of evidence: it is better to say that he is unscientific. Often he estimates the value of an authority extremely justly, and points out its defects with great acuteness, but he does not do so regularly and systematically. His attitude towards his authorities is a little too much that of the advocate who cross-examines hostile witnesses very severely, and tears their evidence to pieces, but is careful to ask no awkward questions of those who testify on behalf of his clients.

Of all the different classes of authorities none need more careful examination than memoirs and autobiographies, and personal narratives of every kind. The net result of the scientific movement in history has been greatly to reduce their value as evidence about historical transactions. Macaulay was well aware of the necessity of circumspection in using this kind of evidence; a story told in Trevelyan's Life illustrates this.

On the fragment of a letter to Mr. Ellis there is mention of a dream he had about his younger niece, 'so vivid that I must tell it. She came to me with a penitential face, and told me that she had a great sin to confess; that Pepys's Diary was all a forgery, and that she had forged it. I was in the greatest dismay. "What! I have been quoting in reviews, and in my History, a forgery of yours as a book of the highest authority. How shall I ever hold my head up again?"'[1]

Most of these authorities, therefore, Macaulay does examine with considerable care, and scattered through his notes are estimates of their value as a whole or of the value of some particular statements they contain. Take as examples, first his criticisms of two memoirs of minor value, and then his criticisms of two of first-rate impor-

[1] ii. 418.

tance. There is the autobiography of Major John Bernardi, who was imprisoned for his share in the Assassination Plot of 1696. Macaulay pronounces it 'not at all to be trusted. It contains some absurd mistakes, and some deliberate falsehoods.'[1] There is the Duchess of Marlborough's vindication of herself, which contains an account of her relations to Anne both before and after her accession, and much about the Duke's relations to William and Anne. This narrative, says Macaulay, 'is to be read with constant suspicion, except when, as is often the case, she relates some instance of her own malignity and insolence.' The Duchess, he asserts in another note, 'was so abandoned a liar that it is impossible to believe a word that she says, except when she accuses herself.' On the next page, he speaks of 'that habitual inaccuracy, which, even when she has no motive for lying, makes it necessary to read every word written or dictated by her with suspicion.' And finally 'she was indeed lamentably deficient in memory, a faculty which is proverbially said to be necessary to persons of the class to which she belonged.'[2] Evidently Macaulay had a certain animus against this witness: he does not sum up the value of her evidence like a judge, but like the counsel for the prosecution. It is rather like Serjeant Buzfuz on the witnesses for that monster Mr. Pickwick.

Take now two more authorities. One of Macaulay's chief authorities was naturally Burnet's History of My Own Time. In chapter vii Macaulay gives a long character of Burnet, pointing out his defects with great frankness, and by no means exaggerating his merits. In a footnote he discusses the question of Burnet's veracity, saying

[1] V, 2590 (xxi).

[2] V, 2127 (xviii); IV, 1819 (xv); V, 2126.

that even the Earl of Dartmouth, who wrote a number of critical notes on the History (printed in all the best editions of that work), did not accuse its author of wilful falsehood.

No person has contradicted Burnet more frequently or with more asperity than Dartmouth. Yet Dartmouth wrote, 'I do not think he designedly published anything he believed to be false.' At a later period Dartmouth, provoked by some remarks on himself in the second volume of the Bishop's history, retracted this praise: but to such a retraction little importance can be attached. Even Swift has the justice to say, 'After all, he was a man of generosity and good nature.'[1]

Macaulay points out in his notes a number of Burnet's errors. Of his account of the death of Thomas Dangerfield, Macaulay says 'Burnet's narrative contains more mistakes than lines.'[2] Again, speaking of the debates on the corporation bill in 1690: 'Burnet's narrative contains more blunders than lines. He evidently trusted to his memory, and was completely deceived by it.'[3] Sometimes, as he shows, Burnet confuses things. He confounds, for instance, two different versions of the abjuration bill.[4]

Nevertheless, in spite of these and other errors, the verdict of Macaulay is, on a view of the whole work, very favourable to Burnet.

It is usual to censure Burnet as a singularly inaccurate historian; but I believe the charge to be altogether unjust. He appears to be singularly inaccurate only because his narrative has been subjected to a scrutiny singularly severe and unfriendly. If any Whig thought it worth while to subject Reresby's Memoirs, North's Examen, Mulgrave's Account of the Revolution, or the Life of

[1] II, 826 (vii).
[2] I, 484 (iv).
[3] IV, 1783 (xv).
[4] IV, 1825 (xv).

James the Second, to a similar scrutiny, it would soon appear that Burnet was far indeed from being the most inexact writer of his time.[1]

In any attempt to estimate the value of a statement in the History of My Own Time, it is necessary to compare the printed version with the original version, written many years earlier, most of which has been preserved. This Macaulay did not fail to do, and he seems to have been the first historian to use the original version to check the other. He terms the original version 'some memoirs written soon after the Revolution', and describes it as follows :

These memoirs will be found in a manuscript volume, which is part of the Harleian Collection, and is numbered 6584. They are, in fact, the first outlines of a great part of Burnet's History of His Own Times. The dates at which the different portions of this most curious and interesting book were composed are marked. Almost the whole was written before the death of Mary. Burnet did not begin to prepare his History of William's Reign for the press till ten years later. By that time his opinions, both of men and of things, had undergone considerable changes. The value of the rough draft is therefore very great : for it contains some facts which he afterwards thought it advisable to suppress, and some judgments which he afterwards saw cause to alter. I must own that I generally like his first thoughts best. Whenever his History is reprinted, it ought to be carefully collated with this volume.[2]

In the interval between the writing of the two versions, Burnet had changed his opinion on many points, both as to men and measures. For instance, as Macaulay points out, he inserted in the first narrative 'an animated panegyric'

[1] II, 826 (vii).

[2] III, 1329-30 (xi). These memories were edited by Miss H. C. Foxcroft and published in 1902 as A Supplement to Burnet's History of My Own Time.

on Walker, the minister who played so large a part in the defence of Londonderry.[1] This he omitted in the second narrative because he thought Walker's merits had been exaggerated. But the most remarkable discrepancy occurs in Burnet's remarks about Marlborough. In the original narrative Burnet frankly stated the reasons for Marlborough's disgrace in 1692. 'The King said to myself upon it that he had very good reason to believe that he had made his peace with King James, and was engaged in a correspondence with France. It was certain he was doing all he could to set on a faction in the army and the nation against the Dutch.' Now, in the published version Burnet suppresses these facts. 'It is curious,' comments Macaulay, 'to compare this plain tale, told when the facts were recent, with the shuffling narrative which Burnet prepared for the public eye many years later, when Marlborough was closely united to the Whigs, and was rendering great and splendid services to the country.'[2]

Another authority much used by Macaulay was the Life of James the Second. Extracts from it were published in 1775 by Macpherson in his Original Papers, and the work itself was printed by J. S. Clarke in 1816. It was a compilation based on autobiographical memoirs written by James himself. The original perished in the French Revolution.[3] This is a very unequal work. Parts of it are of the greatest value, parts of it are worthless. Macaulay pronounces the following verdict upon it:

Several critics have complained that I treat the Saint Germains Life of James the Second sometimes as a work of

[1] IV, 1768 (xv).

[2] V, 2126 (xviii).

[3] Preface to Fox's A History of the Early Part of the Reign of James the Second (1808).

the highest authority, and sometimes as a mere romance. They seem to imagine that the book is all from the same hand, and ought either to be uniformly quoted with respect or uniformly thrown aside with contempt. The truth is that part of the Life is of the very highest authority, and that the rest is the work of an ignorant and silly compiler, and is of no more value than any common Jacobite pamphlet. Those passages which were copied from the Memoirs written by James, and those passages which were carefully revised by his son, are among the most useful materials for history. They contain the testimony of witnesses, who were undoubtedly under a strong bias, and for whose bias large allowance ought to be made, but who had the best opportunities of learning the truth. The interstices between these precious portions of the narrative are sometimes filled with trash. Whoever will take the trouble to examine the references in my notes will see that I have constantly borne in mind the distinction which I have now pointed out. Surely I may cite, as of high authority, an account of the last moments of Charles the Second, which was written by his brother, or an account of the plottings of Penn, of Dartmouth, and of Churchill, which was corrected by the hand of the Pretender, and yet may, with perfect consistency, reject the fables of a nameless scribbler who makes Argyle, with all his cavalry, swim across the Clyde at a place where the Clyde is more than four miles wide.[1]

In another note, he completes this criticism of the Argyle episode. 'The account of the Scotch rebellion in the Life of James the Second is a ridiculous romance, not written by the King himself, nor derived from his papers, but composed by a Jacobite who did not even take the trouble to look at a map of the seat of war.'[2] It is equally untrustworthy, he says, with regard to what happened in Ireland after James himself left it. 'The account

[1] III, 1207 (x). [2] II, 558 (v).

of this attack [on Athlone] in the Life of James, II. 453, is an absurd romance. It does not appear to have been taken from the King's original Memoirs or to have been revised by his son.'[1] Often, too, the documents printed in the Life are garbled.[2] On the other hand, on such a matter as the treasonable relations of some of William's ministers with the exiled king, the Life of James the Second is cited by Macaulay as an authority of the highest value.[3] He also cites it to prove that James was cognisant of the plot to assassinate William in 1696.[4]

Macaulay's employment of Burnet's History and the Life of James shows that he had a just appreciation of the general value of these works, and his criticisms of certain passages show great acuteness. But compared with the modern scientific historian he treats his authorities in a rather superficial fashion. To see this it is only necessary to read the two elaborate studies on Burnet and the Life of James the Second which are contained in the appendix to Volume VI of Ranke's History of England. The German historian, before using either authority, submitted it as a whole to a minute and careful analysis in order to find out how it was put together and exactly what its value was. A rough estimate of its value is not enough : the materials must be carefully weighed and examined that the trustworthiness or falsehood of any statement can be precisely determined. In this way alone can the greatest measure of certainty be obtained by the historian. Further, the process by which the result is arrived at must be made public in order that other historians may estimate the correctness of the process and the justice of the conclusions. A more

[1] IV, 2046 (xvii).

[2] III, 1290 (x), 1480 (xii) ; V, 2608 (xxi).

[3] IV, 1989, 2019 (xvii) ; V, 2444 (xx).

[4] V, 2596, 2608 (xxi).

detailed and systematic examination of the authorities would have saved Macaulay from some serious errors.

Two other classes of authorities must be more briefly treated—namely, the mass of official papers, illustrating the administrative and executive government of the time, which may be generally described as domestic state papers. Macaulay had practically no new information about the debates which took place in Parliament: he used reports of those debates which were already in print, adding here and there a little information from memoirs or letters or foreign despatches. These reports had been very little used, and as the existing histories of William III's reign were obsolete or unreadable, his animated account of proceedings in Parliament had all the air of novelty to his readers. However, he had one set of documents, illustrating parliamentary affairs, which had never been employed by any previous historian, and never printed—namely, the papers of the House of Lords. Papers relating to the proceedings of Parliament tended to be preserved in the archives of the Lords rather than the Commons, because the Lords made it a rule to insist on seeing the originals of communications laid before Parliament and declined to accept copies. Hence many papers which properly should have found their way into the archives of the Lower House are now in those of the Lords. Moreover, bills which failed to pass and amendments not accepted accumulated there, too, till a vast mass of papers for the political and economic history of the seventeenth and eighteenth centuries was brought together. In chapter xi, when Macaulay describes the legislation which followed the Revolution, he mentions the fate of the comprehension bill, which marked the failure of the last effort to bring the Presbyterians within the fold of the Church.

The Toleration Act passed but the comprehension bill failed.

About the same time at which the Toleration Bill became law with the general concurrence of public men, the Comprehension Bill was, with a concurrence not less general, suffered to drop. The Toleration Bill still ranks among those great statutes which are epochs in our constitutional history. The Comprehension Bill is forgotten. No collector of antiquities has thought it worth preserving. A single copy, the same which Nottingham presented to the Peers, is still among our parliamentary records, but has been seen by only two or three persons now living. It is a fortunate circumstance, that, in this copy, almost the whole history of the Bill can be read. In spite of cancellations and interlineations, the original words can easily be distinguished from those which were inserted in the committee or on the report. . . . The bill will be found among the Archives of the House of Lords. It is strange that this vast collection of important documents should have been altogether neglected, even by our most exact and diligent historians. It was opened to me by one of the most valued of my friends, Mr. John Lefevre; and my researches were greatly assisted by the kindness of Mr. Thoms.[1]

This large collection of papers has now been calendared as far as 1710, partly in the reports published by the Historical Manuscripts Commission, partly in the separate volumes published by the House of Lords itself.

Macaulay also used the records of the Privy Council, though to only a slight extent, and, more systematically, the Treasury records. A modern reader, however, misses in his footnotes one reference which he expects to find in all historical works. There is no mention of the Public Record Office, or of documents derived from it. On the

[1] III, 1394-5 (xi).

other hand, there is an occasional reference to the State Paper Office, or to some paper copied from an original in that repository. The explanation of this is very simple. The modern Record Office with all its facilities for research did not exist in Macaulay's time. The building of the present Record Office in Fetter Lane began only in 1851 and it was not till 1859 that the documents now collected there were brought under one roof. Before that date, the records proper—mainly mediaeval or Tudor documents—were in a number of temporary repositories under different authorities. Not till 1837 was the act passed by which they were all placed under the custody of the Master of the Rolls. The more modern documents roughly described as state papers, running from the time of Queen Elizabeth to the eighteenth century and later, were collected in the office known as the State Paper Office, which had been established by Elizabeth in 1578. When Macaulay wrote, they were housed in a building near St. James's Park. In 1854 this separate office was abolished. The papers it contained were placed under the jurisdiction of the Master of the Rolls and transferred in 1862 to the Record Office, thus completing the great collection now accessible in Fetter Lane.

Macaulay's position would have secured him, or did secure him, free access to the documents in the State Paper Office. But there is no evidence that he made much investigation of them. Generally he seems to have contented himself with using the transcripts of papers there which Mackintosh had collected, or the versions of them published in printed books. The modern calendars which do so much to facilitate research did not exist. The first volume of the Calendars of Domestic State Papers was published in 1856. As yet no calendar of the documents of the reign of James II has even been commenced, and that for the reign of William III, commenced in 1895, has reached (1933) 1698. Nor was there in existence then any calendar of the Colonial State Papers.

Thus Macaulay had not at his disposal many documents which are easily accessible to the historians of to-day. Even when they were accessible they were not arranged, catalogued, or calendared so as to make the task of using them as comparatively easy as it is at the present time.

Then, as now, there were outside the Record Office a number of collections of letters and some memoirs or autobiographies in private hands, generally in the possession of descendants of the persons who wrote them. Macaulay's reputation secured him access to many of these collections, and as soon as it was known that he was writing a history of the Revolution people placed at his disposal manuscripts bearing on the time, and librarians hastened to throw open their stores. Dr. Vignoles, the Dean of Ossory, lent him the autobiography of a Huguenot refugee, named Dumont de Bostaquet, who accompanied William of Orange in his voyage to England and fought under him at the battle of the Boyne.[1] Mr. Phippard let him use the manuscript narrative of John Coad, one of Monmouth's followers, who was tried by Jeffreys and transported to Jamaica.[2] Lord Lansdowne allowed him to see some of Prior's papers, Lord Lonsdale some written by his ancestor, Sir John Lowther, who played an important part in William's reign.[3]

[1] IV, 1679 (xiv). Published in 1864 as Mémoires inédits, ed. C. Read and F. Waddington.

[2] II, 640 (v). Published in 1849 as A Memorandum of the Wonderful Providence of God.

[3] III, 1356 (xi).

All these were surpassed in importance by the confidential correspondence of William III with Bentinck, which was in the possession of the Duke of Portland. Macaulay used transcripts of these letters made for Sir James Mackintosh, not the originals, as he owns at the beginning of chapter vii.[1] The papers of Robert Harley, also in the Duke of Portland's possession, Macaulay does not appear to have used, with the exception of one or two copied for Mackintosh.[2] These papers have since been published by the Historical Manuscripts Commission.[3] That commission, appointed to give an account of the collections of papers, in private hands, which relate to public affairs, was not established till 1869. In those reports there is a mass of material, relating to the period, which was not accessible in 1848 or 1856. To compare Macaulay's narrative with the evidence contained in the reports of the Commission and the Calendars issued by the Record Office is one of the tasks which modern historians should undertake. In some cases the result of this examination and comparison would alter his narrative; in some, supplement it; in most, confirm it.

Mr. Gladstone in his essay on Macaulay gave vent to a wish many have shared: 'We sometimes fancy that ere long there will be editions of his work in which his readers may be saved from pitfalls by brief, respectful, judicious commentary, and that his great achievements may be at once commemorated and corrected by men of slower pace, of drier light, and more tranquil, broad-set and com-

[1] II, 811 (vii). These letters were published as Correspondentie van Willem III en van Hans Willem Bentinck, ed. N. Japikse (2 vols.; 1927-8).

[2] V, 2406 (xx).

[3] The Manuscripts of the Duke of Portland (9 vols.; 1891-1923). The papers of Robert Harley are mainly in vols. iii-v. Other papers are in the Manuscripts of the Marquis of Bath, vols. i and ii (1904-7).

prehensive judgment.' Such an edition would have another advantage, because it would save the time of readers who desired to examine Macaulay's sources. In his method, or lack of method, of citing authorities, Macaulay is not a model to be followed. Some people have laughed at one of his characteristic phrases. In chapter iii he says: 'My notion of the country gentleman of the seventeenth century has been derived from sources too numerous to be recapitulated. I must leave my description to the judgment of those who have studied the history and the lighter literature of that age.' [1] In chapter xi he states in a note: 'Here, and in many other places, I abstain from citing authorities, because my authorities are too numerous to cite. My notions of the temper and relative position of political and religious parties in the reign of William the Third, have been derived, not from any single work, but from thousands of forgotten tracts, sermons, and satires; in fact, from a whole literature which is mouldering in old libraries.' [2] He repeats the phrase elsewhere.[3] This however is perfectly legitimate. It is absurd to expect a historian to cite authorities whenever he states the impression he has derived from the whole mass of facts which have come under his notice. His footnotes would be a monstrous list of titles if he did so. Macaulay is blameworthy however in that, when he refers to books for definite facts, he very often fails to state where the passage on which he bases his statement is to be found, and does not cite page or volume or edition. Often he quotes a letter without giving its date or any indication which enables a reader to find the context of the passage. He is capable of citing in the same footnote, Evelyn's Diary with

[1] I, 313 (iii). [2] III, 1324 (xi).
[3] I, 360 (iii).

the date of the entry referred to, and Luttrell's Brief Historical Relation without it. There seems to be quite a chance whether he remembers to give an exact reference or not: no rule can be inferred from his practice. Mr. Andrew Lang commented on the subject as follows:

Monsieur Henri Taine has elaborately traced the methods by which Macaulay made his History so interesting, and to be interesting is a very rare quality in an English writer, says the unprejudiced Frenchman. I think that he overlooks Macaulay's method of reference to his authorities. I open Macaulay at random, in volume I p. 309 (1866). He has a footnote to the remark that, in 1685, 'it was not thought by any means necessary that a divine should be able to read the Gospels in the original Greek.' How does he know that? I expect the footnote to give his proofs with volume and page. But Macaulay only says that 'Roger North tells us, that his brother John, a Greek professor, complained of the general neglect of Greek by the academical clergy'. This is nearly as vague as what Dr. Johnson was once heard muttering to himself. 'Pennant tells us concerning bears . . .' The public likes the vague. . . . For a fact about constitutional etiquette Macaulay offers this useful reference 'See particularly Harrington's Oceana' a work of oceanic dimensions, into which we are to dive without compass. Next North's Life of Guilford is cited in the vague. Barillon and Burnet are quoted, sometimes with no more serviceable minuteness; and sometimes . . . when an important statement is made, there is actually no reference to any authority. At other times strings of references are given with laudable minuteness. It is much to be desired that an able editor should annotate the whole book in this manner even at the risk of making Macaulay uninteresting.[1]

There is at present only one edition of Macaulay's History (in one volume, published in 1907) which attempts to

[1] Morning Post, Aug. 3, 1906.

supply this need. It is edited by Mr. T. F. Henderson, and his notes are numerous and useful, though hardly sufficient. There is still room for an editor who will perform for Macaulay the same office that Professor Bury so admirably executed for Gibbon.

CHAPTER V

MACAULAY'S USE OF LITERATURE

STATE papers, memoirs, and the correspondence of kings and ministers are not the only materials which a modern historian requires. They must be supplemented by unofficial documents of various kinds, but above all by the mass of printed matter, in prose and verse, in which the common ideas and the daily life of a nation find expression, and where small as well as great events are recorded. No one realised this better than Macaulay; he had the great advantage of dealing with a period for which materials of this kind were abundant and easily accessible, without being absolutely overwhelming in their bulk.

One of the characteristics of the History is the extent to which Macaulay uses contemporary newspapers. No English historian before him had devoted much attention to them. Excepting S. R. Gardiner no later historian has so systematically employed this kind of authority. 'There is a noble, and, I suppose, unique Collection of the newspapers of William's reign in the British Museum,' says Macaulay. 'I have turned over,' he adds, 'every page of that Collection.'[1] As a source of historical information, newspapers are far more valuable for William's reign than for the reigns of Charles II or James II. In a well-known passage in chapter iii Macaulay describes what newspapers were at the earlier date. Excepting for the period of the Popish Plot agitation, 1679-1681, they were under

[1] V, 2544, n. (xxi).

such a rigid censorship that they did not dare to print political information of any value.

During the great battle of the Exclusion Bill, many newspapers were suffered to appear, the Protestant Intelligence, the Current Intelligence, the Domestic Intelligence, the True News, the London Mercury. None of these was published oftener than twice a week. None exceeded in size a single small leaf. The quantity of matter which one of them contained in a year was not more than is often found in two numbers of the Times. After the defeat of the Whigs it was no longer necessary for the King to be sparing in the use of that which all his Judges had pronounced to be his undoubted prerogative. At the close of his reign no newspaper was suffered to appear without his allowance and his allowance was given exclusively to the London Gazette. The London Gazette came out only on Mondays and Thursdays. The contents generally were a royal proclamation, two or three Tory addresses, notices of two or three promotions, an account of a skirmish between the imperial troops and the Janissaries on the Danube, a description of a highwayman, an announcement of a grand cockfight between two persons of honour, and an advertisement offering a reward for a strayed dog. The whole made up two pages of moderate size. Whatever was communicated respecting matters of the highest moment was communicated in the most meagre and formal style. Sometimes, indeed, when the government was disposed to gratify the public curiosity respecting an important transaction, a broadside was put forth giving fuller details than could be found in the Gazette: but neither the Gazette not any supplementary broadside printed by authority ever contained any intelligence which it did not suit the purposes of the Court to publish. The most important parliamentary debates, the most important state trials, recorded in our history, were passed over in profound silence.[1]

[1] I, 380 (iii).

The government used the Gazette to publish what political news it thought desirable. But even under the reign of William the Gazette was not much to be relied upon. Describing at length the sufferings of Schomberg's army in Ireland during 1689 Macaulay says: 'The lying of the London Gazette is monstrous. Through the whole autumn the troops are constantly said to be in good condition.'[1] Unofficial journals were prevented by the restrictions of the censorship from publishing news disagreeable to the government. After the expiration of the Licensing Act in 1695, the newspapers became gradually more independent, and in consequence contain at once more news and more truth, but it was a long time before they ventured to comment freely on public affairs and exerted much influence on the formation of public opinion.[2]

The deficiencies of the newspapers were supplied to some extent by the newsletters circulated in manuscript. Of them Macaulay gives the following account:

The newswriter rambled from coffee room to coffee room, collecting reports, squeezed himself into the Sessions House at the Old Bailey if there was an interesting trial, nay, perhaps obtained admission to the gallery of Whitehall, and noticed how the King and Duke looked. In this way he gathered materials for weekly epistles destined to enlighten some country town or some bench of rustic magistrates. Such were the sources from which the inhabitants of the largest provincial cities, and the great body of the gentry and clergy, learned almost all that they knew of the history of their own time. . . . At the seat of a man of fortune in the country the newsletter was impatiently expected. Within a week after it had arrived it had been thumbed by twenty families. It furnished the neighbouring squires with matter for talk over their

[1] IV, 1694 (xiv). [2] V, 2540-4 (xxi).

October, and the neighbouring rectors with topics for sharp sermons against Whiggery or Popery. Many of these curious journals might doubtless still be detected by a diligent search in the archives of old families. Some are to be found in our public libraries; and one series, which is not the least valuable part of the literary treasures collected by Sir James Mackintosh, will be occasionally quoted in the course of this work.[1]

Besides this collection of Sir James Mackintosh, which contains copies of newsletters for the period 1682 to 1688, Macaulay had access to a number of newsletters in the Library of the Royal Institution [2] and to some elsewhere.

One of the authorities of which mention is most often made in Macaulay's notes is Narcissus Luttrell's Diary. This is a compilation based on the newsletters and newspapers of the period, containing many extracts from them, sometimes given at great length, sometimes abridged. Additional information was probably added by the compiler himself, but the work is not a diary in the ordinary sense of the word, for it contains nothing relating to Luttrell personally and is simply a number of items of information about public events, arranged under days. Macaulay speaks of it thus:

A copy of this Diary, from July 1685 to Sept. 1690, is among the Mackintosh papers. To the rest I was allowed access by the kindness of the Warden of All Souls' College, where the original MS. is deposited. The Delegates of the Press of the University of Oxford have since published

[1] I, 381 (iii).

[2] In 1890 the Historical Manuscripts Commission, in a report on the Manuscripts of S. K. Le Fleming of Rydal Hall, printed a valuable collection of newsletters concerning the reigns of James II and William III. Others are contained in Lady Newdigate-Newdegate's Cavalier and Puritan (1901). For 1686-8 there is The Ellis Correspondence, ed. J. J. W. Agar-Ellis, Lord Dover (2 vols.; 1829).

the whole, in six substantial volumes, which will, I am afraid, find little favour with readers who seek only for amusement, but which will always be useful as materials for history.[1]

While newspapers and newsletters are valuable as records of facts, they are inferior to pamphlets as records of opinion, for the political controversies of the time were conducted by pamphleteers of the two parties. There are few historians who have employed the political pamphlets of the period they treat, so constantly and so exhaustively as Macaulay. It is true that earlier historians, such as Kennet, Oldmixon, Ralph, and others, made great use of pamphlets, but they did so largely because the more trustworthy materials such as papers of state and official correspondence were inaccessible at the time when they wrote. Macaulay was able to combine both classes of material.

The pamphlets of the seventeenth century are a mass of historical evidence of very variable and uncertain value. Amongst them there are a number of narratives of fact, relations by eyewitnesses describing historical events, letters, autobiographical narratives of every kind; all these, after due allowance has been made for the personal equation, are evidence of first-rate value. As an instance one might mention the narratives of the various campaigns in Flanders, drawn up by Edward d'Auvergne, a chaplain in the army, to which Macaulay continually refers. Other examples are the Marquis of Caermarthen's Journal of the Brest Expedition (1694), Hamilton's A True Relation of the Actions of the Inniskilling-Men (1690), and Walker's True Account of the Siege of London-Derry (1689). Pamphlets of this kind are just as valuable as memoirs or contemporary history.

[1] II, 612, n. 2 (v).

However, the largest class of pamphlets consists of the controversial tracts in which representatives of some party or section of a party set forth their views on the political situation, or on some particular measure which was before the country, or on the principles of politics in general. These Macaulay uses with great skill as evidence of the feelings and opinions of the people about public questions, and his usual method is to summarise in a rhetorical form the arguments brought forward on either side. The best examples of this are: the arguments for and against requiring the clergy to take an oath of fealty to William and Mary—a measure which led to the non-juring schism; [1] the summary of the arguments for and against opening the East India trade; [2] the account of the 'literary conflict' about the maintenance of a standing army.[3]

It is obvious that all these controversial publications are better evidence for feelings and opinions than for facts, and Macaulay was very well aware of it. More than once he points out the untrustworthiness of the pamphlets as evidence against the government of William III. Discussing the effect of the cessation of the censorship in 1695 he says:

> The pamphleteers were under less restraint than the journalists: yet no person who has studied with attention the political controversies of that time can have failed to perceive that the libels on William's person and government were decidedly less coarse and rancorous during the latter half of his reign than during the earlier half. And the reason evidently is that the press, which had been fettered during the earlier half of his reign, was free during the latter half. While the censorship existed, no tract blaming, even in the most temperate and decorous language, the conduct of any public department, was likely to

[1] IV, 1707-13 (xiv). [2] V, 2106-10 (xviii).
[3] VI, 2736-42 (xxiii).

be printed with the approbation of the licenser. To print such a tract without the approbation of the licenser was illegal. In general, therefore, the respectable and moderate opponents of the Court, not being able to publish in the manner prescribed by law, and not thinking it right or safe to publish in a manner prohibited by law, held their peace, and left the business of criticising the administration to two classes of men, fanatical nonjurors who hated the ruling powers with an insane hatred, and Grub Street hacks, coarseminded, badhearted, and foulmouthed.[1]

On the other hand 'the emancipation of the press produced a great and salutary change. The best and wisest men in the ranks of the opposition now assumed an office which had hitherto been abandoned to the unprincipled or the hotheaded. Tracts against the government were written in a style not misbecoming statesmen and gentlemen ; and even the compositions of the lower and fiercer class of malcontents became somewhat less brutal and less ribald than formerly.'[2]

However, at the beginning of the reign, when party feeling was highest and the censorship was in force, the Jacobite pamphleteers, says Macaulay, 'were, as a class, savagely malignant and utterly regardless of truth.'[3] Everybody knew it and attached little credit to what they wrote. For instance, when they related the story of the massacre of Glencoe, people in England did not believe them. 'The habitual mendacity of the Jacobite libellers had brought on them an appropriate punishment. Now, when, for the first time, they told the truth, they were supposed to be romancing. They complained bitterly that the story, though perfectly authentic, was regarded by the public as a factious lie.'[4]

[1] V, 2544-6 (xxi). [2] Ibid.
[3] V, 2327 (xix). [4] V, 2166 (xviii).

It is natural, argues Macaulay, that William III should not believe the charges which were circulated by these writers against the Master of Stair about the massacre of Glencoe.

> We can hardly suppose that he was much in the habit of reading Jacobite pamphlets; and, if he did read them, he would have found in them such a quantity of absurd and rancorous invective against himself that he would have been very little inclined to credit any imputation which they might throw on his servants. He would have seen himself accused, in one tract, of being a concealed Papist, in another of having poisoned Jeffreys in the Tower, in a third of having contrived to have Talmash taken off at Brest. He would have seen it asserted that, in Ireland, he once ordered fifty of his wounded English soldiers to be burned alive. He would have seen that the unalterable affection which he felt from his boyhood to his death for three or four of the bravest and most trusty friends that ever prince had the happiness to possess was made a ground for imputing to him abominations as foul as those which are buried under the waters of the Dead Sea. He might naturally be slow to believe frightful imputations thrown by writers whom he knew to be habitual liars on a statesman whose abilities he valued highly, and to whose exertions he had, on some great occasions, owed much.[1]

While the evidence of the Jacobite pamphleteers is dismissed as unworthy of belief when they make statements against William, and William was justified in rejecting it when they made charges against the Master of Stair, Macaulay invites his readers to accept it when they make certain statements against Marlborough. Speaking of the campaign in Flanders in 1689 and of Marlborough's victory at Walcourt he says:

> The Jacobites however discovered in the events of the campaign abundant matter for invective. Marlborough

[1] V, 2513 (xxi).

was, not without reason, the object of their bitterest hatred. In his behaviour on a field of battle malice itself could find little to censure: but there were other parts of his conduct which presented a fair mark for obloquy. Avarice is rarely the vice of a young man: it is rarely the vice of a great man: but Marlborough was one of the few who have, in the bloom of youth, loved lucre more than wine or women, and who have, at the height of greatness, loved lucre more than power or fame. All the precious gifts which nature had lavished on him he valued chiefly for what they would fetch. At twenty he made money of his beauty and his vigour. At sixty he made money of his genius and his glory. The applauses which were justly due to his conduct at Walcourt could not altogether drown the voices of those who muttered that, whenever a broad piece was to be saved or got, this hero was a mere Euclio, a mere Harpagon; that, though he drew a large allowance under pretence of keeping a public table, he never asked an officer to dinner; that his muster rolls were fraudulently made up; that he pocketed pay in the names of men who had long been dead, of men who had been killed in his own sight four years before at Sedgemoor; that there were twenty such names in one troop; that there were thirty-six in another. Nothing but the union of dauntless courage and commanding powers of mind with a bland temper and winning manners could have enabled him to gain and keep, in spite of faults eminently unsoldierlike, the good will of his soldiers.[1]

The authority given in the note is 'See the Dear Bargain a Jacobite pamphlet clandestinely printed in 1690.' Anyone who likes can see the Dear Bargain; it is reprinted in the Somers Tracts.[2] The reader will find there charges of just the same kind against William. For instance the pamphleteer accuses him of contriving the death of English soldiers in his army by sending them to

[1] IV, 1702-4 (xiv). [2] X, 349-77.

die of starvation and disease in Holland, where, he goes on to say, 'you might see them sprawling by parcels, and groaning under the double gripes of their bowels and their consciences,' all in order that 'the Dutch, the Danes and other foreigners . . . may possess our country '.[1]

The question the critic of Macaulay has to solve is this: Why does he admit evidence against Marlborough which he would not admit against William? The justice of the character of Marlborough which Macaulay draws in his History is one of those much controverted questions which will require separate and more detailed discussion. Here all that is necessary to observe is that while Macaulay formed a right estimate of the value of a particular class of evidence he did not consistently carry out his own critical principles. When his personal prejudices came into play his vigilance relaxed.

There are pamphlets of another kind which Macaulay employs in a more legitimate fashion; some of them indeed can hardly be called pamphlets. A large amount of ephemeral literature existed which was devoted to describing the social life of the time. Some of it was in verse, some in prose; it mingled fact and fiction; its authors were humourists who sought to amuse their contemporaries by realistic descriptions of low life and sketches of everyday characters; it contributed its share to the development of the novel, and the social essay. Most of the authors of this literature have long been forgotten by all except book collectors, and booksellers class their writings under the general heading of 'Facetiae'. Of these writers Tom Brown and Ned Ward were typical examples. Macaulay used them both. Speaking for instance of the rebuilding of St. Paul's, he says: 'There is

[1] Ibid. pp. 360-1.

an account of the works at Saint Paul's in Ward's London Spy. I am almost ashamed to quote such nauseous balderdash; but I have been forced to descend even lower, if possible, in search of materials.'[1] Tom Brown was a cleverer and better educated writer than Ward, and his works are still readable. Him Macaulay cites to describe the fashion in which criminals were whipped at the cart's tail[2] and to show why the Presbyterian divines of 1689 were not eager for the success of the comprehension bill.[3] In discussing the state of the coinage in 1695 he refers to 'a facetious story, which I do not venture to quote', told by Brown 'about a conversation between the ordinary of Newgate and a clipper'.[4] In describing the distress which prevailed in England in 1693 he takes an illustration of its prevalence from Brown. 'An idle man of wit and pleasure, who little thought that his buffoonery would ever be cited to illustrate the history of his times, complained that, in this year, wine ceased to be put on many hospitable tables where he had been accustomed to see it, and that its place was supplied by punch.'[5]

Any printed stuff of the period was of value to Macaulay, if it threw the smallest light on the topic he was dealing with, and could furnish a touch or a detail for his pictures. Nothing, however, could be of so much use as the dramatic literature of the time, since the object of the stage was to represent men and manners, and its representation of both had been accepted as true by the time itself. There are periods in the history of the stage when the dramas produced have had a direct bearing on contemporary politics. During part of the reign of Charles II—during the national

[1] I, 340, n. (iii).
[2] I, 418 (iii).
[3] III, 1400, n. (xi).
[4] V, 2252 (xix).
[5] V, 2565, n. (xxi).

excitement about the Popish Plot and the exclusion bill—many plays were acted in which the party principles and the party leaders of the day were assailed or defended. But under James II and William III the government was too strong to permit this, and playwrights had to limit themselves to the representation of social types and social phenomena. It is in order to reproduce that side of the life of the age that Macaulay employed the drama. It is therefore to two plays of Shadwell's, The Squire of Alsatia [1] and The Scourers, that he refers as authorities when he is describing the low life in London, and to Farquhar's Beaux' Stratagem as evidence that highwaymen could mix in good society.[2] He goes to Farquhar's Trip to the Jubilee when he wants to show the feeling of the soldiers about the disbanding of the army in 1698,[3] and to Shadwell's Volunteers to prove that in 1691 it became the fashion to serve for a campaign in the army. The last may be quoted as an example.

To volunteer for Flanders became the rage among the fine gentlemen who combed their flowing wigs and exchanged their richly perfumed snuffs at the Saint James's Coffeehouse. William's headquarters were enlivened by a crowd of splendid equipages and by a rapid succession of sumptuous banquets. For among the highborn and highspirited youths who repaired to his standard were some who, though quite willing to face a battery, were not at all disposed to deny themselves the luxuries with which they had been surrounded in Soho Square. In a few months Shadwell brought these valiant fops and epicures on the stage. The town was made merry with the character of a courageous but prodigal and effeminate coxcomb, who is impatient to cross swords with

[1] I, 352-6 (iii). [2] I, 373, n. 2 (iii).
[3] VI, 2747, n. (xxiii).

the best men in the French household troops, but who is much dejected by learning that he may find it difficult to have his Champagne iced daily during the summer. He carries with him cooks, confectioners, and laundresses, a waggonload of plate, a wardrobe of laced and embroidered suits, and much rich tent furniture, of which the patterns have been chosen by a committee of fine ladies.[1]

Even financial and economic questions Macaulay enlivens by using plays to illustrate them. He elucidates the rivalry between the old and the new East India Companies by a quotation from Rowe's comedy, The Biter,[2] and the mania for speculation by a scene in Shadwell's Stockjobbers.

It was in the last drama of Shadwell that the hypocrisy and knavery of these speculators was, for the first time, exposed to public ridicule. He died in November, 1692, just before his Stockjobbers came on the stage; and the epilogue was spoken by an actor dressed in deep mourning. The best scene is that in which four or five stern Nonconformists, clad in full Puritan costume, after discussing the prospects of the Mousetrap Company and the Fleakilling Company, examine the question whether the godly may lawfully hold stock in a Company for bringing over Chinese ropedancers. 'Considerable men have shares,' says one austere person in cropped hair and bands; 'but verily I question whether it be lawful or not.' These doubts are removed by a stout old Roundhead colonel who had fought at Marston Moor, and who reminds his weaker brother that the saints need not themselves see the ropedancing, and that, in all probability, there will be no ropedancing to see. 'The thing,' he says, 'is like to take. The shares will sell well; and then we shall not care whether the dancers come over or no.'[3]

[1] IV, 2029-30 (xvii). [2] V, 2108, n. 1 (xviii).
[3] V, 2280 (xix).

While the legitimate drama of the period was precluded from dealing directly with politics, there was in existence a popular form of drama which escaped, as a rule, from the restriction which limited the freedom of the superior form. The historians of literature think this kind of drama beneath them: to the political historian it is not without its value.

Macaulay quotes even farces, some of which were performed at Bartholomew Fair; that is about equivalent to quoting the dramatic performances of the music halls of to-day. From one called The Late Revolution or the Happy Change he takes a description of the army of the Prince of Orange as it entered Exeter.[1] Another called the Royal Voyage he quotes three times.[2] 'This drama, which, I believe, was performed at Bartholomew Fair, is one of the most curious of a curious class of compositions, utterly destitute of literary merit, but valuable as showing what were then the most successful claptraps for an audience composed of the common people. "The end of this play," says the author in his preface, "is chiefly to expose the perfidious, base, cowardly, and bloody nature of the Irish."'[3] There is a long series of such plays. 'The battle of the Boyne had scarcely been fought,' says Macaulay, 'when it was made the subject of a drama, the Royal Flight, or the Conquest of Ireland, a Farce, 1690. Nothing more execrable was ever written, even for Bartholomew Fair.'[4] But even in this mass of nonsense Macaulay detects a fact of importance; it is that while the Irish soldiers generally were represented on the English stage as a mass of cowards, Sarsfield had a high reputation for

[1] III, 1138, n. (ix).

[2] III, 1455, n. 2; 1490, n. 1 (xii); 1694, n. (xiv).

[3] III, 1455, n. 2 (xii).

[4] IV, 1884, n. 2 (xvi).

courage and conduct amongst the enemies of his race. Another drama of the same kind is a tragicomedy on the siege of Mons in 1691,[1] and, finally, Macaulay cites a political play, performed at St. Bartholomew's Fair in 1693, which expressed the feeling of the people about the maladministration of the navy.

By this time Saint Bartholomew's day drew near; and the great annual fair, the delight of idle apprentices and the horror of Puritanical Aldermen, was opened in Smithfield with the usual display of dwarfs, giants, and dancing dogs, the man that ate fire, and the elephant that loaded and discharged a musket. But of all the shows none proved so attractive as a dramatic performance which, in conception, though doubtless not in execution, seems to have borne much resemblance to those immortal masterpieces of humour in which Aristophanes held up Cleon and Lemachus to derision. Two strollers personated Killegrew and Delavel. The Admirals were represented as flying with their whole fleet before a few French privateers, and taking shelter under the guns of the Tower. The office of Chorus was performed by a Jackpudding who expressed very freely his opinion of the naval administration. Immense crowds flocked to see this strange farce. The applauses were loud; the receipts were great; and the mountebanks, who had at first ventured to attack only the unlucky and unpopular Board of Admiralty, now, emboldened by impunity and success, and probably prompted and rewarded by persons of much higher station than their own, began to cast reflections on other departments of the government. This attempt to revive the license of the Attic Stage was soon brought to a close by the appearance of a strong body of constables who carried off the actors to prison.[2]

These instances show that Macaulay successfully employed the dramatic literature of the period to enliven his

[1] IV, 1984, n. (xvii).

[2] V, 2372-4 (xx).

narrative, to elucidate from time to time the political situation, and to illustrate social facts. There remains the question of its employment as a source for social history. How far is its evidence valid for that purpose? In his third chapter Macaulay draws upon it to prove general propositions about the character of particular classes of men. His notion of the country gentlemen of the time of James II, for instance, is in part based, as he states in a note, on ' the lighter literature of that age ', and anyone who reads it can see how much that notion was influenced by their representation on the stage.[1] The same thing holds good with the description of the country clergy, which follows that of the country gentlemen. Here, too, his conception of their position and his account of their character is largely influenced by the lighter literature and especially by the drama. One of the points he undertakes to show is that the clergy ' were regarded as, on the whole, a plebeian class '.[2] One of his arguments is that ' a waiting woman was generally considered as the most suitable helpmate for a parson.' [3] ' During the several generations accordingly the relation between divines and handmaidens was a theme for endless jest ; nor would it be easy to find, in the comedy of the seventeenth century, a single instance of a clergyman who wins a spouse above the rank of a cook.' In a note, he adds ' Roger and Abigail in Fletcher's Scornful Lady, Bull and the Nurse in Vanbrugh's Relapse, Smirk and Susan in Shadwell's Lancashire Witches, are instances.' [4]

It is well known that Macaulay's characters of these country men and the clergy have been attacked, partly as untrue, and partly on the ground that he relied too much

[1] I, 313, n. (iii). [2] I, 315 (iii).
[3] I, 316 (iii). [4] I, 318 (iii).

on this kind of evidence. The second question is the one that concerns us at present. Clearly the representation of any class of men in the comic drama as frequently results in the creation of figures which are conventional as of figures which are true to nature. We have only to remember the stage Irishman and the stage sailor to see this. The eccentricities of individuals are attributed to a class, certain characteristics are exaggerated and others are softened or omitted to produce a more striking and amusing character. Take these dramatic personages and generalise from them about the class, if you like: but you are not basing your conclusions on facts and it is no good asserting that you are. You are only copying certain fictions which were accepted as facts by the pit and the gallery; you are building on humorous exaggerations of the facts. Macaulay does this far too much in his description of the country gentlemen and the clergy. The general lines of his pictures are correct enough, but individual features are over-coloured and over-emphasised till the result of the process is a caricature, not a portrait. The judgement which should be passed on his description of the clergy and the country gentlemen is not that he employs a kind of evidence which should not be used in such an account, but that he does not recognise that its value is limited, and that it should be employed with more caution.

Another striking characteristic of the History is the extent to which its author utilises the evidence afforded by ballads, satires, lampoons, and the occasional verse of the times generally. Trevelyan remarks that 'Macaulay's predilection for the Muse of the street is, indeed, one of the few personal facts about him which up to this time has taken hold of the public imagination. He bought every halfpenny song on which he could lay his hands; if only it was decent, and a genuine, undoubted, poem of the people.'[1] In the same way Macaulay read every ballad or satire he could come across which was produced in the reigns of James or William. He had access to considerable collections of broadside ballads and used them all. There was first of all the great collection of 1,800 ballads formed by Pepys, which is particularly rich in ballads of those two reigns. In a footnote he acknowledges 'most gratefully the kind and liberal manner in which the Master and Vicemaster of Magdalene College, Cambridge, gave me access to the valuable collections of Pepys.'[2] There was the Roxburghe collection of ballads in the British Museum, since reprinted in the publications of the Ballad Society, but then little known and unindexed.[3] There was also 'an excellent collection formed by Mr. Richard Heber, and now the property of Mr. Broderip, by whom it was kindly lent to me.'[4]

All these were collections of the original broadsides, but Macaulay also quotes and systematically employs the printed collection of satires and political songs published at the beginning of Queen Anne's reign, in four volumes, and known as Poems on Affairs of State. And, finally, he consulted and used a considerable number of manuscript libels and lampoons. He does not state where he found them—probably in the British Museum; but there are also similar collections in the Bodleian, in other libraries, and in private hands.

The question to be considered here is what the precise value of evidence of this kind is for historical purposes. Macaulay has sometimes been accused of over-estimating

[1] Life, ii. 94.

[2] I, 278, n. (iii).

[3] Ibid.

[4] III, 1358, n. (xi).

its importance. There are certainly some instances in which he makes too much of an item of information derived from these sources, but taking the book as a whole the charge is not true. He employs such evidence exactly as it ought to be employed, and that is why his method of using it deserves detailed examination. Popular literature of this kind is poor evidence as to facts, but excellent evidence as to feelings, and it is for the latter purpose that Macaulay uses it.

The popularity of a particular song at a particular moment proves conclusively that the sentiments and opinions it expressed were shared by the multitude. At the beginning of the reign of James the English people were full of loyalty to the Crown and hostility to the Whigs and Exclusionists. In all the convivial gatherings of the time and at the elections to the Parliament of 1685, one song was on every Tory's lips. 'The procession, as it marched,' says Macaulay in his account of the Cheshire election, 'sang "Joy to Great Caesar", a loyal ode, which had lately been written by Durfey, and which, though, like all Durfey's writings, utterly contemptible, was, at that time, almost as popular as Lillibullero became a few years later.'[1] Three years later, in the autumn of 1688, when James was endeavouring to fill the English army with Irish Catholics and to destroy the predominance of the Protestants in Ireland, Lillibullero became the popular song. Macaulay's method of introducing, paraphrasing, and explaining the political significance of this song is worth noting.

Public feeling did not then manifest itself by those signs with which we are familiar, by large meetings, and by vehement harangues. Nevertheless it found a vent.

[1] I, 474 (iv).

Thomas Wharton, who, in the last Parliament, had represented Buckinghamshire, and who had long been conspicuous both as a libertine and as a Whig, had written a satirical ballad on the administration of Tyrconnel. In this little poem an Irishman congratulates a brother Irishman, in a barbarous jargon, on the approaching triumph of Popery and of the Milesian race. The Protestant heir will be excluded. The Protestant officers will be broken. The Great Charter and the praters who appealed to it will be hanged in one rope. The good Talbot will shower commissions on his countrymen, and will cut the throats of the English. These verses, which were in no respect above the ordinary standard of street poetry, had for burden some gibberish which was said to have been used as a watchword by the insurgents of Ulster in 1641. The verses and the tune caught the fancy of the nation. From one end of England to the other all classes were constantly singing this idle rhyme. It was especially the delight of the English army. More than seventy years after the Revolution, Sterne delineated, with exquisite skill, a veteran who had fought at the Boyne and at Namur. One of the characteristics of the good old soldier is his trick of whistling Lillibullero.

Wharton afterwards boasted that he had sung a King out of three kingdoms. But in truth the success of Lillibullero was the effect, and not the cause, of that excited state of public feeling which produced the Revolution.[1]

From similar sources Macaulay illustrates the growth of popular feeling against the policy of James during the three years which intervened between 1685 and 1688; he shows for instance how Mary of Modena after being popular as Duchess of York became unpopular when she was queen,[2] the chorus of jeering ballads which anticipated the birth of the Prince of Wales and predisposed the English nation to regard the royal child as the child of a

[1] III, 1072 (ix). Cf. pp. 1075, 1176. [2] II, 644 (v).

tiler,[1] and the similar chorus which expressed the scorn of the nation for the noblemen and statesmen who turned Catholic to please the King.[2] In similar fashion he traces the revulsion of feeling which took place after the Revolution—the growing unpopularity of William,[3] the distress caused by war and bad harvests,[4] and the attempts of the enemies of the government to foment the general discontent.

Trade was not prosperous; and many industrious men were out of work. Accordingly songs addressed to the distressed classes were composed by the malcontent street poets. Numerous copies of a ballad exhorting the weavers to rise against the government were discovered in the house of the Quaker who had printed James's Declaration. Every art was used for the purpose of exciting discontent in a much more formidable body of men, the sailors; and unhappily the vices of the naval administration furnished the enemies of the State with but too good a choice of inflammatory topics. Some seamen deserted; some mutinied; then came executions; and then came more ballads and broadsides representing those executions as barbarous murders.[5]

Ballads are good evidence as to popular feeling about some particular social or economic grievance. In his third chapter Macaulay uses the Pepysian collection with great effect to prove the unpopularity of the hearth tax—chimney money, as it was called.[6] Often no other evidence is so convincing. Speaking of the fact that in the time of Charles II a shilling a day was regarded as fair wages of

[1] II, 964 (viii); 1012 (viii).
[2] II, 848 (vii).
[3] III, 1371 (xi).
[4] V, 2250 (xix).
[5] V, 2372 (xx). The ballad Macaulay quotes in n. 4 is printed in Naval Songs and Ballads, ed. C. H. Firth (1908), pp. 140-3.
[6] I, 277-8 (iii).

an artisan, Macaulay after quoting a remark made in Parliament says:

> Other evidence is extant, which proves that a shilling a day was the pay to which the English manufacturer then thought himself entitled but that he was often forced to work for less. The common people of that age were not in the habit of meeting for public discussion, of haranguing, or of petitioning Parliament. No newspaper pleaded their cause. It was in rude rhyme that their love and hatred, their exultation and their distress found utterance. A great part of their history is to be learned only from their ballads. One of the most remarkable of the popular lays chanted about the streets of Norwich and Leeds in the time of Charles the Second may still be read on the original broadside. It is the vehement and bitter cry of labour against capital. It describes the good old times when every artisan employed in the woollen manufacture lived as well as a farmer. But those times were past. Sixpence a day was now all that could be earned by hard labour at the loom. If the poor complained that they could not live on such a pittance, they were told that they were free to take it or leave it. For so miserable a recompense were the producers of wealth compelled to toil, rising early and lying down late, while the master clothier, eating, sleeping, and idling, became rich by their exertions. A shilling a day, the poet declares, is what the weaver would have, if justice were done. We may therefore conclude that, in the generation which preceded the Revolution, a workman employed in the great staple manufacture of England thought himself fairly paid if he gained six shillings a week.[1]

As to public events ballads have a very similar value. Sometimes we get rugged verses on a siege or a battle or a seafight, by men who took part in them: oftener the ballads on such incidents are merely rhymed versions of

[1] I, 410-12 (iii).

the accounts in the newspapers or the news circulated in the London streets at the moment. Of this class of ballads Macaulay makes practically no use at all, though he mentions in one of his notes the contemporary ballad on the battle of La Hogue as 'one of the best specimens of English street poetry'.[1]

One more use of the ballads may be mentioned. They are good evidence for popular traditions just as they are for popular feelings. In chapter v, Macaulay has a digression on the fondness with which Monmouth's memory was cherished by the people in the West, the belief that the man who was executed on Tower Hill was not Monmouth but someone else, and that the Protestant hero was still alive and would show himself in the West again. He supports this very aptly by a quotation from a ballad, written after Monmouth's death, which represents him as living and promising that he will come again.

> Though this is a dismal story
> Of the fall of my design
> Yet I'll come again in glory,
> If I live till eighty-nine.[2]

This is from a ballad printed about 1685. In another case Macaulay quotes a ballad handed down by tradition, not printed. Speaking of the trial of the Seven Bishops, and popular feeling in Cornwall in behalf of Trelawney the Bishop of Bristol, he says: 'All over the country the peasants chanted a ballad of which the burden is still remembered.

> "And shall Trelawney die and shall Trelawney die?
> Then thirty thousand Cornish boys will know the reason why."

[1] V, 2190 n. (xviii). Admiral Russell's Scowering the French Fleet: or, The Battle at Sea (Naval Songs and Ballads, pp. 119-20).

[2] II, 622, n. (v).

The miners from their caverns reechoed the song with a variation,

> "Then twenty thousand underground will know the reason why."'

'This fact,' he says in a footnote, 'was communicated to me in the most obliging manner by the Reverend R. S. Hawker of Morenstow in Cornwall.'[1]

Unluckily, the drawback is that it is quite uncertain whether this tradition is really genuine. Hawker was given to inventing Cornish traditions and fictitious historical documents: he wrote a ballad on Trelawney of which this refrain forms part. There is also a certain doubt whether, if the refrain is really genuine, it does not refer to a different Trelawney and a different time. This is an example of the traps into which the historian is liable to fall when he attempts to rely on tradition.

Another pitfall is the uncertain and variable character of the evidence afforded by ballads and the fugitive verses of a particular period as to the character and conduct of public personages. It is necessary to make many reservations and distinctions. For certain purposes ballads and even lampoons are useful. They attest a belief or a feeling but they do not prove a fact. They enable Macaulay to show how much Jeffreys was hated in 1689,[2] why Danby was so unpopular with the Whigs in 1690,[3] and why Sherlock was a mark for general ridicule in 1691.[4] But they supply no proof of the truth of the charges made against these personages, and that they were believed at the time is no sufficient reason for accepting them. Furthermore it is extremely important to distinguish between

[1] II, 1018, n. 2 (viii).
[2] III, 1210 (x).
[3] IV, 1958-9, n. (xvi).
[4] IV, 2018, n. (xvii).

the popular ballad, the printed satire, and the lampoon which circulated privately in manuscript or was clandestinely printed. They are three very different kinds of evidence—witnesses of very different degrees of credibility. The popular ballad is usually the expression of a general feeling, the satire often purely a partisan production or perhaps a literary exercise, the lampoon usually the offspring of private spite. Macaulay refers to the printed and unprinted satires and lampoons of the Jacobites against William III; they are worthless as evidence either of his reputation or his character and serve merely to prove the malignity of party malice at the time and its indifference to truth. Naturally Macaulay does not attach the slightest value to them. 'The Jacobite verses were generally too loathsome to be quoted.'[1] On the other hand, he says, 'The impression which the bluntness and reserve of William and the grace and gentleness of Mary had made on the populace may be traced in the remains of the street poetry of that time,' and he gives a good example.[2] For some notorious trait of a public man's character a line in a ballad may be good evidence. Macaulay attests the arrogance and brutal manners of the Earl of Rochester by a verse from Lamentable Lory.[3] A lampoon may be used to attest the leanness and ghastliness of Danby:

> 'He is stiff as any stake,
> And leaner, Dick, than any rake:
>   Envy is not so pale' says the poet.[4]

But to go a step further and use these touches and traits as materials for building up a conception of a historical character is somewhat dangerous. Macaulay after draw-

[1] III, 1418, n. (xi).
[2] III, 1358, n. (xi).
[3] I, 465, n. (iv).
[4] IV, 1796, n. (xv).

ing the character of Robert Harley says in a note, 'The character of Harley is to be collected from innumerable panegyrics and lampoons, from the works and the private correspondence of Swift, Pope, . . .'[1] The danger is that charges made in these untrustworthy lampoons may be allowed too large a share in forming the historian's general estimate of the personage, may so influence his conception of the character that he may be tempted to accept trifles as confirmation of these charges, and not pay sufficient attention to evidence telling the other way. He may be prejudiced thereby from the outset, and approach the testimony of other witnesses with a biassed mind. Macaulay's estimate of Marlborough's character seems to illustrate this point. In the formation of that estimate Macaulay was far too greatly influenced by contemporary lampoons and satires. In the elaborate character of Marlborough and his wife given in chapter xv, we read: 'In one point the Earl and the Countess were perfectly agreed. They were equally bent on getting money; though when it was got he loved to hoard it, and she was not unwilling to spend it.' The note below mentions only one authority. 'In a contemporary lampoon are these lines:

> "Oh, happy couple! In their life
> There does appear no sign of strife;
> They do agree so in the main,
> To sacrifice their souls for gain.
> The Female Nine".'[2]

A couple of pages later comes another reference to Lady Marlborough (in connection with the quarrel between Queen Mary and the Princess Anne), and we are told that 'if the scandalous chronicle of those times could be

[1] V, 2409, n. (xx). [2] IV, 1817, n. (xv).

trusted,' the Earl of Shrewsbury 'had stood high, too high, in her favour.' Again, the only reference is The Female Nine.[1] The poem in question is a Jacobite libel on the wives of nine Whig statesmen—one of those Jacobite lampoons, which, as Macaulay says, 'in virulence and malignity, far exceed anything that our age has produced.'[2] As evidence it is worthless: the character of the rest of the poem shows that. But since the poem exists only in manuscript, and Macaulay does not say where the manuscript is, the sceptical reader cannot examine the evidence.[3]

If Macaulay sometimes used material of very dubious value without adequate care, it would be unfair to assume that he habitually neglected to discriminate between his literary authorities. No historian more constantly employed the great writers of a period to explain its history. His treatment of Dryden shows this. Whenever he can he connects the events of the time with incidents in the life of Dryden, so that literature and politics are interwoven in the fabric of the History. It is from the career of Dryden that he illustrates the condition of polite literature and the status of men of letters in the days of Charles II.[4] When he recounts the numerous conversions to Catholicism which took place in 1687 Dryden's conversion fills the largest space in the list, and it gives occasion for several pages upon him.[5] In chronicling the ministerial changes which followed the accession of William III Dryden's dismissal from the laureateship is brought in, and leads to another, though shorter, digres-

[1] IV, 1819 (xv). [2] III, 1358 (xi).

[3] Mr. Paget searched for this poem but was unable to find it. New Examen, p. 10. I discovered it by chance in a volume of miscellaneous Jacobite verse once the property of Sir Robert Strange, and now in the possession of Mr. Charles J. Ffoulkes.

[4] I, 392-4 (iii). [5] II, 850-3 (vii).

sion.[1] In explaining the history of the recoinage of 1696 Macaulay cites Dryden's letter to his publisher when Tonson tried to pay him in clipped money.[2] Naturally the publication of the Hind and the Panther affords an opportunity to criticise the poem as well as to show its connection with the controversy then in progress between Catholics and Protestants, and Macaulay skilfully shows how the language of the poet reflects the change which was then taking place in the policy of the King.[3] The non-political works of Dryden are applied to political purposes. Lines from Cymon and Iphigenia exhibit the contempt which the sycophants of James II expressed for the militia, ' in peace a charge, in war a weak defence'.[4]

The dedication of Dryden's Arthur serves to show that by 1690 the war between England and France had become a national war instead of a dynastic quarrel.[5] Dryden's interpolations in his version of the Canterbury Tales are pointed out in order to explain that the doctrine of the indefeasibility of hereditary succession was a seventeenth-century superstition [6] unknown in Chaucer's time, and his play on Aurengzebe is employed to prove conclusively that Englishmen of that time knew nothing about India.[7]

There are many other literary references. Macaulay does not rigidly limit himself to contemporary authors: he quotes eighteenth-century literature as well, either to explain or to illustrate the question he is discussing, or simply to interest his readers. On ten or more occasions he mentions the writings of Addison. When describing the election of 1685 at Chester and, in particular, the singing

[1] III, 1333-4 (xi).
[2] V, 2568 (xxi).
[3] II, 853-4 (vii).
[4] I, 283 (iii).
[5] IV, 1904 (xvi).
[6] IV, 1708, n. 2 (xiv).
[7] V, 2093 (xviii).

of Joy to Great Caesar, he notes: 'See the Guardian, No. 67: an exquisite specimen of Addison's peculiar manner. It would be difficult to find in the works of any other writer such an instance of benevolence, delicately flavoured with contempt.'[1] Describing the sudden fashion for collecting Chinese porcelain, he says, 'Every person who was well acquainted with Pope and Addison will remember their sarcasms on this taste.'[2] He relies on Addison when drawing his portraits of Somers and Wharton, and, to illustrate that the Bank of England was necessarily a Whig body, he notices at length one of Addison's 'most ingenious and graceful little allegories'.[3]

He refers even oftener to the works of Swift, frequently quoting his opinions of the statesmen of the Revolution. He uses him to support the view that in Ireland there was no more danger that the Irishry would rise against the Englishry than that the women and children would rise against the men,[4] and he proves from the Journal to Stella that Elizabeth Villiers' influence over William was due to her powers of mind.[5] Similarly, in his notes he cites Dr. Johnson's opinion on the morality of the Nonjurors[6] and on the government of Ireland,[7] and his theory as to the proper martial policy for England.[8] He quotes Burke as well as Locke, and he has a curious predilection for Sterne. All William's campaigns are illustrated from Tristram Shandy. 'Sterne is an authority not to be despised on these subjects,' Macaulay writes. 'His boyhood was passed in barracks: he was constantly listening to the talk of old soldiers who had served under King

[1] I, 474, n. 2 (iv).
[2] III, 1362, n. (xi).
[3] V, 2396-2404, 2438 (xx).
[4] IV, 2077 (xvii).
[5] V, 2414 (xx).
[6] IV, 1717, n., 1730, n. (xiv).
[7] IV, 2080, n. (xvii).
[8] V, 2393, n. (xx).

William, and has used their stories like a man of true genius.'[1] When Macaulay describes the sufferings of William's army at the siege of Limerick he says: 'The autumnal rain had begun to fall. The soldiers in the trenches were up to their knees in mire. No precaution was neglected: but, though drains were dug to carry off the water, and though pewter basins of usquebaugh and brandy blazed all night in the tents, cases of fever had already occurred.' In his footnote Macaulay quotes Corporal Trim as the authority for this method of curing the flux. In his account of the battle of Steinkirk, Macaulay quotes in a note Corporal Trim's tribute to the valiant behaviour of certain English regiments, and his opinion that they would go to heaven for it.[2] In relating William's defeat at Landen in 1693, Macaulay cannot refrain from referring to Uncle Toby's praise of the courage with which the King strove to rally his broken troops.[3] 'See also the glowing description of Sterne who, no doubt, had many times heard the battle fought over by old soldiers. It was on this occasion that Corporal Trim was left wounded on the field, and was nursed by the Beguine.' Finally when Macaulay, in his narrative of the siege of Namur, has to describe one of the many assaults on the besieged city, he adds in a footnote, 'It was in the attack of July $\frac{17}{27}$. that Captain Shandy received the memorable wound in his groin.'[4]

Macaulay obviously assumed that his readers were familiar with the classics of English literature and needed only to be reminded of what they had read. Hence, instead of using facts of history to make fiction seem true, as a novelist does, he uses fiction to make historical

[1] IV, 1919 (xvi).
[2] V, 2238-40 (xix).
[3] V, 2360, n. (xx).
[4] V, 2525, n. (xxi).

events seem more real and less remote. There are writers in whom such a constant flow of reminiscences, references, and parallels would be tedious, because it would seem affected and strained. In Macaulay's conversation it was sometimes overpowering. 'He should take two tablespoonfuls of the waters of Lethe every morning,' said Sidney Smith. In Macaulay's writings it is the natural outpouring of an exuberant mind stirred with a vast stock of miscellaneous reading. Thackeray, in an incidental panegyric of Macaulay in one of the Roundabout Papers, remarks on the allusiveness of his style. 'Take at hazard,' he says,

> any three pages of the Essays or History: and, glimmering below the stream of narrative, you, an average reader, see one, two, three, a half-score of allusions to other historic facts, characters, literature, poetry, with which you are acquainted. Your neighbour, who has *his* reading and *his* little stock of literature stowed away in his mind, shall detect more points, allusions, happy touches, indicating, not only the prodigious memory and vast learning of this master, but the wonderful industry, the honest, humble previous toil of this great scholar. He reads twenty books to write a sentence; he travels a hundred miles to make a line of description.[1]

In reality, it is not the vastness of Macaulay's knowledge which is so remarkable as the ease with which it is employed. Everything that he had read—state papers and pamphlets, poetry and fiction—was fused together by his glowing memory, and utilised without a sign of effort.

[1] Trevelyan, ii. 216.

CHAPTER VI

MACAULAY'S THIRD CHAPTER

MACAULAY proposed to write the history of the people of England as well as the history of the government. The scheme was to include, he said,

the progress of useful and ornamental arts . . . the rise of religious sects and the changes of literary taste . . . the manners of successive generations . . . even the revolutions which have taken place in dress, furniture, repasts, and public amusements.[1]

He was not the first person to regard these subjects as part of the stuff of English history, and to desire to see them treated side by side with wars and politics. Boswell records a conversation on history between Dr. Johnson and Dr. Robertson, in which Dr. Johnson said : 'I wish much to see one branch well done, that is the history of manners, of common life.' Nor was Macaulay the first historian who attempted to combine these various subjects with narrative history. In the chapters with which Hume concluded the different divisions of his History he systematically surveyed the social, the economic, and the intellectual life of each succeeding period. In the appendix to his account of the reign of James I he said :

It may not be improper, at this period, to make a pause ; and take a survey of the state of the kingdom with regard to government, manners, finances, arms, trade, learning. Where a just notion is not formed of these particulars,

[1] I, 2.

history can be little instructive, and often will not be intelligible.[1]

After his narrative of the reign of Charles II and James II, Hume added : 'We shall subjoin to this general view of the English government, some account of the state of the finances, arms, trade, manners, arts, between the Restoration and Revolution,' [2] and covered in a dozen pages much the same ground as Macaulay does in his third chapter.

What Dr. Johnson had desired and Hume attempted, many others since Macaulay have tried to do, and a comparison of the different ways in which they approached the problem will bring out the characteristics of Macaulay's method. Arrangement is the great difficulty : how is it best to combine the economic and social facts with the political and military facts? Spencer Walpole begins his History of England from 1815 with a description of the social and economic condition of England, which occupies about 400 pages, and is supplemented later by episodes dealing with separate subjects. W. E. H. Lecky prefixes to his History of England in the Eighteenth Century an analysis of the relative strength of the religious and political parties whose action determined the development of the state, and inserts from time to time long chapters describing social, religious, and intellectual changes. He had not attempted, he declared, to write a history of the period year by year. 'It has been my object to disengage from the great mass of facts those which relate to the permanent forces of the nation, or which indicate some of the more enduring features of national life.' As he proceeded, however, he changed his scale and his scheme, combining

[1] David Hume, The History of England from the Invasion of Julius Caesar (1871), iii. 90.

[2] Ibid. p. 775.

in alternate slices a chronological narrative of political and military events with chapters on social history.

Macaulay's arrangement was more skilful. After describing the social, economic, and intellectual state of England at the date when his narrative commences, he strove to weave the social, economic, and intellectual facts into the fabric of his account of political and military events. The description of England in chapter iii was supplemented by descriptions of Ireland in chapter xii and of Scotland in chapter xiii, when the scene of the story shifts from one country to another. It was completed by episodes and descriptive digressions, introduced as occasion served into the course of the narrative, which dealt with topics omitted in chapter iii or incompletely dealt with there. The attack of James II on the Church afforded opportunity for an account of the universities and an estimate of their political influence. The parliamentary debates of 1691 permitted the insertion of an excursus on the history of British trade in the East. Minor changes of manners and customs were incidentally mentioned in a paragraph or a sentence, in connection with political events which they illustrated. In that way Macaulay contrived to tell us when tea-drinking became popular, when a taste for oriental china began, and why a particular kind of lace cravat came into fashion in 1692. But this episodical method of treating social and economic history has many drawbacks. It leads to the omission of certain subjects and to the inadequate discussion of others. The exigencies of the chronological narrative of military and political events determine when and where economic and social facts shall be mentioned, and which of them shall be included. It leads also to the separate and fragmentary statement of facts which should be grouped together, because they explain each other.

Macaulay spoke of the third chapter as the most difficult part of his task. A great part of the difficulty lay in the character of his materials. The economic and social history of England had been very little studied compared with its political history. Some works of solid value were available, such as Eden's State of the Poor, Macpherson's Annals of Commerce, and so on; but there was a great lack of good monographs dealing with various parts of his subject. To-day monographs exist which contain the materials required for the revision of Macaulay's conclusions, and would enable a modern historian to compile an account of England at a given date with greater facility and certainty. Not only was the accessible evidence on social and economic subjects unsifted and undigested when Macaulay wrote, but much evidence of importance which is now in print was then inaccessible. Hence Macaulay had to utilise for his description of England shreds of evidence collected from all sorts of authorities, good, bad, and indifferent. He collected and employed what he termed 'gleanings' and 'fragments of truth', which other historians had deemed of no value.[1] Croker in his review censured this: he said that the third chapter was like an old curiosity shop, into which 'the knick-knacks of a couple of centuries are promiscuously jumbled', and complained that some of Macaulay's references were to eighteenth-century authorities, and therefore not properly applicable to 1685.[2] This criticism is true, but in the absence of adequate contemporary authorities it is legitimate to employ with due caution authorities a little earlier or a little later in date. The question is simply whether the historian employs them with sufficient care.

[1] Miscellaneous Writings (1860), i. 278.

[2] Quarterly Review, lxxxiv. 579.

While Macaulay was open to criticism for relying too much on inferior authorities and generalising too boldly from imperfect data, there could be no two opinions about the artistic skill with which he puts together his facts. With rapid and vigorous touches he brings before us a picture of seventeenth-century England. The arrangement of chapter iii deserves analysis. First he points out the smallness of the population, and the smallness of the revenue of the state, showing how that revenue was raised and expended, and giving an account of the army and navy. Then he passes to an account of the resouces of the nation, its agriculture, its mineral products, and its trade, and under cover of explaining how the rents of the land were divided, takes the opportunity of describing the character of the governing classes of the nation, namely the gentry and the clergy. From the country he passes to the towns, and, sketching in succession the provincial capitals, the manufacturing towns, and the pleasure resorts, finally reaches London, which he describes at length. London is skilfully made the centre of the whole picture, not merely because it was the most populous city in Europe, but because it was the stage on which most of the events he meant to relate took place, because there political opinion was formed, and thence came the impulses which determined the action of the state. To complete his picture it was necessary to describe the intellectual as well as the material condition of the nation, and the transition from one subject to the other was not easy. Macaulay solves the problem by describing the means of communication between the capital and the provinces ; the highways and the methods of travel ; the post and methods of correspondence. As the mails conveyed the newspapers and news-letters which furnished provincials with their political instruction and the books which furnished them with their literary nutriment, it was easy to pass to a discussion of the state of education, literature, and science. But instead of ending his chapter with this picture of the English mind, Macaulay turns back to survey once more the economic condition of England, and winds up by describing the condition of the working classes, the rate of wages, pauperism, the comparative well-being of the lower orders in 1685 and 1848, and the moral and material benefits which civilisation brings in its train for all classes of the people.

The preamble and the peroration of the chapter explain the reasons which dictated its arrangement. In them he sets forth his philosophy of history. The constant progress of physical knowledge and the constant desire of every man to better himself explain the uninterrupted progress of England in wealth during the last six centuries. This progress became portentously rapid about the middle of the eighteenth century and proceeded with accelerated velocity during the nineteenth: 'A change to which the history of the old world furnishes no parallel has taken place in our country.'[1] To bring out the greatness of this change by 'placing before the English of the nineteenth century a true picture of the life of their ancestors' was the subject of chapter iii, and of the History as a whole. Therefore he begins the chapter by showing how thinly inhabited and how poor compared to its neighbours England was then, and contrasts continually the small things of 1685 and the great things of 1848. The peroration of the chapter is intended to prove that the progress of wealth and civilisation has benefited the whole people, and in some ways benefited the poorest class of it most. Macaulay was not unaware of the discontent which existed amongst

[1] I, 272.

the English working classes at the time when he was writing, of the complaint of the unequal distribution of the national wealth amongst the nation, of the defects of the existing social system and the demand for political changes to remedy them. But though the phenomena which moved Carlyle to write Chartism and Past and Present were before his eyes, he under-estimated their seriousness, and they did not shake his optimism. He perceived no flaws in the unrivalled prosperity of England. 'It is, in some sense, unreasonable and ungrateful in us to be constantly discontented with a condition which is constantly improving.'[1] So he describes the England of Charles II and compares it with the England of Queen Victoria, not only to interest his readers, but to impress upon them the lesson of content which he draws from the knowledge of the past.

This tendency is one of the weaknesses of Macaulay. Cotter Morison justly observes :

He was deficient in the true historic spirit, and often failed to regard the past from the really historical point of view. What is the historical point of view? Is it not this : to examine the growth of society in bygone times with a single eye for the stages of the process—to observe the evolution of one stage out of another previous stage—to watch the past as far as our means allow, as we watch any other natural phenomena, with the sole object of recording them accurately? . . . Now what does Macaulay do in his observation of the past? *He compares it, to its disparagement, with the present.* The whole of his famous Third chapter, on the State of England, is one long pæan over the superiority of the nineteenth century to the seventeenth century—as if an historian had the slightest concern with that. Whether we are better or worse than our ances-

[1] I, 420.

tors is a matter utterly indifferent to scientific history, whose object is to explain and analyze the past, on which the present can throw no more light than the old age of an individual can throw light on his youth. Macaulay's constant preoccupation is not to explain his period by previous periods, but to show how vastly the period of which he treats has been outstripped by the period in which he lives. Whatever may be the topic—the wealth or population of the country, the size and structure of the towns, the roads, the coaches, the lighting of London, it matters not—the comparison always made is with subsequent England, not previous England.[1]

A reader who seeks to understand the past is not satisfied with learning that England was a very different place a couple of centuries ago. He wishes to perceive and to comprehend the process by which seventeenth-century England developed into nineteenth-century England. That part of the process which fell within the limits of the period covered by Macaulay should be related and explained in his pages. Take a few of the subjects which ought to be included in any account of the development of England between 1685 and 1702, examine how far they are adequately treated, and see where Macaulay's account needs to be corrected or supplemented.

The Revolution of 1688 and the great war which followed it affected every branch of the national life, sometimes by retarding or accelerating tendencies already in existence, and at other times by setting new forces at work. Begin by considering briefly the position of the labouring classes. In his account of the town and country labourer given in chapter iii, Macaulay omitted one very important fact. He forgot to mention the 'Settlement Act', passed in 1662, which prevented the labourer from migrating from

[1] J. Cotter Morison, Macaulay (1882), pp. 170-1.

one parish to another in search of work. And yet he must have known Adam Smith's denunciation of that law:

> To remove a man who has committed no misdemeanour from the parish where he chuses to reside, is an evident violation of natural liberty and justice. The common people of England, however, so jealous of their liberty, but like the common people of most other countries never rightly understanding wherein it consists, have now for more than a century together suffered themselves to be exposed to this oppression without a remedy. . . . There is scarce a poor man in England of forty years of age, I will venture to say, who has not in some part of his life felt himself most cruelly oppressed by this ill-contrived law of settlements.[1]

Three Acts passed in 1691, 1697, and 1699 rendered the provisions of this law more stringent, and made it still more difficult for a working man to obtain a settlement in a parish. They also obliged persons in receipt of poor relief to wear badges, and increased the penalties imposed on vagrants.[2] In three successive speeches King William called the attention of Parliament to the question of 'setting the poor at work'. In 1699 he said:

> The increase of the poor is become a burthen to the kingdom, and their loose and idle life, does in some measure contribute to that depravation of manners, which is complained of. . . . As it is an indispensable duty, that the poor, who are not able to help themselves, should be maintained; so I cannot but think it extremely desireable, that such as are able and willing, should not want employment; and such as are obstinate and unwilling, should be compelled to labour.[3]

Seventeenth-century statistics are not very reliable, but it seems to be clear that the poor rates for England, which

[1] Wealth of Nations (1904), i. 142.

[2] G. Nicholls, History of the English Poor Law (1904), i. 279, 328, 350, 354.

[3] R. Chandler, The History and Proceedings of the House of Commons from the Restoration to the Present Time (1742), iii. 92, 107, 128.

were estimated at £665,000 for 1685, had risen by 1701 to about £900,000 a year. This alteration for the worse in the position of the labourer was partly due to the war with France, which increased taxation and greatly damaged trade. There was also a series of bad harvests during the reign of William III. Macaulay mentions the distress caused by the failure of the harvest of 1692, but seems unaware that there were seven years of scarcity and high prices, which extended from 1692 to 1698. 'Of these years,' says Thorold Rogers, 'the worst was 1693-4, and the next 1697-8.'[1]

Macaulay, it is clear, had not devoted much attention to agriculture, and it is not given an adequate place in his account of the life of the nation. He begins by saying, in chapter iii, that 'agriculture was in what would now be considered as a very rude and imperfect state'; and adds that half the area of England was moor, forest, and fen, farming was unskilful, the average annual yield of all kinds of grain not more than ten million quarters, the rotation of crops imperfectly understood, and the sheep and oxen of that time diminutive. All this is true, but the comparison of agriculture under Charles II with nineteenth-century agriculture produces too unfavourable an impression; backward though it was, English agriculture was not stationary but progressive; the experiments which Worlidge and other writers on husbandry suggested were beginning to be tried in various parts of the country, and gradually the way was being prepared for the rapid and general improvement which took place during the eighteenth century.[2] One sign of the progress of agriculture

[1] History of Agriculture and Prices in England (1887), v. 240.

[2] R. E. Prothero, English Farming (1917), p. 130; W. Cunningham, Growth of English Industry and Commerce in Modern Times (1919), i. 545-6.

was the great rise in rents which took place during the seventeenth century, a phenomenon not merely due to the greed of landlords, as some writers assert, but also to the increasing yield of the soil and the spread of tillage. The policy of the government was steadily directed to encouraging the production of corn and stock. Under Charles II Irish and Scottish cattle were excluded from England for the benefit of the English farmer, and the export of corn was permitted until it rose above a certain price in England.[1] An Act passed in 1689 established a bounty of 5*s*. per quarter on the export of home-grown corn. This law was, 'by a general consensus of opinion, successful, both in maintaining prices at a steady level, and in giving a stimulus to English agriculture, during the first half of the eighteenth century.'[2] Adam Smith's strictures on the law are well known.

The country gentlemen, who then composed a still greater proportion of the legislature than they do at present, had felt that the money price of corn was falling. The bounty was an expedient to raise it artificially to the high price at which it had frequently been sold in the times of Charles I and II. It was to take place, therefore, till wheat was so high as forty-eight shillings the quarter; that is twenty shillings, or $\frac{5}{7}$ths dearer than Mr. King had in that very year estimated the grower's price to be in times of moderate plenty. If his calculations deserve any part of the reputation which they have obtained very universally, eight-and-forty shillings the quarter was a price which, without some such expedient as the bounty, could not at that time be expected, except in years of extraordinary scarcity. But the government of King William was not then fully settled. It was in no condition to refuse any thing to the country gentlemen, from whom

[1] Cunningham, op. cit. i. 371-3, 540, 546.

[2] Ibid. ii. 723; cf. i. 541.

it was at that very time soliciting the first establishment of the annual land-tax.[1]

It is hardly fair, however, to regard the measure merely as an example of class legislation: it was part of a deliberate national policy for the development of the nation's resources, which both the landed interest and the commercial interest agreed in holding expedient. A similar desire to develop and protect the manufactures and trade of the country inspired the commercial policy of the government, and was generally accepted by all parties. Macaulay gives neither an adequate nor a definite account of British trade and its progress during the period which the History covers. In chapter iii he tells us that the cotton trade was still in its infancy, that Leeds was the chief seat of the woollen manufactures in Yorkshire, and that Norwich was the chief seat of the cloth trade, which was the 'great staple manufacture of England'. In a later chapter we are told of the efforts necessary to prevent wool from being smuggled out of the kingdom, and of the suppression of the attempt to establish the woollen manufacture in Ireland in the session of 1698. 'It was in that age,' says Macaulay, 'believed by all but a very few speculative men that the sound commercial policy was to keep out of the country the delicate and brilliantly tinted textures of southern looms, and to keep in the country the raw material on which most of our own looms were employed.'[2] But nowhere does he explain how great the volume of this trade was compared to other trades. In 1688, for instance, the woollen goods exported were valued at about £2,000,000 out of a total export trade of about £4,300,000. During the years 1699-

[1] Adam Smith, op. cit. i. 196-7. The bounty was suspended in famine years such as 1698.

[2] VI, 2768-75 (xxiii).

1701, the value of the woollen goods exported rose to an average of about £2,250,000 a year, but the general export trade was proportionately much larger.

The foreign trade of England was mainly in the hands of half a dozen great companies, of which the chief was the East India Company. Macaulay gives a full and interesting account of the rise of British trade with India, of the rivalry between the Old Company and the New, and of the effects of the struggle on English politics. He also gives a sketch of the beginning of British trade with Russia, and mentions the Russia Company, when he relates Peter the Great's visit to England. But though he mentions the Turkey Company he gives no account of trade with the Levant and in the Mediterranean, and mentions the other great companies simply as presenting loyal addresses to James II.

The greatest omission of all is the neglect to discuss England's American and colonial trade. The Navigation Act, which was the basis of that trade and secured to English merchants the sole possession of it, is never named, nor is the reader told that 'the Plantation trade' was as great and as profitable as the East India trade. According to Davenant's estimate the net profits of our foreign trade amounted at the end of William's reign to an average of about two millions per annum, of which the Plantation trade and East Indian trade represented each about £700,000, and the remainder was derived from the European, African, and Mediterranean trade.[1]

The growth of this great foreign trade was the most remarkable feature in the economic history of England during the latter half of the seventeenth century. The total imports and exports at the beginning of Charles II's reign

[1] Charles Davenant, Political and Commercial Works (1771), ii. 18.

were estimated at about £7,750,000. In the year of the Revolution they had risen to about £11,500,000, and by 1701 to £13,500,000. During the war, the progress had suffered a check: in 1696-7 the total sank to only £7,000,000; but after the peace of Ryswick it at once rose again. English shipping increased with equal rapidity. It was agreed that the mercantile marine was practically doubled between 1660 and 1688, and though it fell during the war, by 1700 it was about three times as large as it was at the Restoration.[1]

During the reign of William the vicissitudes of English commerce and English agriculture affected the success of the war, and it was the pressure of the commercial interests rather than concern about the balance of power that led the nation to engage in the War of the Spanish Succession. For England, as Seeley points out, was becoming a predominantly commercial state and the transformation began at the Revolution and was completed at the peace of Utrecht.[2] Contemporaries were very conscious of this change in the character of the British state. 'Trade,' says Addison, in his account of Mr. Spectator's visit to the Royal Exchange, 'without enlarging the British territories, has given us a kind of additional empire'; and he describes the Exchange as 'making this metropolis a kind of emporium for the whole earth'.[3]

There is one side of the economic history of the time to which Macaulay devotes special attention—that is, public finance. At the close of Charles II's reign the annual revenue of the Crown was about £1,400,000, and Macaulay

[1] W. R. Scott, Constitution and Finance of English, Scottish and Irish Joint-Stock Companies to 1720 (1912), i. 306, 361; G. L. Beer, The Old Colonial System, 1660-1688 (1912), i. 13-14; Cunningham, op. cit. ii. 932.

[2] J. R. Seeley, Growth of British Policy (1895), ii. 353, 367, 379.

[3] Spectator, May 19, 1711.

describes in detail how it was raised and how it was expended. Of that only about one-seventh was raised by direct taxation, namely the hearth tax or chimney money, which produced about £200,000 per annum. Under James II the revenue was increased to a little over two millions, by imposing additional duties on wine, sugar, tobacco, and other commodities. The King preferred indirect taxes because they did not involve an annual application to Parliament, as they were usually granted for a term of years or for life; and the Members of Parliament preferred them because they were landowners. The Earl of Ailesbury, who proposed the new taxes in the House, tells us the instructions he received from James.

> He would not have one farthing laid on land. 'That,' said he (and like a true English king), 'is the last resource if God Almighty should afflict us with a war. . . . Lay it . . . on luxury, as chocolate, tea, coffee, Indian commodities as not necessary for the life of man, and' (with warmth) 'on wine'; (for he was a most sober prince). 'Who obliges people to make themselves drunk? But if they will drink, let them pay for it.'[1]

This is a compendious statement of the Tory theory of taxation just before the Revolution.

When William III became king the hearth tax was abolished because it was unpopular, but it had to be replaced by a window tax in 1695, when money was needed to pay the cost of the re-coinage. The war with France at once made it necessary to revert to direct taxation, in the shape of poll taxes and assessments on property, such as had existed during the Civil War, in the days of Cromwell, and during the Dutch wars of Charles II. During the

[1] Memoirs of Thomas, Earl of Ailesbury, ed. W. E. Buckley (2 vols.; Roxburghe Club, 1890), i. 105.

Williamite war between four and five millions a year was raised by taxation, of which the part raised by direct taxes was rather more than half the total. The land tax, imposed in 1692, was a property tax of four shillings in the pound, which brought in finally about two millions a year, and was reduced to three shillings in the pound when peace returned. Macaulay makes the imposition of the land tax an occasion for a brilliant digression on the history of direct taxation, and the changes which took place in the rate of this particular tax till it was made permanent by Pitt in 1798.[1]

As in spite of the new taxes, the income of the state was still insufficient to meet the expenditure caused by the war, the balance had to be met by raising loans, and so the national debt came into being. When William died England was burdened with a debt of about £12,500,000 (or according to another account, of over £16,000,000).[2] Macaulay in another digression traces the later history of the debt down to his own day, discusses the opinions of economists and statesmen about it, and refutes their predictions that the nation would sink under the burden. 'We find it as easy,' he says, 'to pay the interest of eight hundred millions as our ancestors found it, a century ago, to pay the interest of eighty millions. . . . A long experience justifies us in believing that England may in the twentieth

[1] V, 2272-4 (xix).

[2] George Chalmers, in his Estimate of the Comparative Strength of Great Britain (1794), stated that the principal of the public debt on December 31, 1701, amounted to £16,394,701, whereon was due an annual interest of £1,109,123, and that on December 31, 1697, it had amounted to £21,515,743 (pp. 80, 85; cf. p. 64). The blue book on Public Income and Expenditure (Parliamentary Papers, session 1868-9: House of Commons, vol. xxiv), compiled by Mr. H. W. Chisholm, states (pt. ii, p. 298) that the national debt amounted to £15,445,416 in 1698 and to £12,552,486 in 1701. It also gives the amount of the debt in 1714 as about 36 millions, while Chalmers, whom Macaulay followed, put it at about 50 millions at that time.

century be better able to pay a debt of sixteen hundred millions than she is at the present time to bear her present load.' But even his optimism would probably have given way if he had anticipated a debt of about seven and a half thousand millions.

The result of the system of borrowing was the foundation of the Bank of England, the origin and development of which Macaulay traces with great clearness, relating in detail its struggle with the Land Bank and its final triumph over all its enemies. By the aid of the Bank the government was able to raise money at a reasonable rate during the rest of the war, and to carry through the re-coinage of 1696. The restoration of the currency is the last great financial question of the time which Macaulay has to treat, and he recounts it with the same skill, but at rather excessive length.

A later historian, Thorold Rogers, who went over the same ground as Macaulay and used nearly the same authorities, has borne testimony to the fairness and accuracy of this portion of Macaulay's work.

> I have found him scrupulously just. In many cases he could with perfect historical honesty have pourtrayed persons, who played a conspicuous part in the financial history of the time, in far darker colours than he thought proper to employ. After going through the particulars of this period, I feel, even though the facts are nearly two centuries old, almost as much loathing towards Sir Charles Duncombe, whose existence in London was a perpetual conspiracy against the Bank of England and public credit, as every right-minded person feels towards Oates and Fuller.... I think Macaulay over-rated the political genius of William the Third, great as it was. I think he over-rated the financial genius of Montague, great as it was. I think he might have given greater credit to those honest,

God-fearing, patriotic men, who really founded the Bank of England, watched over its early troubles, relieved it, by the highest shrewdness and fidelity, from the perils it incurred, and established the reputation of British integrity. For in point of fact, the history of the Bank of England during its first years is in no slight degree the history of the settlement of 1689, and of the new departure which that great event makes in the politics of the civilised world.[1]

Turning from economic and financial to social questions let us consider the various factors which influenced the political development of the society Macaulay describes. First of all, what does the phrase ' people ' mean? Taken in its largest sense it signifies five or six millions, including the million or so who were in receipt of poor relief. Politically it signifies that portion of the population whose votes or opinions determined the action of the state. It was estimated that there were then about 200,000 persons in England entitled to exercise the franchise. About a century later, in 1782, the number of electors was said to be about 300,000. Burke in 1796 tried ' to compute those who, in any political view, are to be called the people ', and, taking England and Scotland together, calculated that they were about 400,000 persons.[2]

The most powerful sections of the people in 1685 were the country gentry and the clergy, and Macaulay gives an account of the composition and character of these two classes. He has been accused of unfairness and injustice, and critics have not hesitated to say that he was prejudiced against both classes, because they were the main

[1] J. E. Thorold Rogers, The First Nine Years of the Bank of England (1887), pp. xi-xii.

[2] Parliamentary History, ed. William Cobbett (36 vols. ; 1806-20), xxii. 1344 ; Edmund Burke, Works (1852), v. 284 ; cf. Carl von Noorden, Europäische Geschichte in achtzehnten Jahrhundert (1870), i. 55.

props of the Tory party then and in his own time. Croker, in his articles on Macaulay's History, in the Quarterly Review, made both charges. He devoted six pages to the defence of the country gentlemen, and nine to the defence of the clergy. The clergy were also defended at greater length by Churchill Babington (a Fellow of St. John's College, Cambridge) in Mr. Macaulay's Character of the Clergy in the Latter Part of the Seventeenth Century Considered, with an Appendix on the Character of the Gentry (1849). Mr. Gladstone, in an article on Sir George Trevelyan's Life of Macaulay,[1] held the refutation conclusive, but that is going too far. Babington succeeds in showing that Macaulay sometimes misinterprets and sometimes overstrains the evidence of the authorities he quotes, and that he omits to take into account much evidence that tells against his view, but he does not overthrow his main position as completely as devoted churchmen assume. The clergy were much poorer then than they were in Macaulay's time, but their political influence was very much greater. The educated and the learned clergy were mostly to be found in the towns; many of the country clergy were extremely ignorant, and domestic chaplains often occupied a somewhat servile position. But when Macaulay said that 'the clergy were regarded on the whole as a plebeian class', and that 'for one who made the figure of a gentleman ten were menial servants', he weakened his case by his rhetorical extravagance. Lecky's judgement on the dispute is very just. After citing some fresh evidence on the position of the clergy he concludes:

It is clear that Macaulay greatly understated the number of men of good family that entered the Church, and his picture is, perhaps, in other respects a little over-coloured,

[1] W. E. Gladstone, Gleanings of Past Years (1879), vol. ii.

but the passages I have cited are, I think, quite sufficient to establish its substantial accuracy.[1]

In several respects, the position of the clergy was seriously affected by the Revolution and its consequences. The non-juring schism, due to the refusal of Sancroft and other bishops and clergymen to swear allegiance to William III, caused a division which diminished the moral authority of the Church. That authority was further impaired by the quarrels between the High and Low Church parties, and between the Lower and Upper Houses of Convocation. During the same period the Toleration Act, by the comparative freedom which it gave to the Nonconformists, allowed them to increase in numbers and strength,[2] and to attain municipal and civil offices from which they had previously been excluded. Finally, the whole tendency of the speculative movement of the time was to undermine the political influence of the clergy by weakening their spiritual influence. Burnet bitterly complains of the attacks of ' profane wits ' upon the Church :

> It is a common topic of discourse, to treat all mysteries in religion as the contrivances of priests to bring the world into a blind submission to them ; *priestcraft* grew to be another word in fashion, and the enemies of religion vented all their impieties under the cover of these words.[3]

Jeremy Collier, in his Short View of the Profaneness and Immorality of the English Stage (1698), defended the clergy against the dramatists, by claiming that ministers of religion in general ought to be immune from attack.[4]

[1] W. E. H. Lecky, History of England in the Eighteenth Century, i. (1919), 97 n.

[2] At most they did not number 5 per cent of the population.

[3] Gilbert Burnet, History of My Own Time, ii. 211-12.

[4] Macaulay, IV, 1722 (xiv).

He did much to purify the stage, but did not strengthen the position of the Church. The bitter struggle between the Church and the Nonconformists in Queen Anne's reign, which ended in the passing of the Occasional Conformity Act and the Schism Act, secured the political privileges of the Church at the expense of its national character.

Macaulay's account of the country gentlemen is open to the same objections as his account of the clergy. It is exaggerated, it is undiscriminating, and accuracy is sometimes sacrificed to rhetorical effect. At the period of which he wrote the class as a whole was much larger than it is now; the land was divided amongst more owners, and large properties were fewer. Gregory King estimated that the landed gentry consisted of about 16,000 families, and the class included rich knights and baronets, whose ancestors for generations had represented the county, and the 'little gentlemen of two hundred a year' that a dramatist laughs at.[1] The level of culture varied as greatly as the average amount of wealth. The smaller gentry were naturally less cultivated than those who could afford to spend liberally on the education of their children, and to travel. In the remoter parts of the country the gentry were less educated and less civilised than those who lived nearer to the capital. In the picture which Macaulay draws of the class as a whole these shades of difference are suppressed; he generalises too much from the lower half of the class and makes no adequate allowance for the large number of educated and intelligent men it contained. 'From this description,' he says, 'it might be supposed that the English esquire of the seventeenth century did not materially differ from a rustic miller or alehouse keeper of our

[1] Davenant, Works, ii. 184.

time,'[1] and the fact that it produces this impression shows that the description is a caricature. Any one familiar with the domestic correspondence of the period will form a more favourable impression of the manners and intelligence of the country gentry. Collections of correspondence such as that contained in the Memoirs of the Verney family, or those calendared in the volumes of the Historical Manuscripts Commission,[2] prove that there were many families with habits and ideals as high as those of the corresponding class in Macaulay's own time.

Macaulay also omits to state clearly the nature and the importance of the public services which the country gentry performed. He speaks of them as magistrates dispensing to those who dwelt near them 'a rude patriarchal justice', but says nothing of the functions of the magistrates in quarter-sessions. Yet the whole system of local administration depended upon the efficiency with which they discharged their multifarious functions,[3] and generally speaking they did so with considerable energy and a fair amount of success. Since Macaulay wrote, the publication of various calendars of the quarter-sessions records, and the researches of local historians, have elucidated this

[1] I, 311.

[2] Notably the Harley papers in the Duke of Portland's MSS., vols. iii-vi (1894-1901), and the Le Fleming MSS.

[3] 'The repairing of bridges, the maintenance of the king's gaols, the building and management of the newer houses of correction, the fixing of wages, prices and rates of land carriage, the licensing of various kinds of traders, the suppression of disorderly houses, the sanctioning of special levies for various parish needs, the confirmation or disallowance of the orders of individual justices or pairs of justices on every conceivable subject, were among the multifarious civil functions of Quarter Sessions.' S. and B. Webb, The Parish and the County (1906), pp. 296-7. This admirable work deals with the period after the Revolution, but conditions were much the same during the second half of the seventeenth century as during the first part of the eighteenth.

side of English history, and provided evidence which was not accessible in Macaulay's day for rightly estimating the share of the country gentry in the development of the state.

The great defect of the gentry was their indifferent education. Burnet severely described them as 'for the most part the worst instructed, and the least knowing of any of their rank I ever went amongst', and compared them unfavourably with the Scots of the same class.[1] The schools of the time were bad, and sport was more attractive to young men brought up in the country. But Macaulay exaggerates when he says:

> Few knights of the shire had libraries so good as may now perpetually be found in a servants' hall, or in the back parlour of a small shopkeeper. An esquire passed among his neighbours for a great scholar, if Hudibras and Baker's Chronicle, Tarlton's Jests and the Seven Champions of Christendom, lay in his hall window among the fishing rods and fowling pieces.[2]

The seventeenth-century libraries which occasionally come into the market, bills for books, references in letters, and other indications show that there was more reading done in the country houses than Macaulay admitted, and the state of the English book trade refutes the view that neither the country gentry nor the country clergy bought books.

Macaulay says that the power of the country gentlemen and the clergy in the rural districts was in some measure counterbalanced by the power of the yeomanry. They were not less than 160,000 in number, but the class of small landowners was already beginning to diminish, and

[1] Own Time, ii. 64.

[2] I, 384.

was destined to a rapid decrease in the next century.[1] The really important change in the social balance was the rise of the mercantile class and moneyed interest, which became the backbone of the Whig party. It had been rapidly growing in wealth between the Restoration and the Revolution. Sir Josiah Child, who was a good authority, said that in 1688 there were more men on 'Change worth ten thousand pounds than there were in 1650 worth a thousand. The war with France, the great loans, the creation of the national debt, and the foundation of the Bank of England gave those who possessed money many opportunities for investing their capital safely and accumulating more. Wealthy merchants and newly enriched speculators began to contend with the squirearchy for the representation of the boroughs, and to carry the day by the expenditure of money. The landed interest strove to protect itself by a law enacting that all Members of Parliament must possess property in land of a certain value. As Macaulay points out, the first bill for this purpose was vetoed by William in 1696, the second rejected by the House of Lords in 1697.[2] By the middle of Queen Anne's reign, the moneyed interest seemed to have permanently established its political position. 'Power,' wrote Swift in 1710, 'which according to the old maxim, was us'd to follow land, is now gone over to money.'[3] But in February 1711 the Tories succeeded in passing

[1] Davenant, Works, ii. 184. Cf. A. H. Johnson, The Disappearance of the Small Landowner (1909), pp. 82, 136. The latter notes 'a very general consensus of opinion among contemporaries that the closing years of the seventeenth century and the first fifty years of the eighteenth century were fatal to the small owner'.

[2] V, 2621 (xxi); VI, 2688-9 (xxii).

[3] Examiner, Nov. 2, 1710. On the rise of the moneyed interests, see Lecky, op. cit. i. 239-51.

their property-qualification bill, which required county members to possess £600 a year in land and borough members £300 a year, and this law remained in force till 1838.[1]

Macaulay related only the first stage of the struggle; if he had completed his History he would probably have dwelt on the social as well as political results of the rise of the commercial class. A Swiss who visited England in 1694 remarked on the difference between English and foreign merchants.

> They seem to me to differ from other merchants in many things; they are neither in so much haste as the French to grow rich, nor so niggardly as the Dutch to save; their houses are richly furnished, and their tables well served; none can out-do a merchant in good eating, if he makes it his business, and 'tis, no doubt, this sumptuous way of living that obliges them to sell their goods at dear rates, for being accustom'd to great expenses, they despise small gain. There's something very singular in their character, and which, in my opinion, distinguishes them still more from other merchants; no sooner do they acquire wealth, but they quit traffick, and turn country gentlemen.[2]

In this way, the ranks of the landed gentry were continually recruited from the cities as they long had been from the law courts: there was no permanent barrier between one section of the community and another, and this blending of interests made the governing classes more representative of the nation, strengthened the basis of the state, and assured the gains of the Revolution.

[1] F. W. Wyon, History of Great Britain during the Reign of Queen Anne (1876), ii. 283; Examiner, Mar. 29 and June 7, 1711; E. and A. G. Porritt, Unreformed House of Commons (1903), i. 166-81.

[2] B. L. Muralt, Letters Describing the Character and Customs of the English (tr. 1726), p. 9. Cf. Burnet, Own Time, ii. 652: 'As for the men of trade and business, they are, generally speaking, the best body in the nation, generous, sober, and charitable.'

In his review of Sir James Mackintosh's History of the Revolution in 1688,[1] Macaulay discusses what the permanent gains of the Revolution were. He mentions five—the Toleration Act, the final establishment of the Presbyterian Kirk in Scotland, the alteration in the mode of granting supplies, the purification of the adminstration of justice in political cases, and the full establishment of the liberty of unlicensed printing. He dwells at length on the last, which he regarded as the most important. During the greater part of the reign of Charles II the press had been fettered by the rigorous censorship established in 1662. From 1679 to 1683 it regained its freedom, but only to fall under the severe control of the law courts when Charles II triumphed over the Whigs.[2] James II's Parliament revived the system of censorship;[3] and the Licensing Act of James II continued in force till 1693, and, when it expired, was renewed for a couple of years. But the new licensers employed fell into discredit, and in 1695, when the Act expired, the House of Commons refused to renew it. Macaulay somewhat over-emphasises the emancipation of the press.

> Meanwhile events which no preceding historian has condescended to mention, but which were of far greater importance than the achievements of William's army or of Russell's fleet, were taking place in London. A great experiment was making. A great revolution was in progress. Newspapers had made their appearance.[4]

It is certainly true that other historians of the reign,

[1] Edinburgh Review, July 1835 (reprinted in Essays, ii. 104-9).

[2] Macaulay, I, 237, 260 (ii), 380 (iii).

[3] Ibid. II, 574 (v), 762 (vi), 854 (vii), 910.

[4] Ibid. V, 2540-8 (xxi).

whether contemporaries or not, did not appreciate the importance of the event in question. But the emancipation was brief and imperfect. The Stamp Act in the reign of Queen Anne, the paper taxes in the reign of George III, and the legal doctrines adopted in the law courts for more than a century, made freedom from the need of a licence a somewhat illusory gain for journalists.

There are other aspects of the intellectual development of England, after the Revolution, that Macaulay leaves in obscurity. The theories, the beliefs, and the arguments which influenced the minds of men deserve just as much attention as the machinery by which they were circulated. To the history of political thought, 'the noble science of politics' as Macaulay calls it in one of his articles, he pays curiously little attention. In chapter i he gives an account of the doctrine of divine right, as it was formulated by Filmer, and in chapter iii refers to the political theories of Harrington, treating both with equal contempt. Aversion to any abstract theory of politics probably accounts for his neglect of Locke. He tells us a certain number of trivial facts about him: that he was ejected from his studentship at Christ Church, dedicated one of his books to Lord Pembroke, and perhaps drew up a paper against the Licensing Act. But though he remarks incidentally that Locke's famous treatise excluded Roman Catholics from toleration, the only one of his writings deemed worthy of more than a line is a little pamphlet on the currency: 'It speedily became the text-book of all the enlightened politicians in the kingdom.' Why not state that his greater works also became text-books for the politicians of the time? 'Locke,' says the historian of English Thought in the Eighteenth Century, 'expounded the principles of the Revolution of 1688, and his writings became the political bible of the following century.'[1] The Two Treatises of Government Locke published in August 1689 were written, as Locke himself declares in the Preface, 'to establish the throne of our great restorer, our present King William', and 'to justify to the world the people of England'. He undertook in them the task Milton had undertaken forty years earlier in his Tenure of Kings and Magistrates, and his Defensio pro Populo Anglicano, and achieved his purpose with more success than Milton did. Locke's other writings exerted so great an influence on the development of English ideas on religion, politics, and philosophy that no history of the nation should have omitted them. To analyse at length the drivellings of Dodwell and the charges of the pamphleteers against Sherlock is an inadequate compensation for so serious an omission.

Macaulay's treatment of Dryden, and of the literature of William's reign in general, is open to similar objections. He mentions Dryden often but makes no attempt to bring out the significance of his writings in the development of English life. The period which follows the Revolution of 1688 has a character of its own. In foreign relations it is marked by the triumph of a national over a dynastic policy, in domestic affairs by the triumph of self-government. The nation through its representatives takes the management of its affairs into its own hands. The fashion is to regard the Revolution too much as if it were the triumph of aristocracy. Contemporaries saw more truly which way things were going. At the beginning of William's reign Tories like Evelyn complained that there was a republican spirit abroad; at the end the Whig Burnet lamented that we 'were become already more than half a common-

[1] Leslie Stephen, History of English Thought (1876), ii. 135.

wealth', and were 'falling insensibly into a democracy'.[1] This tendency appears in other writings of the times too. There is no revolution in English literature, but there is a definite development in a new direction. English literature becomes by degrees more independent of foreign influences, and characteristically national in the ideas it expresses and in the manner of expressing them. And as the statesmen henceforth seek habitually to secure the support of the people (or of that part of it possessing political rights), so the men of letters seem henceforth to appeal to a larger constituency than their predecessors had reached. They seek a wider audience than the Court and the universities. This had for some time been apparent in the case of writers on politics: it now becomes evident in the case of writers on philosophy and religion,[2] and even in the case of poets and critics. Dryden is an illustration. In his translations, his adaptations, and his critical writings he began to appeal to a larger public, and to seek to popularise literature.

In one of his essays Dryden says: 'Every age has a kind of universal genius, which inclines those that live in it to some particular studies.'[3] Part of the purpose of a history of England should be to bring out the unity of spirit which pervades the different manifestations of the national life. Macaulay's plan comprehended this. He purposed to combine a picture of all sides of the nation's life with a narrative of the events which happened between

[1] John Evelyn, Diary, Apr. 12, July 19, 1689; T. E. S. Clarke and H. C. Foxcroft, Life of Gilbert Burnet (1907), p. 385.

[2] Mark Pattison's essay on Tendencies of Religious Thought in England, 1688-1750, brings this out very clearly. Essays, ed. Henry Nettleship (1889), ii. 42 ff.

[3] An Essay of Dramatic Poesy, in W. P. Ker, Essays of John Dryden (2 vols.; 1926), i. 36.

the death of Charles II and the accession of the House of Hanover. He failed not only because of the inherent difficulties of the task, but also because he had to leave untold the story of half the thirty years he hoped to cover. The prologue contained in chapter iii was never completed by the epilogue which should have followed the close of the drama.

CHAPTER VII

ARMY AND NAVY

A CIVILIAN who undertakes to write the history of his country during the time when it was engaged in a great war has peculiar difficulties to overcome. Personally he may be most interested in the development of government or society, and best qualified to treat them : he is obliged nevertheless to enter unfamiliar fields, and to master a new series of problems. In relating military and naval affairs he is constantly liable to blunder. For that reason Marshal Schomberg advised Bishop Burnet 'never to meddle in the relation of military matters. He said, some affected to relate those affairs in all the terms of war, in which they committed errors that exposed them to the scorn of all commanders.' On the other hand soldiers and sailors are not as a rule accustomed to weigh authorities, and their accounts of historical events are often based on bad evidence or on a curious mixture of good and bad evidence. And, besides that, they often do not possess the art of making technical questions intelligible to the non-professional reader. Swift's comment on Schomberg's warning to Burnet was : 'Very foolish advice, for soldiers cannot write.'[1] Encouraged, no doubt, by Swift's dictum, Macaulay faced the risks which Schomberg had pointed out. One part of the task, however, was made easier for him by his political career. From 1839 to 1841 it had been his duty, as Secretary at War, to introduce the Annual Army

[1] Burnet, Own Time, i. 49.

Estimates, and in 1846, as Paymaster-General, he was again concerned with military finance. He had thus become interested in military questions, had acquired some knowledge of them, and had made the acquaintance of officials capable of helping him when he needed further information.

Macaulay made good use of these advantages. Military affairs are more adequately treated in his pages than in previous histories of the same time. He does not confine himself either to relating campaigns and battles, or to tracing the development of the army, but endeavours to show the relation of the army to the nation. He takes a broad and comprehensive view of the whole subject, which compensates for errors of detail.

It was necessary to take a broad view, for the history of an army cannot be understood if it is regarded apart from the history of the nation. The period with which Macaulay had to deal was a decisive one both for the development of our military institutions and the development of our political institutions. Both alike reflected the political conditions of the age in which they took shape. The British army grew up in the midst of the struggle against absolute monarchy, and every vicissitude in the struggle influenced its growth.

As Macaulay frequently points out, hostility to the existence of an army was a fundamental principle with the politicians of the latter part of the seventeenth century. This was the result of the Civil War. The twelve years' military rule which followed it had 'left deep and enduring traces in the public mind. The name of standing army was long held in abhorrence.'[1] The nation was sick of the very name, and held that a standing army was fatal to freedom and unnecessary for defence.

[1] I, 136 (ii); 283 (iii).

For protection against invasion or rebellion the country depended on the militia : 'the only army which the law recognised '.[1] Macaulay dwells at length on its popularity. Its full strength was supposed to be 130,000 men, but they were drilled only for fourteen days in the year at most, and in reality much less frequently, and were undisciplined as well as unexercised. Against rebellion they were practically useless : 4,000 of them were routed by Monmouth at Axminster and many deserted to him.[2] At Sedgemoor these deserters, still wearing their red-and-yellow uniforms,[3] were conspicuous in the ranks of the rebels. After Monmouth's rebellion it had been admitted that the militia was not in a satisfactory state, and on November 12, 1685, Parliament resolved that a bill should be brought in to make it more efficient.[4] But in reality the resolution was directed against the continuance of the standing army which James insisted on maintaining after the rebellion had been suppressed. That it would have been followed by any effective reforms is improbable, and as James never let Parliament meet again after the prorogation of November 20 no such bill was ever introduced.

When there was a threat of invasion the militia was full of zeal. The men called out in 1690 and 1692 assembled in thousands at the shortest possible notice and were eager to fight the French.[5] 'No man accustomed to war,' says Macaulay, could doubt that the trained soldiers of Louis XIV could easily have scattered three times their number of militia men. But the average Member of Parliament knew nothing of war, and believed, to use Macaulay's phrase, 'the spirit of the English people was such that

[1] I, 282 (iii).
[2] II, 570 (v).
[3] II, 582 (v).
[4] II, 686 (vi).
[5] IV, 1899-2900 (xvi) ; V, 2176 (xviii).

they would, with little or no training, encounter and defeat the most formidable array of veterans from the continent.'[1] Hence the treaty of Ryswick was followed by the immediate reduction of the army, first to 10,000 and then to 7,000 men. The formula adopted by the House of Commons in 1698 was that all forces raised since September 1680 were to be disbanded.[2] Macaulay summarises with great skill the arguments employed in the controversy between the opponents and the supporters of a standing army, and agrees with William III in holding that 7,000 men were far too few to secure the safety of the nation. He blames William for pressing for the retention of the Dutch guards instead of asking for an additional number of English troops instead, which he thinks the King might have succeeded in obtaining from Parliament.[3] On the other hand it is hardly fair to the opposition not to mention the facts that, besides the 7,000 men in England, about 7,000 more in Scotland and 12,000 in Ireland were retained in pay.[4] Even so, in the condition of Europe at the time, the army was far too small for its purpose. The treaty of Ryswick, like the treaty of Amiens, was merely a truce. Parliament in its ignorance of foreign affairs provided just enough men to maintain the peace of the kingdom against internal foes, but deprived the government of the striking force it needed in order to fulfil the foreign obligations of England and defend her European or colonial interests. In 1701 war broke out again, and the government was called upon to furnish 10,000 men for the defence of Holland (under the treaty of 1677) and was required at the same time to send a force to the

[1] VI, 2738 (xxiii).
[2] VI, 2743 (xxiii).
[3] VI, 2881-6 (xxiv).
[4] Charles Dalton, English Army Lists (6 vols.; 1892-1904), iv. pp. xviii, 216, 301; J. W. Fortescue, History of the British Army (1910), i. 388-9.

West Indies. It was only with the greatest difficulty that these men could be provided. Ireland was denuded of troops, fresh regiments were raised in a hurry to fill their places, and foreign troops were hired to complete the English contingent to the army of the coalition.

It does not seem to have occurred either to William or to his advisers that the reduction of the army made the proper organisation of the militia a measure of the first necessity. The opponents of a standing army praised the militia but they did nothing to make it an efficient weapon against foreign invaders. That was not effected till the elder Pitt carried his militia bill in 1757.[1] Mr. Fortescue terms that measure 'the one truly great military reform which marks our history in the eighteenth century'. The militia, he says in another passage, was 'the salvation of the country in the Napoleonic wars'.[2] Nevertheless, as soon as these wars ended, its services were forgotten. 'The annual training was suspended in 1829; and though the statutory machinery for raising, organising, and training such a force still existed nothing more was heard of the militia till after the Revolution of 1848.' It was revived and re-organised by Lord Derby's ministry in 1852. During Macaulay's tenure of the post of Secretary at War the militia had been nothing but a name; judging from the references to that institution in his History he doubted the possibility of making any militia an effective part of the national defences. Hence his treatment of the disbanding controversy is somewhat one-sided: he echoes, with complete conviction, all the contemporary arguments against the militia, and treats the arguments against a standing

[1] Basil Williams, Life of William Pitt (2 vols.; 1913), i. 277-9, 295, 403-7.

[2] J. W. Fortescue, The British Army, 1783-1802: Four Lectures (1905), pp. 26, 59.

army as mere claptrap. The true solution of the controversy was a compromise between the two systems : a combination of a well-trained militia with a nucleus of professional soldiers. A modern reader, with the example of the national armies of to-day before his eyes, can see this clearly ; Macaulay did not, though had he possessed a larger knowledge of military history he might have perceived it.

If, however, Macaulay's experience of military administration caused him to underestimate the value of the militia and to concentrate his whole attention on the standing army, at least he was led to familiarise himself with its history. He traces its development briefly but very exactly throughout the period. He proudly reminds his readers that 'the little army formed by Charles the Second was the germ of that great and renowned army which has, in the present century, marched triumphant into Madrid and Paris, into Canton and Candahar.'[1] He notes its growth in numbers. At the close of Charles II's reign the English army numbered about 7,000 foot and 1,700 horse. It was raised by James II in 1685 to 20,000 men[2] and by 1688 to about 34,000.[3] Under William it increased to 65,000 men in 1692, was 83,000[4] in 1694, and rose to 87,000 in 1697. By the disbanding which followed the peace of Ryswick it was reduced to 7,000.

This computation is but a rough one. At the close of Charles II's reign, the forces in Ireland numbered about 10,000 and those in Scotland nearly 3,000. After the disbanding of 1698 about 12,000 men were maintained in Ireland and about 7,000 in Scotland, so that the total for the three kingdoms was about 21,000 in 1685 and about

[1] I, 284 (iii).
[2] II, 664 (vi).
[3] III, 1106 (ix).
[4] V, 2426-7 (xx).

26,000 in 1698. And besides this there were in 1698 about 3,000 marines.[1] Taking either basis of comparison, it is clear that in the space of fifteen years a little army which was merely sufficient to keep the peace at home developed into one strong enough, if skilfully used, to determine the fate of a European war. In his reflections on the capture of Namur, Macaulay points out the significance of the change.

> During several generations our ancestors had achieved nothing considerable by land against foreign enemies. We had indeed occasionally furnished to our allies small bands of auxiliaries who had well maintained the honour of the nation. But from the day on which the two Talbots, father and son, had perished in the vain attempt to reconquer Guienne, till the Revolution, there had been on the Continent no campaign in which Englishmen had borne a principal part. At length our ancestors had again, after an interval of near two centuries and a half, begun to dispute with the warriors of France the palm of military prowess.[2]

Any author who undertakes to narrate the growth of the army must note the origin of the different regiments comprising it, and their successive incorporation in it. Macaulay does not fail to do this, and by devoting a few words to their history seeks to show the descent of existing regiments and to link the army of the seventeenth century to that of the nineteenth. Mr. Fortescue in his History of the British Army designates by their modern numbers old regiments which still survive. But it was not usual to do this when Macaulay wrote, and it was not so easy. No good account of the early history of the army existed, and Mr. Dalton's invaluable Army Lists had not been pub-

[1] VI, 2748 (xxiii).

[2] V, 2536-8 (xxi).

lished. Before 1751 regiments were generally designated by their commanders' names rather than by numbers, and their early history was often obscure. Fortunately for Macaulay a series of regimental histories began to be published in 1837. He writes: 'Most of the materials which I have used for this account of the regular army will be found in the Historical Records of Regiments, published by command of King William the Fourth, and under the direction of the Adjutant General.'[1] These official compilations had many defects, and in the case of most of the regiments included they have now been superseded by better books, but they sufficed to supply Macaulay with the data he needed. Supplementing them by the authorities published since, the regimental history of the army up to the disbanding of 1697 can be satisfactorily traced, and Macaulay's account corrected when necessary.

The formation of the army dates not from the year of the King's restoration but from 1661. Its nucleus consisted of three troops and three regiments. The three troops were the King's, the Duke of York's, and the Duke of Albemarle's troops of life guards, which are now represented by the First and Second Life Guards. The three regiments were the Earl of Oxford's regiment of horse, known later as the Blues; the King's own regiment of Foot Guards, now the Grenadier Guards; and one regiment of foot from the Cromwellian army, which became known as the Coldstream Guards. Other regiments were raised from time to time as occasion demanded and disbanded again when the need was over. Five of them are still to

[1] I, 288 (iii). Between 1837 and 1852 there were published, in all, 71 volumes, which included records of all the existing regiments of cavalry and of 42 regiments of infantry of the line. They were edited by Richard Cannon, principal clerk of the Adjutant-General's office, excepting the history of the Royal Horse Guards, which was written by Captain Edmund Packe.

be found in the Army List. Of these five, two were regiments which had served under foreign flags and were recalled to fight under their own. The first regiment of foot—the Royal Scots—had been raised in 1633 for service in France, and was permanently transferred to the English establishment in 1678. The third regiment of foot—the Buffs—consisted of Englishmen in the Dutch service who returned to England in 1665 when Charles declared war on the United Provinces. The three remaining regiments were formed from the garrison which had held Tangiers against the Moors till its evacuation in 1684. Two were infantry regiments and are now the Second and the Fourth of the Line; the other is the First Dragoons.

James II's army is represented by nineteen existing regiments. Nine regiments of infantry of the line, from the seventh to the fifteenth inclusive, and the cavalry regiments now known as the first six regiments of Dragoon Guards and the third and fourth Hussars, were raised to suppress Monmouth's rebellion. Two other existing regiments of infantry, the sixteenth and seventeenth, were raised to meet the threatened invasion of William of Orange. James also called into England in 1688 various regiments from Scotland and Ireland, and, of these, three Scottish and one Irish regiment were after the Revolution incorporated in the English army. One was the Scots Guards; the others were the Second Dragoons or Scots Greys, and Twenty-first Foot or Royal Scots Fusileers. The Irish regiment added at the same time was the Eighteenth Foot or Royal Irish.

Though the great army William created was disbanded in 1698 he left his mark permanently on the Army List. When he sailed from Holland he brought over with him the English regiments then in the Dutch service. One of these became the Fifth Foot or Northumberland Fusileers, the other is the Sixth or Royal Warwickshire Regiment. The Nineteenth and Twentieth Foot and the Seventh Dragoon Guards, represent regiments raised by William's English supporters after he landed. Eight regiments owe their existence to the struggle with James and his supporters in Scotland and Ireland. The Twenty-second, Twenty-third, and Twenty-fourth Foot were raised to reconquer Ireland and formed part of the unlucky expedition which served under Schomberg. The Twenty-fifth and Twenty-sixth Foot—the King's Own Scottish Borderers and the Cameronians—were raised to fight Dundee.[1] The forces which the Protestants of Ulster raised to defend themselves survive in the Twenty-seventh Foot or Inniskilling Fusileers, in the Fifth Lancers, long known as the Royal Irish Dragoons, and in the Sixth or Inniskilling Dragoons.

Between the commencement of the war with France and the treaty of Ryswick, many more new regiments were raised. According to Macaulay, four new regiments of dragoons, six of horse, and fifteen of infantry were voted by the House of Commons in December 1693.[2] The only permanent additions to the Army List were the two regiments now known as the Seventh and Eighth Hussars, one a regiment of dragoons formed in Scotland about 1690, the other a regiment of dragoons formed in Ireland about 1693.[3] The rest of the new regiments were disbanded in 1698, but at the close of 1701 it became evident that the

[1] Cf. A Ross, Old Scottish Regimental Colours (1885), pp. 39, 42.

[2] V, 2426-7 (xx).

[3] Fortescue, History of the British Army, iv. 368, 376 ; Dalton, English Army Lists, iv. 3, 61, 62 ; Ross, op. cit., p. 49 ; C. R. B. Barrett, History of the Seventh Hussars (1914).

renewal of the war was merely a question of weeks, and in February 1702, a month before William's death, nine new regiments of infantry and six of marines were ordered to be raised. Of these fifteen regiments eleven are still represented in the British army, the Twenty-eighth to the Thirty-seventh Foot and the Thirty-ninth Foot. Three of these, the Thirtieth, the Thirty-first, and the Thirty-second, were originally marines.[1]

Macaulay is less satisfactory when he deals with the equipment of the army. He states briefly that infantry regiments continued to be composed of both musketeers and pikemen, that the pike was giving way to the musket, but that there was still at the end of Charles II's reign 'a large intermixture of pikemen'.[2] By that time, he says, the musketeer was generally provided with a new weapon, viz. a dagger to be inserted in the muzzle of his piece, known from William III's time by the name of bayonet. In a later passage he mentions Mackay's introduction of the ring-bayonet, which could be fixed upon the barrel, in place of the plug bayonet.[3] He does not however mention the nature of the musket in use or the improvement which took place in the armament of the infantry during William's reign.[4] The researches of Colonel Clifford Walton have made these points clear. We now know that while at the commencement of Charles II's reign a third of a regiment consisted of pikemen, the proportion was reduced to about a fourth by 1692, and to about a fifth in 1698, while the pike was definitely abandoned by the infantry about

[1] Fortescue, History of the British Army, i. 400 ; Dalton, op. cit. iv. pp. xxi, 10.

[2] I, 286 (iii).

[3] IV, 1640-2 (xiii).

[4] See Hugh Mackay, Memoirs of the War Carried On in Scotland and Ireland, 1689-1691 (Bannatyne Club, 1833), p. 52.

1705. During the same period the matchlock was superseded by the fusil, firelock, or flintlock. At first only a small number in each regiment had firelocks; by the end of Charles II's reign all the Guards were armed with them; by the Revolution about half of the soldiers in other regiments carried them, and there were some regiments known as fusileers entirely armed with them. The proportion of fusils in use continued during the war with France, though the matchlock was not entirely disused at the close of the century. 'Under William's rule,' concludes Colonel Walton, 'the English infantry became perhaps the best armed in Europe.'[1]

Another subject on which the History must be corrected and supplemented from Colonel Walton's book is the administration of the army. Macaulay tells us emphatically that it was bad, but nothing more. 'Under James the courtiers took bribes from the colonels; the colonels cheated the soldiers; the commissaries sent in long bills for what had never been furnished: the keepers of the magazines sold the public stores and pocketed the price. But these evils, though they had sprung into existence and grown to maturity under the government of Charles and James, first made themselves severely felt under the government of William.'[2] Instances of various abuses are given later. Nowhere however is there an account of the manner in which the army was organised and governed. Indeed, when Macaulay wrote, the subject had been so little investigated that there would have been difficulty in putting together a good account of it from printed sources, though the War Office papers would have supplied the

[1] Clifford Walton, History of the British Standing Army, A.D. 1660 to 1700 (1894), pp. 427, 428, 431, 433.

[2] III, 1368-9 (xi).

necessary materials. Hence Macaulay is inclined to attribute to the iniquity of the age or the corruption of individuals, failures and evils really due to defective organisation.[1]

As a military historian Macaulay's chief defect is the propensity to substitute a vague and rhetorical description for a statement of the facts. There are some serious omissions in his narrative. The strength of the force with which William of Orange landed in England is very material. It is the first question which a soldier who was writing an account of the campaign would seek to determine. Macaulay however tells us that James had at his disposal in England about forty thousand men,[2] and that the army he assembled at Salisbury on the news of William's landing, 'though inferior in discipline to that of William, was superior in numbers'. But he does not mention the numbers in either army.[3] He describes picturesquely the entrance of William's army into Exeter. First came two hundred gentlemen under the Earl of Macclesfield, 'glittering in helmets and cuirasses' and 'mounted on Flemish war horses'. There followed 'a squadron of Swedish horsemen in black armour and fur cloaks'. Then came 'a long column of the whiskered infantry of Switzerland'—and so on.[4] With all these details there are no figures. Bishop Burnet had no pretensions to being a military historian, but he does tell us that

[1] A good illustration of the defects of the military administration of the time is supplied by Mr. Fortescue's account of the expedition sent to the West Indies in 1695. The British Army, pp. 24-26. The administration is dealt with at length by Col. Walton.

[2] III, 1106 (ix).

[3] According to Mr. Fortescue, James got together about 24,000 men at Salisbury. History of the British Army, i. 306.

[4] III, 1132-8 (ix).

the Prince resolved to bring 9,000 foot and 4,000 horse and dragoons, and the statement is approximately correct.[1] With a force not much more than half that which James assembled at Salisbury, William did not hesitate to march against him. By a statement of the exact figures, Macaulay would have better explained the campaign, and enhanced the merit of William's achievement.

Again a reader of the History is surprised and somewhat disagreeably impressed by what appears to be the inactivity of William's government during the first six months of his reign. He accepted the crown on February 13, 1689, but Londonderry was not relieved till July and Schomberg did not land in Ireland till August. The complaints of the Whigs against William's government and their attacks on the minister who was held responsible for this delay, seem at first sight justifiable. But Macaulay does not explain the military situation properly. Immediately after his accession William had been obliged to send back to Holland most of the Dutch troops he had brought with him.[2] They were urgently needed for the defence of their own country against the French. Macaulay does not mention this. He explains that 'France had declared war against the States General: and the States General had consequently demanded from the King of England those

[1] Burnet, Own Time, i. There is a list of the regiments and their strength given in a contemporary broadside printed in the Somers Tracts, ix. 270. Their nominal strength was 14,352 (3,660 horse and 10,692 foot), their real strength apparently about 12,000. See also Abel Boyer, History of King William the Third (3 vols.; 1702-3), i. 227.

[2] Narcissus Luttrell, A Brief Historical Relation of State Affairs (6 vols.; 1857), i. 503-4, 507-9. See also P. L. Müller, Wilhelm III von Oranien und Georg Friedrich von Waldeck (2 vols.; 1873, 1880), ii. 126-7, 143, 147, 164. According to Mr. Fortescue four battalions of guards and six of the line were sent. By treaty 10,000 men should have been sent, but the regiments were not up to their proper strength. History of the British Army, i. 334.

succours which he was bound by the treaty of Nimeguen to furnish,' and he adds that William 'had ordered some battalions to march to Harwich, that they might be in readiness to cross to the Continent.'[1] But the fact that in consequence of the demand of the States-General nearly 10,000 of the best troops in the English army were actually dispatched abroad in March 1689 is not stated. The picturesque account of the mutiny of the Royal Scots which Macaulay gives does not adequately replace the figures which would have made the military situation intelligible.[2]

Similarly in his accounts of battles, where a military historian would give a definite statement of the regiments engaged and their movements, Macaulay substitutes a general description of the fighting.[3] This is not due to the defects of the authorities he employs; they contain sufficiently precise information to enable him to be more exact. In his desire to produce a picture he suppresses details, sometimes those details which are necessary to explain the events he is relating. It is difficult for a civilian to know what the really important details are. A movement which he passes over in silence may be, to the eye of a soldier, the turning point of a battle or the decisive stroke of a campaign. The best thing he can do is to

[1] III, 1346-7 (xi).

[2] The late king's army besides being mutinous and disaffected is said to have been reduced by wholesale desertion to about half its numbers. Luttrell, i. 494, 505. This is perhaps an exaggeration, but the army was certainly much reduced in numbers and had to be completely reorganised before it could be employed. New regiments had to be raised before Schomberg's expedition could take place. Small detachments such as the two regiments sent to Londonderry under Cunningham in April and three under Kirke in June were all that could be spared. Walter Harris, History of the Life and Reign of . . . William III (1749), pp. 204, 207.

[3] Compare for instance Macaulay's accounts of the battles of Steinkirk and Landen (V, 2232-8 [xix], 2355-62 [xx]) with Mr. Fortescue's (History of the British Army, i. 361, 370).

present the facts as clearly as possible and leave judgements on strategy and tactics to persons better qualified to form them. Macaulay avoids the mistake of showing how battles ought to have been fought, but does not always state with sufficient clearness how they were fought. In this respect he has been compared, to his disadvantage, with Thiers. A critic of the historian of Napoleon's campaigns observes :

> L'art de M. Thiers, ici comme dans son style, se cache si bien, qu'on est en danger de ne pas assez le sentir. On a besoin, pour apprécier tout le talent déployé par l'auteur, d'appeler à son aide la réflexion et la comparaison. Prenons, par example, l'un des plus brillants de nos historiens modernes ; ouvrons Macaulay, et parcourons ces tableaux pâles et confus qu'il retrace dès qu'il s'agit de décrire des opérations militaires : lisons sa victoire de La Boyne ou sa défaite de Nerwinde, et nous reconnaîtrons aussitôt la supériorité de l'écrivain francais.[1]

One cannot agree that Macaulay's battles are colourless, but they are certainly less clear than those of Thiers because the details are not given with equal precision. Macaulay regarded such details as dull. 'I turned over,' he writes in his diary, 'the new volumes of Thiers's book ; the Austrian campaign of 1809. It is heavy. I hope that my volumes will be more attractive reading.'[2]

Macaulay does not deal comprehensively with the story of the army's revolt against James II. In the strictest sense of the words it was not a military revolt. It was not dictated by professional interests ; no desire for laxer discipline or more pay had any part in producing it, nor were the

[1] Edmond Scherer, Etudes critiques sur la littérature contemporaine (1863), i. 145-6.

[2] July 1852. Trevelyan, ii. 315.

officers inspired by personal ambition. The feelings which moved officers and soldiers were the feelings which moved the majority of the nation: their revolt was part of a national movement.

Macaulay insists on this aspect of the revolt. He dates the commencement of the disaffection from the winter of 1685-1686, when James showed his intention of overriding the laws against the employment of Roman Catholics. 'Already began to appear the first symptoms of that feeling which three years later impelled so many officers of high rank to desert the royal standard.'[1] This disaffection was not confined to the officers. When James established his camp at Hounslow, 'he hoped that his army would overawe London; but the result of his policy was that the feelings and opinions of London took complete possession of the army.'[2] When he imprisoned the Seven Bishops in the Tower the sentries asked the blessing of their prisoners:[3] when the bishops were acquitted the regiments in camp shouted for joy.[4] 'The army was scarcely less disaffected than the clergy and gentry. . . . The force he relied on as the means of coercing the people shared the opinions of the people . . . It was plain that if he determined to persist in his designs he must remodel his army.'[5] Accordingly James attempted to coerce the English by appealing to the aid of the Irish. He brought over some regiments from the Irish army and endeavoured to incorporate Irish recruits in English regiments. 'Of the many errors James had committed none was more fatal than this.' The sight of 'armed columns of Papists just arrived from Dublin' inflamed the national

[1] II, 674-5 (vi).
[2] II, 758 (vi).
[3] II, 1006 (viii).
[4] II, 1031 (viii).
[5] III, 1066-8 (ix).

antipathy of the English people against the Irish race. 'These were the men who were to hold England down by main force while her civil and ecclesiastical constitution was destroyed. The blood of the whole nation boiled at the thought.'[1] When the officers of an English regiment refused to obey the order to admit Irish recruits, and were cashiered by a court martial for their disobedience, 'the whole nation applauded the disgraced officers.'[2]

At this crisis the invasion of William of Orange took place. A number of colonels and other officers deserted to William. Few soldiers followed them, but their action was fatal to discipline. 'That prompt obedience without which an army is merely a rabble was necessarily at an end.'[3] The material strength of the army was little diminished, but its moral strength had been destroyed. Unable to fight, James withdrew his army as William advanced, and finally ordered it to disband, and fled from England.

Macaulay narrates these events, and condemns the treachery of certain individual officers, but does not examine the question whether the policy of James justified the refusal of the officers to obey him. Yet that was a question which every officer in the army must have been obliged to ask himself. The great difference between the politics of the seventeenth century and those of the next age is that Englishmen, whether citizens or soldiers, were continually debating whether it was right to resist their government by arms, and if so, when. For nearly a century the controversy about right of resistance or the duty of passive obedience filled pamphlets, sermons, and constitutional treatises. It was a practical, not a theoretical, problem. Macaulay discusses it at length, and shows that

[1] III, 1068-9 (ix).
[2] III, 1071-2 (ix).
[3] III, 1150 (ix).

the clergy and the gentry who formed the Tory party were led by the policy of James to abandon the doctrine of non-resistance. He concludes, as they did, that there were cases in which rebellion was justifiable. Yet he never considers the question in relation to the army, but only in relation to the nation. Admitting that there are cases in which a citizen is justified in resisting the government, are there cases in which a soldier is justified in doing it? He answers by a general maxim: 'Of all the maladies incident to the body politic, military insubordination is that which requires the most prompt and drastic remedies. If the evil be not stopped as soon as it appears, it is certain to spread; and it cannot spread far without danger to the very vitals of the commonwealth.'[1] No one will dispute this, but are there no limits to military obedience? It is only when he is discussing the responsibility for the massacre of Glencoe that Macaulay touches the question. He says that if the soldiers are ordered to 'lay a thriving town in ashes' or 'shoot a whole gang of banditti', the responsibility lies with the officer who gives the order, not with the men who obey it. The soldiers of Captain Campbell of Glenlyon were not to be punished for obeying the orders of their captain, nor was he to be punished for obeying the orders of Lieutenant Colonel Hamilton. On the other hand 'the orders given to Glenlyon were of so peculiar a nature that if he had been a virtuous man, he would have thrown up his commission, would have braved the displeasure of Colonel, General, and Secretary of State, would have incurred the highest penalty which a court martial would inflict, rather than have performed the part assigned to him.' In this case 'disobedience was assuredly a moral duty.'[2]

[1] III, 1351 (xi). [2] V, 2511-2 (xxi).

How do these pronouncements apply to the political situation in 1688? Like Macaulay, the Whigs did not discuss the abstract question, but they had no doubt that there were limits to military obedience, and that the refusal of the officers to obey the orders of the King was justifiable. One of the first acts of the Convention was to vote that 'the thanks of this House be given to the officers, soldiers, and mariners, in the army and fleet, for having testified their steady adherence to the Protestant religion, and being instrumental in delivering this kingdom from popery and slavery.' [1]

In this vote the navy was coupled with the army. Many officers and sailors were opposed to the King's policy but circumstances prevented the open manifestation of their hostility and kept their plots from coming to a head. Hence the action of the malcontents was retarded and the defection of the navy followed that of the army instead of accompanying it. In the summer of 1688 James sent out a squadron of twenty ships under Sir Roger Strickland to observe the motions of the Dutch fleet, but Strickland's fleet was only half-manned, and the celebration of the mass on board his flagship nearly caused a mutiny. On October 1 Strickland was superseded by Lord Dartmouth, and at the same time the fleet was raised to about forty ships. It was however very doubtful whether the fleet would fight. William hoped it would not. 'You must be already sensible,' said his letter to the officers and sailors, 'that you are only made use of as instruments to bring both your selves and your country under popery and slavery. . . . And therefore wee hope that God will put it in your hearts at this time to redeeme your selves, your

[1] Feb. 1, 1689. Architell Grey, Debates of the House of Commons (1763), ix. 41.

countrey, and your religion.'[1] To attract their support, the Prince placed his fleet under the command of Admiral Herbert, and many English sailors served under him. Through Herbert and Captain Edward Russell, who also sailed in the expedition, he worked on the malcontents. According to Russell, eight of Dartmouth's captains were resolved to come over to the Prince, and this statement is confirmed from other sources. The malcontents were the ablest and most influential officers in the fleet, and their defection would have been followed by that of others. Dartmouth's own loyalty was above suspicion. Despite the inferiority of his numbers, he was prepared to fight the Dutch fleet whenever he could meet it. But during the passage of the expedition down the Channel the weather prevented him from getting out of harbour. Through Pepys the King expressed his conviction that Dartmouth had done 'all that a prudent and careful admirall could doe', considering, as he said, 'the place in which you were then hooked and the wind that then blew to the benefit of the Holland's fleet, and disadvantage of yours'.[2] After the landing of the expedition at Torbay, Dartmouth put to sea intending to attack the Dutch fleet there, but was driven back by a storm and his ships were much damaged. 'I am sorry you have been so roughly used by the winds at sea,' wrote James. 'This is a bad tyme of

[1] English Historical Review, i. 523, 527. One of the chief actors in the conspiracy was George Byng, afterwards Earl of Torrington, then first lieutenant of the 'Mordaunt' under Captain John Ashby. Extracts from his life were printed by Sir John Dalrymple, in his Memoirs of Great Britain and Ireland (2 vols.; 1771, 1773); and in 1889 the life as a whole was edited by Sir John Laughton under the title of Memoirs Relating to the Lord Torrington (Camden Society). This is supplemented by the selection from Herbert's correspondence printed by Sir E. M. Thompson in the English Historical Review.

[2] Hist. MSS. Comm., Dartmouth MSS., i (1887), 186. Nov. 7, 1688.

yeare for any action upon that inconstant element. The preservation of the squadron under your command is of the last consequence.'[1] Negotiations prevented further attempts to fight. On November 30 James issued a proclamation announcing that a new Parliament would be called for January 15. Next day all the captains in the fleet signed an address of thanks to the King declaring that a Parliament was the only means left to quiet the minds of the people, and trusting that it would lead to 'the settlement in this realm both in Church and State, according to the establish'd laws of the kingdom.' Dartmouth signed it too, apologising to the King because the officers were so unanimous that he could not help himself, and hoping that it would be 'no offence nor disservice' to his Majesty.[2] Dartmouth's obedience had its limits. He would not join William of Orange, but he refused to obey the King's repeated orders to carry the Prince of Wales to France. It 'will be of fatal consequence', he told James, to your person, crown, and dignity, and all your people will (too probably) grow so much concerned at this your great mistrust, as to throw off their bounden allegeance to you. . . . Can the Prince's being sent to France, have other prospect than the entailing a perpetual war upon your nation and posterity; and giving France always a temptation, to molest, invade, nay hazard the conquest of England. . . . I will not be instrumental in, nor suffer him to be carried into France, if by any means I can prevent it.[3]

James yielded to this remonstrance and ordered the Prince to be sent to London instead. Dalrymple prints

[1] Ibid. p. 219. Nov. 29, 1688. Dalrymple (op. cit. ii. 319-31) printed several of Dartmouth's letters. Since then the whole correspondence has been printed in Dartmouth MSS., i.

[2] Dartmouth MSS., i. 275. The address is printed in the Second Collection of Papers Relating to the Present Juncture of Affairs in England (1688).

[3] Dalrymple, op. cit. ii, App. pt. i, 328-30. Cf. Macaulay, III, 1171-4 (ix).

this letter and another in which Dartmouth expressed his despair at learning the King's own intention to fly to France, but he does not print the letter in which the King announced his intentions and ordered Dartmouth to take what ships he could to Ireland and place them at the disposal of Tyrconnel. It was dated Whitehall, December 10.[1]

My affairs are, as you know, in so desperat a condition that I have been obliged to send away the Queene and the Prince, to secure them at least, what so ever becoms of me, that am resolved to ventur all rather than consent to anything in the least prejuditial to the Crowne or my conscience, and having been basely deserted by many officers and souldiers of my troups, and finding such an infection gott amongst very many of those who still continu with me on shore, and that the same poysone is gott amongst the fleett, as you yourself owne to me in some of your letters, I could no longer resolve to expose myself to no purpose to what I might expect from the ambitious Prince of Orange and the assosiated rebellious Lords, and therefore have resolved to withdraw, till this violent storme is over, which will be in God's good tyme, and hope that there will still remaine in this land seven thousand men which will not bow downe the knee to Baal and keep themselves free from assosiations and such rebellious practices. I know not whether any of the fleett under your command are free to continu serving me; if they are, their best course will be to go to Irland, where there are still some that will stick to me. If any are free to go order them thither to follow such orders as they shall receve from Lord Tyrconnel. If they will not there is no remedy, and this I may say, never any Prince took more care of his sea and land men as I have done, and been so very ill repayd by them.

This was too much for even the loyal Dartmouth. He preferred to obey the orders he received from the council

[1] Dartmouth MSS., i. 226.

of peers which assembled at the Guildhall when the King's flight was discovered. Like them, there being now no government in existence, Dartmouth addressed himself to the Prince of Orange. As he said in 1691, 'After the King was withdrawn, I could not think the fleet under my command belonged to any but my country, to whom I brought it by God's blessing safe home, without making any capitulations with the then Prince of Orange.' [1]

This episode has been dwelt on at some length partly because it is interesting to compare the conduct of the army and the navy and partly because the new materials published since Macaulay wrote have made the action of the navy and its commander much clearer. In dealing with the history of the navy, Macaulay had none of the advantages which he possessed when he treated military affairs. He started with less knowledge of the subject and he had imperfect materials at his disposal. There were two books of some little merit to which he frequently referred. One was The Naval History of England in All Its Branches, from the Conquest to the Conclusion of 1734, by Thomas Lediard: a compilation in a couple of folio volumes, which Sir John Laughton says is, for its date, both comprehensive and accurate. It was published in 1735. The other was the valuable contemporary history called Memoirs of Transactions at Sea during the War with France Beginning in 1688 and Ending in 1697. This was by Josiah Burchett, Secretary to the Admiralty from 1695 to 1742, and was published in 1703. For the personal history of the commanders, Macaulay had at his disposal Charnock's Biographia Navalis, published in 1794. There was a number of contemporary pamphlets about naval affairs, but hardly any documents relating to

[1] Ibid. p. 290.

them were then available in print. Since that time, not only a large amount of documentary materials but several valuable books based on those materials have been printed. Events have been more exactly ascertained and retold, while the strategy and tactics of the naval commanders on both sides have been explained and criticised by competent writers. Macaulay wrote when the facts of the war had not received this critical treatment, and when the principles of naval warfare had neither been scientifically worked out nor clearly stated. Under these conditions it was impossible for any historian to write an adequate and satisfactory account of the war at sea unless he could devote some years to preliminary investigations.

The new evidence which has been printed since Macaulay wrote is mainly to be found in the Calendar of State Papers, Domestic, and the Manuscripts of the House of Lords. The first contains abstracts of the official correspondence of the Admiralty (up to 1697) and the second the evidence laid before the various committees appointed from time to time to enquire into the administration of the navy or the conduct of its commanders. A few scattered documents are also to be found in the reports of the Historical Manuscripts Commission, and for the reign of Charles II there is the invaluable calendar of the Pepys Manuscripts in Magdalene College, Cambridge, edited by Dr. J. R. Tanner and published by the Navy Records Society.

The narrative and critical works in which the theory of naval warfare is illustrated by reference to this particular period are: Admiral Mahan's Influence of Sea Power upon History (1890), Admiral P. H. Colomb's Naval Warfare (1891), and Sir Julian Corbett's England in the Mediterranean (1904). The second volume of the History of the Royal Navy edited by W. Laird Clowes, which appeared in 1898, deals with the period covered by Macaulay. Finally, the numerous articles contributed by Sir John Laughton to the Dictionary of National Biography have superseded Charnock's lives of the naval commanders of the seventeenth century. In the light of these later authorities it is not surprising to find that the naval part of Macaulay's History needs rewriting. To produce a satisfactory account of naval affairs from 1688 to 1697 would necessitate consulting not only these authorities, but the mass of unprinted naval documents now in the Public Record Office. All that can be done here is to elucidate a few of the more important points.

In the third chapter of his History Macaulay describes the condition of the navy at the close of Charles II's reign. 'It had sunk', he says, 'into degradation and decay such as would be almost incredible were it not certified to us by the independent and concurring evidence of witnesses whose authority is beyond exception.'[1] But it is not just to lay the blame entirely on the King. Macaulay says that Parliament had always been 'bountiful to profusion when the interests of the navy were concerned,' but that the 'liberality of the nation had been made fruitless by the vices of the government.' But the fact is that the sum voted by Parliament during the first four years of the King's reign was never sufficient to defray the cost of the navy, and then the Dutch war came and overwhelmed the navy with debts which hampered it for the rest of the reign. The fanaticism of the nation was more detrimental to the navy than the vices of the King. Immediately after the Restoration the administration of the navy was bad; thanks to the Duke of York and Mr. Pepys, it was greatly

[1] I, 289 (iii).

improved; in 1673 the Duke of York was deprived of the post of Lord High Admiral by the Test Act; in 1679 Mr. Pepys was removed from the Secretaryship of the Admiralty on the suspicion of popery. The board of experts to whom Pepys had been secretary was replaced by a board of politicians selected for their popularity and their influence in Parliament. It was under this board, which lasted from 1679 to 1684, that the navy sank into the condition which Macaulay describes.[1]

In May 1684, Charles II dismissed this incompetent board and took the government of the navy into his own hands, with the advice and assistance of the Duke of York. 'His Majesty', wrote James to the Prince of Orange, 'declared at the Cabinetcouncell that he thought it for his service to recalle the Commission of the Admirality and, without making me admiral, to lett me have the managing of it.'[2] On June 10, 1684, Pepys was appointed 'Secretary for the Affairs of the Admiralty of England' by letters patent and set to work to reform the administration. On his recommendation, a special commission 'for the recovery of the navy' was named in April 1686, and during the next two and a half years put the ships into thorough repair and reorganised the dockyards. The story of the decay and the restoration of the navy is told by Pepys in a vindication of his administration which he published in

[1] 'If the naval administrations of the period from the Restoration to the Revolution are viewed as a whole, it is difficult to avoid the conclusion that they are not quite as black as they have been painted . . . except during the period 1679 to 1684 there was no abject incompetence, and something was effected from time to time in the way of solid reform.' A Descriptive Catalogue of the Naval Manuscripts in the Pepysian Library at Magdalene College, Cambridge, ed. J. R. Tanner, i (Publications of the Navy Records Society, vol. xxvi; 1903), 244-5.

[2] G. Groen van Prinsterer, Archives ou correspondance inédite de la Maison d'Orange-Nassau, Ser. II, vol. v (1861), 586.

1690. It is entitled Memoires Relating to the State of the Royal Navy of England for Ten Years Determined December 1688.[1] Macaulay frequently refers to it, and terms Pepys 'the ablest man in the English Admiralty.'[2]

After the Revolution the Admiralty was once more put in commission, as it had been from 1673 to 1684. Under the commissioners of the Admiralty were the Navy Office, the Victualling Board, established in 1683, and a Transport Board, established in 1689. Ships were built and repaired in the six great dockyards under the control of the Navy Office; disabled seamen were pensioned from the Chatham Chest, or after 1696 provided for through Greenwich Hospital. To ensure its proper working this system of administration required a strong and competent Admiralty Board. Unhappily the Commissioners of the Admiralty came more and more to be politicians, without any practical knowledge of naval affairs, and often with no experience of administration. Pepys was removed at the Revolution and no secretary of equal ability replaced him. Expert knowledge was supposed to be provided by the Commissioners of the Navy and other subordinates. Under those conditions the administration of the navy fell into disorder. Macaulay lays the blame on a man whom he particularly detested rather than on the system to which the maladministration was due.[3] Arthur Herbert, created Earl of Torrington on June 15, 1689, was made First Lord of the Admiralty on March 8, 1689, and resigned that post on January 6, 1690. As he was at sea most of the summer

[1] I, 294 (iii). A reprint edited by Dr. J. R. Tanner was published by the Clarendon Press in 1906. His introduction should be compared with vol. i of the Catalogue of the Naval Manuscripts, pp. 65-98.

[2] I, 289 (iii); 440 (iv); III, 1106 (ix).

[3] IV, 1696-8 (xiv).

he cannot fairly be held responsible for faults which his colleagues should have corrected. During the winter he endeavoured to remedy some of them, but without success. According to Burnet, 'he tried to dictate to the Board; and, when he found that did not pass upon them, he left it: and studied all he could to disparage their conduct; and it was thought he hoped to have been advanced to that high trust alone.'[1] He was opposed not only by his five colleagues, none of whom had any naval experience, but also by the principal Secretary of State, the Earl of Nottingham. When he urged many reasons for strengthening the fleet, Nottingham only answered, 'You will be strong enough for the French.' 'My Lord,' replied Torrington, 'I know my business, and will do my best with what I have; but pray remember it is not my fault that the fleet is no stronger. I own I am afraid now, in winter, whilst the danger may be remedied; and you will be afraid in summer, when it is past remedy.'[2] From these facts it is obvious that when Macaulay censures Torrington for the inefficiency of the fleet, he is unjust. On Torrington's resignation, Thomas, Earl of Pembroke, was made First Lord, but three out of the five old commissioners remained in office till March 1692. Why Pembroke was appointed is not clear. Burnet describes him as

> a man of eminent virtue, and of great and profound learning, particularly in the mathematics: this made him a little too speculative and abstracted in his notions: he had great application, but he lived a little too much out of the world, though in a public station; a little more practice among men would give him the last finishing: there was something in his person and manner that created him

[1] Burnet, Own Time, ii. 5.

[2] P. H. Colomb, Naval Warfare (1891), p. 112.

an universal respect; for we had no man among us whom all sides loved and honoured so much as they did him.[1]

Under this peer of immense respectability but little practical ability, the administration of the navy does not seem to have been any better than it was when Torrington was First Lord. In March 1692, Pembroke was replaced by Lord Cornwallis, and on his death in April 1693, he was succeeded by Anthony, Viscount Falkland. He had been treasurer of the navy in 1681 and one of the Admiralty commissioners since January 1691, so that he had some experience of naval administration. In December 1693 the House of Commons charged him with peculation, for which he was censured and lost his place.[2] On May 2, 1694, Edward Russell (created in 1697 Earl of Orford) became First Lord and held the post till June 1699. According to Macaulay, 'from the time he became first lord of the admiralty there was a decided improvement in the naval administration.' The men who served under him 'had better food and drink than they ever had before.' But in another passage, when speaking of the causes which led to Russell's retirement from office in 1699, Macaulay comes to the conclusion that while Russell may have spent the public money better than his predecessors, he embezzled a great deal of it.[3] These charges of embezzlement may or may not be true; but they prove conclusively that the finances of the navy were very badly managed. Torrington was probably not far wrong when he described the commissioners of the admiralty as a set of 'insipid ignorants'.[4] It was true of most of them, but perhaps

[1] Burnet, ii. 199.

[2] Grey, Debates, x. 348-56.

[3] V, 2454 (xx); VI, 2887-8 (xxiv).

[4] Epistolary Curiosities, ed. Rebecca Warner, 1st Ser. (1818), p. 157.

there was a good deal of corruption in their incapacity. Until the history of the naval administration of the period has been more minutely investigated, it is impossible to decide.

The sea-fights of the period are a more attractive subject. The strategic aspects of the war as a whole have been admirably summarised by Admiral Mahan. He points out the initial mistake made by Louis XIV in not preventing the conjunction of England and Holland. At the moment of William's expedition, Louis 'could control the sea if he would.' He should have sent his navy into the Channel and attacked Holland by land. In this way he would have kept William at home. But instead of that he turned his armies against Germany, and left the road to England open instead of using his navy to bar it.[1] After the Revolution Louis, having a decided superiority at sea, failed properly to support James II in Ireland. Ireland was the weakest point in William's frontier, and as long as it was unsubdued his power was not secure in England. Louis ought to have used his fleet during 1689 and 1690 to prevent the transport of William's forces to Ireland or to cut the communications between William's forces there and their base in England. 'There is nothing more striking than the carelessness shown by both the contending parties, during the time that Ireland was in dispute, as to the communications of their opponents with the island; but this was especially strange in the French, as they had the larger forces, and must have received pretty accurate information of what was going on from disaffected persons in England. . . . The English communications were not even threatened for an hour.'[2]

[1] A. T. Mahan, Influence of Sea Power upon History (1890), pp. 177-97.
[2] Ibid. p. 181.

In 1690 Tourville gained at Beachy Head 'the most conspicuous single success the French had ever gained over the English', but used it only to make fruitless demonstrations against the south coast. In 1692, the definite plan of Louis XIV for the invasion of England was defeated at La Hogue, the last general action fought by the French fleet during the war. After that the French navy seemed to dwindle away, but its decay 'was not due to any one defeat, but to the exhaustion of France and the great cost of the continental war.'[1] The expense of the continental war prevented Louis from maintaining great French fleets at sea. Instead the French devoted their energies to privateering and commerce destroying. They sent out small squadrons of cruisers or privateers and caused great loss to English trade, but did not dispute the command of the seas. Meanwhile the sea power of the English and Dutch brought a quiet, steady pressure to bear upon France and maintained it in all quarters. As the war went on and as the administration of the navy improved in efficiency commerce destroying was brought within bounds. 'The cruisers were more and more controlled as the great French fleets disappeared.'[2]

To sum up, the French were stronger than the English and Dutch at the beginning of the war, but they misdirected their naval superiority, and lost it. At the beginning of the war, it was 'possible, as it will usually be possible, for a really fine military navy of superior force to strike an overwhelming blow at a less ready rival; but the opportunity was allowed to slip, and the essentially stronger, better founded sea power of the allies had time to assert itself.'[3]

[1] Ibid. p. 191. [2] Ibid. p. 196.

[3] Ibid. p. 197.

Macaulay does not appreciate the meaning of the naval operations he relates, or realise how much stronger the French navy was at the beginning of the war than that of England and Holland. For both these reasons he is unjust to Torrington, whom he condemns as an admiral as well as an administrator. He describes him as personally brave, but afraid of responsibility.[1] Nothing could be further from the truth. At Bantry Bay, on May 1, 1689, Torrington did not hesitate to engage Châteaurenault, though he had only nineteen men of war against the French commander's twenty-four. He was worsted but does not appear to have shown himself wanting either in skill or courage.[2]

Torrington's conduct next summer gave rise to a controversy famous in the history of naval strategy. He took command of the fleet in the Downs on May 30; it consisted of fifty Dutch and English men-of-war, but seven ships under Sir Cloudesly Shovell were cruising in the Irish Sea, and seventeen under Vice-Admiral Killigrew were on their way back from Cadiz. The French fleet under Tourville, consisting of about seventy men-of-war, sailed from Brest on June 13 and stationed itself off the Isle of Wight and between Torrington and the two detached squadrons. Torrington and his captains agreed that the French fleet was too strong to be engaged with any prospect of success. His plan therefore was to endeavour to get past the French fleet to the westward, and join the

[1] IV, 1857 (xv).

[2] A list of Torrington's fleet and a good account of the engagement are given in Memoirs Relating to the Lord Torrington, pp. 37-8. A list of the French fleet is given in Calmon-Maison's Le Maréchal de Châteaurenault (1903), pp. 118, 319. The French lost 40 men killed and 93 wounded, the English 90 killed and 270 wounded. For comment, see Colomb, Naval Warfare, p. 246. See also Hist. MSS. Comm., Le Fleming MSS., pp. 240, 241.

two detached squadrons. If that could not be done he meant to retreat eastward, take up a position north of the Thames off Harwich, and, secure amongst the shoals, avoid fighting till he was stronger. The strength of the French fleet, he wrote to Lord Nottingham, 'puts me beside the hopes of success, if we should fight, and really may not only endanger the losing of the fleet, but at least the quiet of our country too; for if we are beaten, they being absolute masters of the sea, will be at great liberty of doing many things they dare not attempt whilst we observe them, and are in a possibility of joining Vice-Admiral Killigrew and our ships to the westward. If I find a possibility, I will get by them to the westward to join those ships.'[1] King William was away in Ireland, and the council of regency completely lost its head. Its members could not understand Torrington's reasoning or accept his conclusions. They were afraid that Killigrew's and Shovell's squadrons would be destroyed or that Tourville would land a force in England, and they believed that the French fleet was much weaker than it really was. Instigated by Nottingham, who, having been First Lord of the Admiralty, regarded himself as an expert in naval affairs, they sent Torrington a peremptory order to fight. He remonstrated once more. 'Whilst we observe the French, they cannot make any attempt either upon ships or shore, without running a great hazard; and if we are beaten, all is exposed to their mercy. 'Tis very possible I reason wrong, but I do assure you I can, and will, obey.'[2] Accordingly on June 30 he engaged the French off Beachy Head, was worsted, and retreated with his shattered fleet to the Nore. In the battle and the retreat he lost six ships. As Tourville had not completely disabled

[1] Colomb, pp. 115-6. [2] Ibid. p. 120.

Torrington's fleet his victory was without solid results. He took some prizes, and burnt Teignmouth, but he neither destroyed the two detached squadrons nor effected a serious landing anywhere. Torrington was dismissed from his command and tried, in deference to the popular clamour against him. It was alleged that he deliberately refused to risk his own ships and exposed the Dutch squadron to destruction by deserting it. In his defence he said that his conduct was justified by the result.

> The French made no great advantage of their victory, tho' they put us to a great charge in keeping up the militia; but had I fought otherwise, our fleet had been totally lost, and the kingdom had lain open to an invasion. What then would have become of us in the absence of His Majesty, and most of the land forces? As it was, most men were in fear that the French would invade; but I was always of another opinion; for I always said, that whilst we had a fleet in being, they would not dare to make an attempt.

Torrington was unanimously acquitted by the court which tried him. Macaulay[1] and many historians have condemned his conduct, but it has been lately vindicated by a series of writers on naval strategy. Admiral Colomb was the first and his Naval Warfare contains the fullest account of the battle and its preliminaries.[2] Sir Cyprian Bridge sums up the controversy by saying: 'Most seamen were at the time, have been since, and still are in agreement with Torrington. . . . Both as a strategist and as a tactician Torrington was immeasurably ahead of his contemporaries. The only English admirals who can be placed above him are Hawke and Nelson. He paid the penalty of his pre-eminence: he could not make ignorant men and dull men see the meaning of the advantage of his

[1] IV, 1856-8 (xv); 1955-7 (xvi). [2] Pp. 110-23.

proceedings.'[1] Macaulay's narrative faithfully reflects the passions of the time, but he does not perceive the significance of Torrington's acquittal by a body of competent naval officers, and accepts the popular verdict too implicitly. This is not a case in which the discovery of new evidence has invalidated Macaulay's views, but one in which he interpreted the evidence wrongly.

Macaulay's account of the battle of La Hogue is not open to the same criticism. The facts were well ascertained and there was no controversy about their meaning. The aim of the French was to obtain the mastery of the Channel and land an army of twenty thousand men in England. But the English fleet was ready and was concentrated by the middle of May, and when the Dutch joined it Russell found himself in command of ninety-nine ships of the line besides smaller vessels. Tourville, on the other hand, could not collect more than forty-five; twelve ships under d'Estrées which ought to have joined him from Toulon were retarded by a storm, and twenty more were kept in Brest for want of men. Forced by the orders of his government to put to sea without them and to fight a force so vastly superior to his own, he was defeated on May 29 off Barfleur and in the running fight which followed, fifteen of his ships were burnt, three at Cherbourg and twelve at La Hogue.[2] There was great grumbling in England because Russell did not also destroy the twenty

[1] Sir Cyprian Bridge, Sea Power and Other Studies (1910), pp. 47-51; J. R. Thursfield, Naval Warfare (1913), pp. 31-48; J. S. Corbett, Some Principles of Maritime Strategy (1911), pp. 215-26.

[2] For accounts of the battle see Burchett, pp. 128-50; Colomb, Naval Warfare, pp. 123-30; and Sir John Laughton's article in the Quarterly Review for Apr. 1893. The fullest French account is La Bataille de la Hougue, by G. Toudouze (1899); Ranke (v. 45-51) writes a longer account than he usually devotes to battles. Macaulay (chap. xviii) rather understates the numbers of Russell's fleet.

French ships which took refuge in St. Malo, but his council of war agreed that the design was impracticable.[1]

In one way, the battle of La Hogue resembles that of Beachy Head. In each case the admiral who was defeated was forced by the order of his government to fight in spite of his better judgement, and the result was what usually happens when professional opinion is overruled by politicians. According to Colomb the 'complete failure of strategy' on the French side led to their being obliged to fight under the most disadvantageous conditions, and made disaster inevitable. Mahan praises Tourville's tactics in the battle. On the other hand he asserts that 'considered tactically' the battle 'possesses little importance, and the actual results have been much exaggerated, but popular report has made it one of the famous sea battles of the world.'

Yet, in spite of the success he achieved, Russell has not obtained a great reputation amongst naval historians.

> Credit is due to Russell for the promptitude with which, in face of difficulty, he arranged his junction with the Dutch ; but it can scarcely be contended that at Barfleur, and during the subsequent movements, he could, with his greatly superior fleet, have well done much less than he did. He won a victory of vast importance, yet of no particular brilliancy. Tourville lost a very small amount of reputation in the encounter, and Russell gained as little.[2]

Beachy Head and La Hogue too long monopolised the attentions of historians. The importance of Russell's

[1] See Manuscripts of the House of Lords, 1692-1693 (1894), pp. 181-4, 198-214. Macaulay is mistaken in saying that Rear Admiral Carter was killed at the very beginning of the battle (V, 2187 [xviii]). He was killed during the pursuit, some hours after it ended. Manuscripts of the House of Lords, 1692-1693, p. 212.

[2] William Laird Clowes, The Royal Navy (7 vols. ; 1897-1903), ii. 356.

operations in the Mediterranean, 1694-1695, escaped their notice. Macaulay devotes a couple of paragraphs to this expedition.[1] He relates how the progress of the French arms in Spain was stopped by the appearance of the English fleet in 1694. Palamos and Gerona had fallen before the combined action of the French armies and squadrons. 'Barcelona would in all probability have fallen, had not the French Admirals learned that the conqueror of La Hogue was approaching. They instantly quitted the coast of Catalonia, and never thought themselves safe till they had taken shelter under the batteries of Toulon.' Instead of returning home early in the autumn, the English fleet wintered at Cadiz and returned to the Mediterranean again in the spring of 1695. 'During the whole summer Russell was the undisputed master of the Mediterranean, passed and repassed between Spain and Italy, bombarded Palamos, spread terror along the whole coast of Provence, and kept the French fleet imprisoned in the harbour of Toulon.'[2] But though Macaulay states these facts he does not appreciate or explain their strategic significance. That was pointed out by Admiral Colomb[3] and is developed in Julian Corbett's book on England in the Mediterranean.

Mr. Corbett's conclusions[4] are as follows: The naval strategy of the first few years of the reign must be condemned. During the early period of the war the English fleet was employed in trying to obtain the command of the Narrow Seas in order to secure the English coasts from invasion and to recover Ireland. Even after Russell's victory at La Hogue had given William the command of the Narrow Seas, it was only used in the old way—in

[1] V, 2442 (xx), 2452-4; 2538 (xxi).
[2] V, 2538 (xxi).
[3] Naval Warfare, p. 271.
[4] Chap. 26.

attacks on the French Channel ports and raids on the French coasts. For William the war was at the beginning a military war and the fleet was kept subsidiary to the military operations. The fifth year of the war was starting before William discovered the power which the English navy gave him. The concentration of the French fleet under Tourville and d'Estrées in the Mediterranean, in 1693, opened his eyes; in May 1694 he resolved to send Russell and the main English fleet there. This resolution was entirely the King's own; he took all the responsibility on his own shoulders. His too was the resolution to keep the fleet out during the winter of 1694-1695 instead of letting it return home as usual. The King's own Council was afraid of such a new departure. 'I do not know if I rightly comprehend,' he wrote to Shrewsbury on August 2, 1694,

> but it appears that the Committee are of opinion that Admiral Russell should winter at Cadiz, but dare not declare that opinion, through fear of being responsible for the event. I do wish that they had spoken more clearly on this occasion, and indeed they ought to have done, so as to prevent my being exposed to the supposition of acting solely from my own opinion. But as there is no time to deliberate, I am reduced to the necessity of coming to some determination, and I have accordingly resolved to order Admiral Russell to winter with his whole squadron at Cadiz.[1]

William saw that the orders were so positive that they left Russell no discretion in the matter. For that admiral was opposed to the King's strategy, and hated the idea of being kept in the Mediterranean. He lamented loudly and talked about putting 'an end to a troublesome life'.

[1] Corbett, England in the Mediterranean, ii. 169.

'Could I have imagined this expedition would have been detained here so long, I would much rather have chosen to live on bread and water. . . . The business of the conducting part is so terrible . . . that I am at present under a doubt with myself whether it is not better to die.'[1]

The details of the operations of Russell's fleet during 1694 and 1695 in the Mediterranean are given by Corbett. He sums up thus their main features and their results:

> So ended the two campaigns—the type of so many that were to succeed them. How often were their main features to recur! The French fleet helpless in Toulon—not blockaded, but refusing to stir; the fitful operations on the Spanish coast hampering in greater or less degree the military operations of the French army; the fruitless efforts to achieve something on the coast of Provence by the help of preoccupied or faint-hearted allies. Nor was this the whole. As always, beneath the apparent failures and disappointments there was still, unseen and almost unnoticed, the silent pressure of the chafing fleet that was felt to the farthest borders of the war.[2]

In his account of these events Macaulay relied almost exclusively on Burchett's History, and on the letters of Russell in the Shrewsbury correspondence. Since he wrote, further letters of Russell's have come to light, calendared in the Report of the Historical Manuscripts Commission on the Manuscripts of the Duke of Buccleuch at Montagu House.[3] Manuscripts of the House of Lords also contains a number of documents relating to the expedition.[4] The most important additions to our knowledge of these events consist of the official correspondence contained in the Calendars of Domestic State Papers for

[1] Ibid. pp. 171-3.
[2] Ibid. p. 182.
[3] Vol. ii (1903).
[4] 1693-1695 (1900), pp. 458-98.

1694 and 1695. But all these original authorities needed interpreting by men who understood naval strategy; a historian without professional or technical knowledge could hardly have understood their meaning even if they had been accessible in print. It required Mahan, and Colomb, and Corbett to set the facts in their true light and show the conclusions to be drawn from them.

CHAPTER VIII

MACAULAY'S TREATMENT OF SCOTTISH HISTORY

ONE of the merits of Macaulay is that he treats the Revolution broadly and comprehensively, connects throughout the history of England with that of Ireland and Scotland, and shows how the change of government in one country affected the fortunes of the other two. It was a more difficult task than his readers realise, for there was at that time no good history of either Ireland or Scotland in existence, nor were there available many of those monographs on particular subjects which help to replace consecutive narratives. Take, for instance, Scotland. Malcolm Laing's verbose and obsolete History of Scotland from the Union of the Crowns to the Union of the Kingdoms was the best available account. Tytler's excellent history stopped short in 1603; Hill Burton's was not yet published. However, the first instalment of Burton's book, which covered the period from 1689 to 1745, appeared in 1853, and was much used by Macaulay in his account of William III's reign. At present a historian of the period has at his service, Hill Burton's revised and completed history, the books of Professor Hume Brown, Mr. Andrew Lang, and Mr. W. L. Mathieson, besides a number of biographies of particular persons or treatises on particular subjects. Take into account also the new evidence made accessible during the last sixty years, the documentary publications of the government, the reports of the Historical Manuscripts Commission, the volumes issued by the Scottish History Society and other societies, and the matter contained in

N

the Scottish Historical Review.[1] With little assistance from previous writers, and from imperfect materials, Macaulay put together his vigorous and vivid narrative of events in Scotland from 1685 to 1701. It contains many errors, and there are some serious omissions, but he deserves the credit which belongs to a pioneer, and should for that reason be more leniently judged. Perhaps the fact that this portion of the History has been more minutely scrutinised than the rest makes it seem comparatively more inaccurate.[2]

The chief omission is, that Macaulay gives no adequate account of the state of Scotland at the end of the seventeenth century. A clear conception of the social and economic conditions under which the political life of Scotland developed is essential, in order to appreciate the policy of statesmen and the strength of the forces with which they had to deal. Without it the meaning of events and their true proportions are obscured.

Macaulay begins his narrative of the reigns of James II and William III by an account of the state of England in 1685, but there is no similar account of the state of Scotland. We get incidental glimpses of the country during the reign of King James. In chapters ii and iv there is some account of the persecution of the Covenanters, in chapter v a narrative of Argyle's rebellion, and in chapter vi an account of the attempt made to carry out the ecclesi-

[1] An Index to the Papers Relating to Scotland Described or Calendared in the Historical MSS. Commission's Reports, published by Professor C. S. Terry in 1908, and the same author's Catalogue of the Publications of Scottish Historical and Kindred Clubs and Societies (1909)—continued for 1908-27 by Cyril Matheson (1928).

[2] Mr. John Paget devoted three articles to the Scottish part of the History in his New Examen. Mr. T. F. Henderson, in the annotated edition of Macaulay, published in 1907, points out a large number of minor errors.

astical policy of James II in Scotland. But chapter xiii is the first one devoted entirely to Scotland, and while it contains a lengthy description of the condition of the Highlands, there is not anywhere an equally full account of the condition of the Lowlands.

Macaulay introduces this description of the condition of the Highlands in order to explain the rising of the clans on behalf of James II. Its correctness has been vehemently denied, and a section of Paget's New Examen is devoted to its refutation. 'We cannot allow', says Mr. Paget, 'this gross caricature, this shameless libel, this malignant slander, this parricidal onslaught by a son to pass unnoticed. Lowlanders as we are, it moves our indignation.'[1] He then examines Macaulay's authorities in detail, and has no difficulty in showing that some of them are of very little value, and that others do not say what they are represented as saying. However, the errors in Macaulay's description of the Highlands are less serious than his omissions. The Lowlanders were the makers of the Scottish nation: their ideas and their institutions moulded its character, shaped its future, and determined its place in the British Empire. Anyone who reads Macaulay's narrative of the events which followed the Revolution in Scotland should supplement it by reading the chapter entitled Scotland on the Eve of the Union, in Professor Hume Brown's History of Scotland.[2] It summarises in a masterly fashion the state of agriculture, trade, industry, and commerce during the later part of the seventeenth century. Incidentally it corrects some of Macaulay's errors. For instance, Macaulay somewhat

[1] New Examen (1860 ed.), p. 80.

[2] P. Hume Brown, History of Scotland (3 vols.; 1911), iii. chap. 2. This should be taken in connection with volume ii. pp. 350-8, describing the Social Condition of the Country (1625-1689).

exaggerates the result of the Act for the Settling of Schools passed by the Scottish Parliament in 1696.[1] In Scotland, even before that date, 'education was more widely spread among all classes than in any other nation,' and the Act marked no new departure, though it was doubtless more effective than its predecessors.[2] In another passage, Macaulay dwells on the influence of commercial considerations in modifying the stubborn attachment of the Scots to their independence, and in preparing the way for the union of the kingdoms. He exaggerates the importance of the freedom of trade which existed during the Cromwellian union, and the extent of the prosperity resulting from it as factors in producing these results.[3] Hopes for the future, not reminiscences of 'the golden days of the usurper', influenced the Scots. The failure of the Darien scheme showed that the development of a national trade was impossible without a closer union with England.

Much evidence illustrating the social and economic history of Scotland has been published since Macaulay wrote. To begin with, there are four volumes containing descriptions of Scotland, written by English and foreign travellers during the seventeenth century.[4] The accounts

[1] VI, 2698 (xii).

[2] Brown, ii. 357, iii. 56-7, 209; cf. Lecky, History of England in the Eighteenth Century, ii. 44.

[3] IV, 1540-42 (xiii). Macaulay was led into this error by Hill Burton. Whatever advantages the Scots then derived from freedom of trade were neutralised by the weight of taxation. See C. H. Firth, The Last Years of the Protectorate (2 vols.; 1909), ii. 113-15, 119; and Miss Theodora Keith's article on Scottish Trade with the Plantations before 1707, in Scottish Historical Review, vi. 32-48.

[4] Early Travellers in Scotland (1891); Scotland before 1700, from Contemporary Documents (1893); Tours in Scotland, by Thomas Kirk and Ralph Thoresby (1892). All three collections were edited by Professor Hume Brown. There is also C. Lowther's Journey into Scotland in 1629, edited in 1894 by William Douglas

by French visitors are much more favourable than those by Englishmen. Half the English travellers were excessively hostile, and many laboured to make the country and its people ridiculous. Their descriptions of the Lowlands remind one of Macaulay's description of the Highlands. It is clear, however, that their tempers were soured, not merely by religious or political animosity to the Scots, but by the discomforts of travelling in Scotland. 'I must confess, I was too impatient at the Scotch victuals,' said Thoresby.[1] 'They have neither good bread, cheese, or drink,' complained Ray.[2] 'They cannot make them, nor will they learn.' 'The sluttishness and nastiness of this people is such', reported an earlier tourist, 'that I cannott ommitt the particularizeing thereof.'[3] The fact is the poverty of Scotland produced a lower standard of living than in England, not merely different manners, and both were obstacles to the intercourse of the two nations.

Other evidence of a more impartial but duller nature is supplied by books of household accounts,[4] by judicial records,[5] by local records of various kinds,[6] and by private correspondence. There are also collections of extracts and documents arranged either in the form of annals or

[1] Tours in Scotland, 1677 and 1681, p. 50.

[2] Memorials of John Ray (1846), p. 153.

[3] Journal of Sir William Brereton, 1635, in North Country Diaries (1915), ii. p. 32.

[4] Account Book of Sir John Foulis of Ravelston, 1671-1707, ed. A. W. C. Hallen (1894); The Household Book of Lady Grisell Baillie, 1692-1733, ed. R. Scott-Moncrieff (1911).

[5] The Records of the Proceedings of the Justiciary Court, Edinburgh, 1661-1678, ed. R. Scott-Moncrieff (2 vols.; 1904-5).

[6] The Court Book of the Barony of Urie, 1604-1747, ed. D. G. Barron (1892); Records of the Baron Court of Stitchell, 1655-1807, ed. C. B. Gunn (1905); Records of the Convention of Royal Burghs of Scotland, 1295-1738, ed. J. D. Marwick (6 vols.; 1866-90); and the Publications of the Scottish Burgh Records Society.

under subjects in order to illustrate social history.[1] The development of Scottish trade and manufactures during the seventeenth century is now being investigated with great thoroughness.[2] All these various contributions to the national history have made it possible 'to relate the history of the people as well as the government', as Macaulay wished to do.

This history of the government of Scotland has also been made clearer. Macaulay's account of it is vague and rhetorical. In chapter iv he tells us that the legislature of Scotland 'was as obsequious as those provincial Estates which Lewis the Fourteenth still suffered to play at some of their ancient functions in Brittany and Burgundy', that 'none but an Episcopalian could sit in the Scottish Parliament, or could even vote for a member', and that it could 'pass no law which had not been previously approved by a committee of courtiers'.[3] Of the composition and powers of this legislature, either before or after the Revolution of 1688, no precise account is given. Macaulay mentions the abolition of the Lords of the Articles, but does not explain the magnitude of the change which the Revolution made in the position of the Scottish Parliament.[4] William's difficulty in governing Scotland was caused by the fact that he had to deal with an assembly which was no longer subservient to the Crown, but almost as independent as an English Parliament.[5] And the

[1] Robert Chambers, Domestic Annals of Scotland (3 vols.; 1859-61); E. D. Dunbar, Social Life in Former Days (2 vols.; 1865-66).

[2] The Records of a Scottish Cloth Manufactory at the New Mills, 1681-1703, ed. W. R. Scott (1905). Dr. Scott's Joint Stock Companies contains much new information (ii [1910], 207-27, 377-8; iii [1911], 123-95).

[3] I, 488-90.

[4] IV, 1933 (xvi).

[5] See Professor C. S. Terry's The Scottish Parliament: Its Constitution and Procedure, 1603-1707 (1905); and, as an introduction to that work, Professor R. S. Rait's The Scottish Parliament before the Union of the Crowns (1901).

King could not play off one House of Parliament against another, since the Scottish Parliament consisted of a single chamber, in which nobles, barons of the shires, and burgesses all sat together. Under Charles II and James II the government of the country had been conducted by the Privy Council;[1] after the emancipation of Parliament from the control of the Lords of the Articles, the importance of the Council diminished.

It was the Council which conducted the repressive measures, against the ecclesiastical or political opponents of the government, which fill so large a place in Scottish history during the reigns of Charles II and James II. Macaulay mentions the beginnings of this repression in chapter ii, when he describes the administrations of Lauderdale and of the Duke of York. Incidentally he charges James with exceptional cruelty.

> The Scottish Privy Council had power to put state prisoners to the question. But the sight was so dreadful that, as soon as the boots appeared, even the most servile and hard-hearted courtiers hastened out of the chamber. . . . The Duke of York, it was remarked, seemed to take pleasure in the spectacle . . . He not only came to Council when the torture was to be inflicted, but watched the agonies of the sufferers with that sort of interest and complacency with which men observe a curious experiment in science.[2]

[1] The Calendars of the Register of the Privy Council of Scotland now cover the period from 1473 to 1689 (1933). Its action during the reign of Charles II is fully explained in Professor Hume Brown's introductions to the post-Restoration volumes, and by those of Robert Kerr Hannay.

[2] I, 260 (ii). See Mr. T. F. Henderson's note at p. 71 of his edition of the History. In one of his letters James expresses his satisfaction that a prisoner, after torture by the boot, has begun to speak. When the Privy Council proposed that contumacious rebels, who were let off with transportation, should be 'stigmatised by having one of the ears of everyone of them cut off', he warmly approved of the measure. Hist. MSS. Comm., MSS. of the Duke of Buccleuch at Drumlanrig, i (1897), 105, 205.

This charge, which Macaulay repeats three or four times, rests solely on the authority of Burnet, and is not confirmed by other evidence. James was not humane: he had no objection to the employment of torture; but there is no proof that he took any special delight in it.

In another passage Macaulay says that the 'fiery persecution, which had raged when he ruled Scotland as vicegerent, waxed hotter than ever from the day on which he became sovereign.' For illustrations of this persecution he relies mainly on Wodrow's History of the Sufferings of the Church of Scotland from the Restoration to the Revolution, published in 1721-1722,[1] and on the Cloud of Witnesses, which is a collection of the last speeches and testimonies of the sufferers, published about 1720. Both were partisan works, but there was no impartial authority available.[2]

In legend and history the accumulated odium of all the persecutions and executions of the 'killing time' had been heaped on Claverhouse, and Macaulay accepts the popular tradition with too little discrimination, exaggerates his misdeeds, and credits him with the crimes of other men. 'Preeminent', writes Macaulay, 'among the bands which

[1] It is to be regretted that a critical edition of Wodrow has never been published, though his correspondence and papers furnish materials for the purpose. Patrick Walker's lives of Peden, Cameron, and other worthies have been carefully edited by D. Hay Fleming, under the title of Six Saints of the Covenant (2 vols.; 1901). Similarly the collection of epitaphs at the end of the Cloud of Witnesses has been reprinted, with additions, in Mr. J. H. Thompson's The Martyr Graves of Scotland (1903), though these stories are not critically examined.

[2] Unluckily the records of the Privy Council for these years are imperfect. Macaulay says that the Acts during almost the whole administration of the Duke of York are wanting, and adds that the hiatus extends from Aug. 1678 to Aug. 1682. The missing volume has been since recovered, and is now in the Register House, but there is still a gap from the beginning of 1686 to May 1689. See The Register of the Privy Council of Scotland, 3rd Ser., xi (1929), Introduction.

oppressed and wasted these unhappy districts were the dragoons commanded by John Graham of Claverhouse. The story ran that these wicked men used in their revels to play at the torments of hell, and to call each other by the names of devils and damned souls.' [1] Wodrow, however, who is the authority cited, appears to attribute these diversions to Grierson of Lag and his men.[2] Macaulay terms Claverhouse 'the chief of this Tophet', though even Wodrow does not accuse him of taking part in the alleged revels.

Another famous figure amongst the persecutors was Sir George Mackenzie, Lord Advocate from 1674 to 1685. One of Scott's characters terms him 'the bloody advocate Mackenzie, who for his worldly wit and wisdom had been to the rest as a god.' Another calls him 'the man that has the blood of the saints at his fingers' ends'. Lawyer, essayist, novelist, and historian, his accomplishments attracted the admiration of Mr. Andrew Lang, who came to the conclusion that the charges against him were not warranted by the facts, and that he was a much maligned man.[3] But the vindication is by no means convincing.

Amongst the opponents of the government persecuted by Mackenzie was the ninth Earl of Argyle, who was condemned for high treason in 1681 on a scandalously unjust accusation, but succeeded in escaping to Holland. In May 1685 he returned to Scotland, was made prisoner

[1] I, 492 (iv). The charges against Dundee are examined in detail in chapter xi.

[2] See Col. Alexander Ferguson, The Laird of Lag: A Life Sketch (1886).

[3] Sir George Mackenzie, King's Advocate, of Rosehaugh: His Life and Times (1909). The account of Mackenzie's career and character given in Mr. G. W. T. Omond's Lord Advocates of Scotland (1883), i. 200-34, appears to be substantially just.

on June 18, and was executed on June 30. In chapter v Macaulay gives a full account of his rebellion, basing his narrative mainly on Wodrow, and on the narrative of Sir Patrick Hume, who accompanied Argyle.[1] Since then, the journal of another of his companions, John Erskine of Carnock, has been published. Erskine left his studies at the University of Leyden 'to join in that design of endeavouring . . . the delivery of our native land from being again drowned in popish idolatry and slavery'. Like Hume he makes it clear that divided counsels were one cause of the failure of the expedition: others were 'the lukewarmness and little zeal' of gentlemen and people in the Lowlands, and the desertion of Argyle by the 'irreligious and cowardly Highlanders' when he crossed the Clyde.[2] Outside his own clan Argyle was personally unpopular, and he possessed neither military skill nor the gifts of a leader. Macaulay lays the blame for the failure on Hume and the Committee, but it does not appear that if Argyle's hands had been entirely free he would have been more successful.

After the suppression of the rebellions headed by Monmouth and Argyle the position of King James was so much stronger that he could attempt to carry out his plans

[1] Hume's narrative is printed in vol. iii (1831) of the Papers of the Earls of Marchmont, ed. Sir George Rose. Macaulay also used the Memoirs of Mr. William Veitch and George Brysson, ed. Thomas McCrie (1825).

[2] Journal of the Hon. John Erskine of Carnock, 1683-1687, ed. Walter Macleod, in Publications of the Scottish History Society, vol. xiv (1893), 113, 124, 130. Other new evidence may be found in the Hist. MSS. Comm., Athole MSS. (1891), pp. 12-24. One of these letters gives a detailed account of Argyle's capture which differs from that followed by Macaulay. The Manuscripts of the Duke of Argyle, calendared in the Sixth Report of the Hist. MSS. Comm. (1877), contain very little new information. A biography of Argyle, entitled A Scots Earl in Covenanting Times: Being Life and Times of Archibald, 9th Earl of Argyll, by Rev. John Willcock, was published in 1907.

in favour of the Catholics. The laws against them in Scotland were so severe that justice demanded their mitigation,[1] but, as in England, the King aimed at something more than toleration, and to carry out his policy he had to change his ministers and coerce those who ventured to oppose it. William Douglas, first Duke of Queensberry, was Lord Treasurer, and had been for some years considered first minister. No man had been more trusted by James whilst he was still Duke of York. He was now suspected of promoting the anti-Catholic riots which took place in Edinburgh, and was not disposed to turn Catholic himself. The two Drummonds, James Earl of Perth, who was Chancellor, and John Earl of Melfort, the Secretary of State, were not men to stick at such trifles. Both had abjured their creed, and had for some time been plotting to overthrow their rival. 'Duke Queensberry', said Perth to the King, 'was an atheist in religion, a villan in friendship, a knave in business, and a traitor in his carriage to him.'[2] This was effective: in February 1686 Queensberry lost the treasurership and, instead, was made president of the Council. In June he lost that post too.

William Douglas, third Duke of Hamilton, was more compliant than his kinsman, but even he would not go as far as the King desired. In February 1688 James asked him whether he would support the repeal of the penal laws and tests, demanding a positive answer in three days. Hamilton declined to pledge himself. 'I have been ever and am still of the opinion that none should suffer for consience sake and that every peaceable subject should

[1] See A. Bellesheim's History of the Catholic Church in Scotland, translated by D. O. Hunter Blair (4 vols.; 1887-90).

[2] Hist. MSS. Comm., Hamilton MSS. (1887), p. 171.

be alloued the exercise of their one religion, but how this is to be done with securety to the Protestant religion, our laws, and oaths, is in my humble opinion, what will desairve serious consideration, and is above what I can presently determine myself in.' [1]

When the Revolution came Hamilton declared against James, was chairman of the assembly of Scottish lords and gentlemen which requested the Prince of Orange to call the Convention, was elected president of the Convention when it met, and was appointed High Commissioner when it was turned into a Parliament. Macaulay speaks rather slightingly of Hamilton's abilities; Burnet is still more depreciatory. 'He wanted all sort of polishing: he was rough and sullen, but candid and sincere. His temper was boisterous, neither fit to submit nor to govern. He was mutinous when out of power, and imperious in it.' Burnet confesses that Hamilton 'seemed always to have a regard to justice, and the good of his country,' but adds that his 'narrow and selfish temper' rendered him unfit for great affairs.[2] In spite of his defects Hamilton's importance made him indispensable, and his correspondence during the first eighteen months of William's reign is an authority of great value.[3]

The conversations with William III, which the Marquis of Halifax recorded in his journal, contain a number of references to Scottish politics during those months. Scotland was one of William's difficulties. Before he became king he told the Marquis of Halifax that Scotland by its divisions 'would give him more trouble than any-

[1] Ibid. p. 175.

[2] Own Time, i. 103.

[3] Hamilton MSS., pp. 176-94. Parts of the correspondence are printed in the Leven and Melville Papers, 1689-1691 (Bannatyne Club, 1843), and were used by Macaulay, but there are many letters which he never saw.

thing', and Halifax noted that the 'Scotchmen by their several stories distracted his mind'.[1] Though William employed Hamilton, he had no great confidence in him. 'Upon my best observation', wrote Halifax, 'Duke Hamilton was never well with the King from the beginning. . . . He was too pressing at first, and earnest in his own particular concerne, which gave the King an ill impression of him.' William promised Hamilton that 'he should be the first man in Scotland', but the Duke grumbled because he was not made Lord Treasurer.[2] The Scottish Parliament demanded the abolition of the Lords of the Articles, a veto on judicial appointments, and the incapacitation of the ministers of the late government. William refused: in Scotland as in England he meant to maintain all the prerogatives of the Crown. He told Halifax that he would not agree to take away the Lords of the Articles but would reform them, and when Halifax said that would not satisfy the Parliament, he replied, 'hee could not help it, he would yield no more, neither there nor here, and if the Parliament in Scotland did not like it, hee would dissolve it, and get another.' Privately he said that 'Duke Hamilton was at the bottom of all the opposition in Scotland,' and 'all the Scotch Lords both friends and enemies agreed, that he might have hinder'd some votes if he would.'[3]

William was not much better satisfied with his Secretary of State. It had been customary to have two Secretaries of Scotland, but William declared that he would not have two, 'to have one advise him one thing, and the other to another.'[4]

[1] H. C. Foxcroft, Life and Letters of the First Marquis of Halifax (2 vols.; 1898), ii. 202.

[2] Ibid. pp. 205, 234.

[3] Ibid. pp. 223, 236, 237, 239.

[4] Ibid. p. 218.

Accordingly on May 15, 1689, he appointed Lord Melville sole Secretary. 'A very unhappy step', says Burnet, 'for, as he was by his principle bigoted to presbytery, and ready to sacrifice every thing to their humours, so he proved to be in all respects a narrow hearted man, who minded his own interest more than either that of the King or of his country.'[1] Halifax noted that, whereas William spoke well of Lord Melville when he made him Secretary, he subsequently 'changed his style of him as to his abilityes.' He complained that Melville was very slow and very timorous, and by July 1689 he was looking round for another secretary. Halifax proposed Lord Tweeddale. William cried, 'Pish; hee cannot bee,' thinking him too old.[2] The King solved one of his problems in 1690, by appointing Melville High Commissioner in place of Hamilton, and the other in 1691, by appointing as Secretary for Scotland Sir John Dalrymple, Master of Stair, till then Lord Advocate.[3]

The feuds of Scottish parties and Scottish statesmen gave William more trouble than the armed opposition of the Jacobites. He said in June 1689 that 'hee did not know whether he was not to wish King James might come into Scotland,' adding 'wee shall never bee quiet, till wee have a brush for it.'[4] The brush was not long in coming: in April Dundee[5] had raised the standard of James II, on July 27 the battle of Killiecrankie was fought, on August 21 the Highlanders were repulsed at Dunkeld, and finally, on May 1, 1690, Sir Thomas Livingstone routed Buchan and what was left of the Jacobite forces at the Haughs of

[1] Own Time, ii. 24.

[2] Foxcroft, ii. 217, 224.

[3] Macaulay, IV, 1932 (xvi); V, 2142-3 (xviii).

[4] Foxcroft. ii. 220.

[5] Mark Napier's Memorials and Letters was published in 1859-62 (3 vols.). It is rather difficult to discover from Macaulay's narrative whether he really knew the letters of Dundee published by the Bannatyne Club in 1826.

Cromdale. Since Macaulay's narrative of these events was put together some new evidence has come to light. Most of the letters collected by Mark Napier in his life of Dundee were written before the Revolution, but there are some of this period in his book. Napier translates also long passages from the Latin epic on Dundee, named the Grameid, which was one of Macaulay's authorities.[1] This poem was edited by Mr. Alexander Murdoch for the Scottish History Society in 1888. Macaulay also employed Memoirs of the War Carried On in Scotland and Ireland, 1689-1691, by Major-General Hugh Mackay, which was published by the Bannatyne Club in 1833, and the Life of Major-General Mackay, by John Mackay of Rockfield, published by the same club in 1836. But many letters of Mackay's have been lately printed in the reports on the Manuscripts of the Dukes of Hamilton and Athole.

The study of the campaign has resulted in a number of controversies. Historians disagree about the site of the battle of Killiecrankie. Macaulay fixes on one spot, Mark Napier on another, Professor Terry on a third. Professor Terry says: 'Mackay's very minute topography leaves me no room to doubt that the sites which hitherto have been accepted for the battle are wrong. . . . Macaulay imagined that the battle was fought in the field where "Claverhouse's Stone" is marked upon the accompanying map. That site has the sanction of the Ordnance Map of 1900. The most cursory reading of Mackay's narrative is sufficient to prove that that was the spot on which Mackay halted, and not that on which the battle was fought.' He then takes the site preferred by Mark Napier, and gives various reasons

[1] IV, 1607 (xiii). Macaulay's criticisms (pp. 1597-8) of the Memoirs of the Life of Sir Ewan Cameron and the Historical and Genealogical Account of the Clan Maclean also deserve attention.

for believing that the battle was not fought there. Finally he gives his own theory of the position, illustrating it by a plan, and proving that it is the only reasonable one. Two years later Mr. Andrew Lang took up the question again, and pronounced in favour of Mark Napier's theory.[1] Thus all three writers agree in rejecting Macaulay's view. The opinion of a competent military critic on the issue would be of interest.

A second controversy concerns the manner of Dundee's death and the nature of his wound. Was he killed by a shot in the left eye or a shot in the side? Did he die on the spot, or at the Castle of Blair after the battle? Did he write the letter to James II which was printed in his name? After examining the evidence, I have no doubt that he died on the field, and that the letter is fictitious, but there is not the slightest proof that it was forged by Macpherson, as Macaulay insinuates.[2]

After the Jacobite rising had been defeated, the settlement of constitutional and ecclesiastical disputes became more easy. William wisely gave up the attempt to maintain the Lords of the Articles, and accepted in ecclesiastical affairs arrangements which satisfied the main body of the Presbyterians. In effecting this settlement, the chief instruments were Melville, as High Commissioner, and the Earl of Crawford, who was President of the Parliament. Macaulay describes Crawford as a Presbyterian zealot, needy, greedy, and canting, with a steady eye to the main chance.

[1] C. S. Terry, John Graham of Claverhouse, Viscount of Dundee (1905), pp. 336-7; Andrew Lang, History of Scotland (1907), iv. 17; Mark Napier, Life and Times of John Graham of Claverhouse, Viscount Dundee, iii (1862), 630.

[2] IV, 1634 (xiii); Napier, iii. 647-72. Michael Barrington, Claverhouse's Last Letter, in Scottish Historical Review, v. 505-9; answers by C. S. Terry and John Anderson, ibid. vi. 63-70.

The view is based on Crawford's letters in the Leven and Melville papers; other letters of his have been published since.[1] Judging from them he seems to have been an honest zealot, as merciless as such men usually are, but faithful to his principles, and not without ability.

Behind Melville and Crawford was Carstairs (or, as he signs himself, Carstares), an adviser who, as Macaulay says, 'deserved and possessed more influence than any of the ostensible ministers.' He goes on to say that Carstairs 'united great scholastic attainments with great aptitude for civil business, and the firm faith and ardent zeal of a martyr with the shrewdness and suppleness of a consummate politician. In courage and fidelity he resembled Burnet; but he had, what Burnet wanted, judgment, selfcommand, and a singular power of keeping secrets.'[2] Burnet barely mentions Carstairs, and was evidently jealous of his influence.[3] That influence is difficult to define, but clearly attested both by the correspondence addressed to him and by his letters to other people.[4] His policy was temperate and cautious: we see him inspiring the King, reconciling the quarrels of William's supporters, restraining the zeal of the fanatical, confirming the waverers, and securing the triumph of the moderate Presbyterianism which the majority of the Scottish people desired. 'Use all endeavours', he wrote to a friend, 'to keep people from extravagances upon the account of changes that are made.' The counsel

[1] Macaulay, IV, 1578 (xiii); Hist. MSS. Comm., Hope Johnstone MSS. (1897).

[2] IV, 1580 (xiii).

[3] See Foxcroft, Supplement to Burnet's Own Time, p. 541.

[4] See J. McCormick's State Papers and Letters Addressed to William Carstairs (1774); see also the letters of Carstairs to Crawford, 1689-91, in the Hope Johnstone MSS., those to Lord Polwarth in the Marchmont MSS. (Hist. MSS. Comm., Fourteenth Report, App. iii [1894]), and those to the Duke of Hamilton in the Hamilton MSS.

might have been given by Burnet, but Carstairs saw clearly what Burnet failed to perceive—that, good or bad, the ecclesiastical settlement must be the work of Scotland itself. 'The more I consider the temper of this nation and their notions of government, . . . the more I dread the thoughts of any of the English being much concerned in our affairs.' [1] Since Macaulay wrote, Principal Story's life of Carstairs has thrown new light on his career, and it has been further elucidated by the letters published more recently.

More prominently employed, and working generally in close co-operation with Carstairs, were the two Dalrymples, Sir James, first Viscount Stair, President of the Court of Session, and his son Sir John, afterwards first Earl of Stair. Macaulay draws the characters of both at full length.[2] Admitting the great ability of the father, and his moderation during the ten years in which he held office in Charles II's reign, he charges him with hypocrisy and insincerity. No man was more unscrupulously attacked by contemporary libellers, and Macaulay, complains Stair's biographer, 'has drawn chiefly from these satirists all the charges his enemies made against Stair, and without examining their truth has insinuated others for which even satire gave no foundation.' [3] As the satires referred to have been reprinted, their value can easily be estimated. Macaulay employs them to supply picturesque and romantic touches to his account of the house of Stair, and this is legitimate enough.[4] But he

[1] R. H. Story, William Carstares : A Character and Career of the Revolutionary Epoch (1874), pp. 188, 195, 206, 225.

[2] IV, 1548-51 (xiii).

[3] Aeneas J. G. Mackay, Memoir of Sir James Dalrymple, First Viscount Stair : A Study in the History of Scotland and Scotch Law during the Seventeenth Century (1873), p. 286.

[4] See A Book of Scotish Pasquils, 1568-1715, ed. J. Maidment (1868), pp. 174, 221, 370.

appears to allow them to influence his judgement too much, and proceeds to suggest charges, against the founder of the house, which rest on hypotheses rather than facts, and are the more difficult to meet because they are not directly made. In short the character is unfair.

The Master of Stair had been made Lord Advocate by James II, when Mackenzie refused to support that king's claim to the dispensing power, but held the post for only a year.[1] He was one of the Commissioners who on behalf of the Scottish Convention offered the crown to William III and was reappointed Lord Advocate, May 23, 1689. In January 1691 he became the colleague of Melville as Secretary of State. Macaulay terms him 'the prime minister for Scotland', and this is a fair description of his position from 1691 to the summer of 1695. Sir John was the ablest debater in the Scottish Parliament: 'there was none in the parliament capable to take up the cudgels with him,' says Lockhart. Bold, able, clear-sighted, free from prejudices, either ecclesiastical or secular, and equally free from scruples, he was a curious contrast to men such as Melville, Crawford, and Hamilton. But the massacre of Glencoe has permanently stained his fame, and his national services have been forgotten.

Macaulay's account of the Glencoe episode has led to more controversy than almost any other passage in the History, because it affects the character of the King as well as that of his minister. Paget, Mackay, Lang, and many other writers have minutely examined the evidence on which Macaulay's story is based. This is not a case in

[1] From Jan. 21, 1687, to Jan. 19, 1688. Macaulay says (IV, 1571 [xiii]) he had been an accomplice in some of the misdeeds he arraigned after the Revolution. But Sir John had been himself fined and imprisoned by the government of Charles II, and during the period when he was Lord Advocate persecutions had almost ceased.

which the discovery of fresh facts has invalidated a historian's verdict, but a question of the conclusions to be drawn from well-known facts and documents.[1] Macaulay tries to exonerate the King at the expense of the Secretary. In this he follows the example of the Commission of Enquiry appointed by the King in 1695. Both the report of the Commission and the address of Parliament based on it, in the words of a contemporary, 'loaded to purpose' the Master of Stair, but 'the King is most justly relieved of all the aspersions raised in that affair of Glenco.'[2] William in turn exonerated Stair, and laid the blame on Glenlyon and the inferior agents employed. He declared that the manner of the execution of the men of Glencoe was contrary to the laws of hospitality and humanity, but that Viscount Stair, being 'many hundred miles distant', 'could have no knowledge of nor accession to the method of that execution,' and was therefore pardoned for 'any excess of zeal, as going beyond his instructions.'[3] To a limited extent this distinction is justifiable. Stair did not suggest the treachery which preceded the massacre: he merely ordered the massacre. He ordered that 'the thieving tribe in Glencoe' should be 'rooted out', and that the attack should be 'secret and sudden'. But after the massacre he wrote, 'All I regret is that any of the sect got away'; and this subsequent approval of the measures taken to carry out his directions fixes the responsibility upon him.

William's position is clearer. His orders were: 'If

[1] Paget, Paradoxes and Puzzles, chap. ii, Lord Macaulay and the Massacre of Glencoe (originally published as an article in Blackwood's Magazine for July, 1859).

[2] Ogilvie to Carstares, in State Papers and Letters Addressed to William Carstares, p. 258. The report is printed; ibid. pp. 236-54.

[3] See John Murray Graham, Annals and Correspondence of the Viscount and the First and Second Earls of Stair (1875), i. 160, 193-200.

M'Ean of Glencoe and that trybe can be well separated from the rest, it will be a proper vindication of the public justice to extirpate that sect of thieves.' These orders, evidently drafted by Stair, do not sanction either treachery or breach of faith, and it is improbable that all the details of the affair were known to William.[1] Stair decided with promptitude that a distinction could be made between the MacIans and the rest, and ordered the extirpation to be effected. When subsequent inquiry revealed the details, William, as we have seen, condoned the massacre and pardoned Stair. He treated Stair's act as an error, not as a crime, and, regarding Highland thieves as 'two-footed wolves', was not much moved by their fate.[2] The extirpation by fire and sword of a turbulent and intractable clan was no new thing in Scottish history: the novelty was that it excited so much popular indignation amongst Lowlanders. This was not entirely due to humanity: opponents of the government seized the opportunity to discredit it, and the enemies or rivals of the Secretary utilised it to overthrow him.[3]

One of these rivals was Stair's colleague, Secretary Johnstone, who had succeeded Melville about the end of 1691. James Johnstone was the son of Sir Archibald Johnstone of Warriston. His cousin, Burnet, described him as a man of 'a very good understanding, and a great dexterity in managing business,' and also 'of an entire virtue'. He adds that though his descent obliged him 'to espouse the Presbyterian interests', yet he had 'none of their narrow notions', and was even a little 'too loose as to the

[1] Mr. Paget considers that 'no reasonable doubt can be entertained' that William knew that Glencoe had taken the oath (pp. 55-7). The evidence he adduces does not prove the point.

[2] The phrase was used by William in conversation with Breadalbane. Story, Carstares, p. 218.

[3] See Brown, History of Scotland, iii. 16-17.

doctrinal part of religion.' In the first draft of his history Burnet gave many particulars about Johnstone which are omitted in the final version.[1] His character, his political views and his influence have been made clearer by the publication of a number of his letters, now scattered through various collections but worth assembling and editing.[2] The difference between Johnstone and Stair was not entirely personal: what Burnet[3] terms Johnstone's 'principles with relation to public liberty' enabled him to work more harmoniously with popular assemblies, and in Parliament he not only showed great skill in debate, but great dexterity in the conduct of business. William dismissed him in February 1696, and Sir James Ogilvy, afterwards Earl of Seafield, became Secretary in his place, and held that office till the end of the reign. His correspondence, lately published by the Scottish History Society, is a valuable addition to our knowledge of the last years of William's reign.[4] Johnstone had been dismissed for his part in the passing of the Act for a Company Trading to Africa and the Indies (June 26, 1695), against which the English Parliament had protested. This Act led to the attempt to found the colony at Darien, established in November 1698 and abandoned in June 1699. Macaulay's account of the inception and failure of the scheme is based mainly on the volume of Darien Papers edited by Hill Burton in 1849 for the Bannatyne Club, but recent investigations have shown that his narrative is in many points inaccurate. Originally

[1] Foxcroft, Supplement to Burnet, pp. 370-3, 392, 415. See also pp. 542-4, Additional Note on Burnet's Original Account of Scotch Affairs after the Revolution.

[2] See Hope Johnstone MSS., Marchmont MSS., Buccleuch MSS. at Montagu House, vol. ii, and Hamilton MSS.

[3] Supplement, p. 415.

[4] Seafield Correspondence from 1685 to 1708, ed. James Grant (1912).

the company was to have been a British rather than a Scottish enterprise; half the capital was to be raised in one country, half in the other. The London subscribers raised their money at once, but the English Parliament intervened, forced them to withdraw their subscriptions, and put an end to the operations of the company in England. It then became a purely Scottish enterprise, and was doomed to failure because its capital was insufficient and its directors inexperienced. Macaulay inverts the order of events; the subscription in London took place in October 1695, that in Edinburgh began in February 1696. The intervention of the English Parliament occurred in December 1695, more than two months before any capital had been raised in Scotland; and the promoters must have been well aware that they could expect no support from the English government.[1] The disaster which overtook the colony at Darien emphasised the fact that without English protection it was impossible for Scotland to develop its foreign or colonial trade. Ex-Secretary Johnstone—a shrewd observer—pointed out to the Earl of Annandale that the best that could be hoped from any success was that it would 'produce an union in trade betwixt the two kingdoms.'[2]

The reign of William III prepared the way for the union. The ecclesiastical settlement made it possible, the commercial difficulty made it indispensable. William began his reign by recommending it to the Scottish Convention, and ended it with a similar recommendation to the English Parliament. 'On the twenty eighth of February', says Macaulay, the Commons listened with uncovered heads to the last message that bore William's sign manual. An unhappy

[1] See J. S. Barbour, A History of William Paterson and the Darien Company (1907).

[2] Hope Johnstone MSS., p. 108.

accident, he told them, had forced him to make to them in writing a communication which he would gladly have made from the throne. He had, in the first year of his reign, expressed his desire to see an union accomplished between England and Scotland. He was convinced that nothing could more conduce to the safety and happiness of both. He should think it his peculiar felicity if, before the close of his reign, some happy expedient could be devised for making the two kingdoms one; and he, in the most earnest manner, recommended the question to the consideration of the Houses.[1]

The Seafield Correspondence supplies a fresh proof of William's eagerness for the completion of the union. The King sent for Seafield four days before he died. 'My lord', wrote the Countess of Seafield, 'had a short adiens of him on Wadsenday, when he spok very kyndlie to him and of the Scots nashion and mighty fordvard for the uneion. I am shour ther is no honast or Cristien Scotsman bot will be senseabell of this ireparabell loss.'[2]

This regret was not universal. One Scottish historian says bluntly that the Scots were 'glad to be rid of King William.'[3] Another confesses that when William died, 'he was not a popular king in Scotland . . . There was no class among his subjects to whom his rule had given entire satisfaction; and the fact may be put to the credit of his general policy.' However, 'the main body of his Scottish subjects gladly recognised that he had fulfilled the chief objects for which he had been invited to become their king. He had saved Protestantism, given to the nation a church which the majority desired, and substituted a constitutional monarchy

[1] From a fragment on the death of William III (VI, 3000-2 [xxv]). On the attitude of the English Parliament see Marchmont MSS., pp. 152, 154-5, and James Mackinnon, The Union of England and Scotland (1896), pp. 57-9.

[2] Seafield Correspondence, p. 349.

[3] Mackinnon, p. 65.

for a despotism.'[1] A third writes: 'William was the only Scottish sovereign since the Reformation who had governed the country in an entirely reasonable spirit; and, however little appreciated by his English subjects, as the champion of Protestantism who had overthrown the wretched government of the Stewarts, he enjoyed the popularity in Scotland which was little obscured by the shadow of Glencoe, and which his enforced attitude on the Darien question did not seriously impair.'[2]

My own view is that William was not really popular in either Scotland or England, and could not be. The Scots wished to be governed according to Scottish ideas, the English according to English ideas: in both countries William sought to impose ideas of his own. The King, wrote Secretary Johnstone, 'has his rules and often verry hidden ones, if you can comply with them, you can serve him; if not, you can not, he will not part with them.'[3] In each country he endeavoured to be the king of the nation, not the king of a party: in England he governed sometimes through the Whigs, sometimes through the Tories, sometimes through a combination of both. In Scotland he tried to follow a similar plan. But in neither was he thoroughly a national sovereign; the Scots felt that he sacrificed Scottish to English interests, the English that he sacrificed English to European interests. The larger community came first in his mind. Such a king by the breadth of his views might render great services to the nations he ruled, but was not likely to give satisfaction to all classes or to win popularity.

[1] Brown, History of Scotland, iii. 33-4.

[2] W. L. Mathieson, Scotland and the Union (1905), p. 70.

[3] Hope Johnstone MSS., p. 97.

CHAPTER IX

MACAULAY'S TREATMENT OF IRISH HISTORY

MACAULAY devoted the latter part of the sixth chapter of his History to the government of James II in Ireland, and the whole of the twelfth and nearly all the sixteenth and seventeenth chapters to the history of its reconquest by William. The narrative was brought down to the siege and treaty of Limerick, but thenceforth there is no systematic account of Irish affairs and such episodes as are mentioned are dealt with from the point of view of English politics.

Macaulay had a great disadvantage to contend with. There was no good history of Ireland in existence. Above all, there was no adequate account of the years 1660 to 1685 which would have supplied a solid foundation for the study of the years which followed. There were available Carte's Life of James Duke of Ormond, a collection of the state letters of the Earl of Orrery, the letters written by the Earl of Essex in 1675, and some other materials, but they left many points obscure. The few paragraphs Macaulay devotes to describing the aboriginal peasantry and aristocracy are very vague and rhetorical, and his account of the state of the English colony is vitiated by the failure to explain how or when English and Scotch settlers came to Ireland and how their ascendancy was maintained. He is content to assume that the dominion which the English population exercised over the Irish 'was the dominion of wealth over poverty, of knowledge over ignorance, of civilised over uncivilised man.'[1]

[1] II, 786 (vi).

The modern historian, unlike Macaulay, has at his disposal a number of valuable secondary works and new sources. Robert Dunlop contributed a good account of Ireland, 1660-1700, to the Cambridge Modern History, vol. v. Much more detailed is Richard Bagwell's Ireland under the Stuarts, vol. iii, 1660-1690 (1916). Four other books worth mentioning are J. P. Prendergast's Ireland from the Restoration to the Revolution (1887), which contains much information about some aspects of the period, Fitzmaurice's Life of Sir William Petty (1895), valuable for all questions connected with the land settlement or the economic condition of Ireland, A. E. Murray's the Commercial Relations between England and Ireland (1903), and George O'Brien's The Economic History of Ireland in the Seventeenth Century (1919). These works enable the student to check and supplement Macaulay's rather inadequate account of the social and economic condition of Ireland at James's accession; and, in particular, the omission of any analysis of the Cromwellian land settlement and of the subsequent acts of Charles II can be supplied.

For the years 1689-1702, Robert H. Murray's Revolutionary Ireland and Its Settlement (1911) is indispensable. Two sources of extreme importance have appeared since Macaulay wrote: A Calendar of the State Papers Relating to Ireland in the English Public Record Office, which covers the seventeenth century up to 1670 (after that the Irish state papers are included in the English Calendar of State Papers, Domestic); and the Historical Manuscripts Commission Reports on the papers of the Duke of Ormonde at Kilkenny Castle.

James began his government by dismissing the Duke of Ormonde from the post of Lord Lieutenant and appointing the Earl of Clarendon to succeed him. Clarendon held office till February 1687, when Tyrconnel took his place. Macaulay had the advantage of Clarendon's own letters, printed in the Diary and Correspondence of Henry Earl of Clarendon, edited by S. W. Singer, but for the period of Tyrconnel's rule there are no materials of equal value and authority. One of the authorities Macaulay used was 'Sheridan MS. among the Stuart Papers.'[1] The memoirs of Thomas Sheridan, Chief Secretary and First Commissioner of the Revenue in Ireland, have been printed by the Historical Manuscripts Commission, Stuart Papers, vi (1916). Of Tyrconnel's letters few have been preserved. Those calendared by the Historical Manuscripts Commission (Eighth Report, pp. 494-7) are few in number and mostly relate to the military operations which followed the Revolution. Some concerning 1688 are printed in Analecta Hibernica, No. 1 (1930; pp. 38-44). Nothing, however, in the scraps of new evidence which have come to hand about the years 1687 and 1688 vindicates the policy or the administration of Tyrconnel from the censure Macaulay has pronounced upon it. It was well known, he wrote, that Tyrconnel had set his heart on the extermination of the English colony in Ireland.[2] By the end of 1688 both civil and military power had been transferred from the Saxon to the Celtic population.[3] Tyrconnel's violent policy had aroused the wildest hopes of the Irish. It was natural therefore that the Irish should refuse to recognise the English settlement of the Revolution, and adhere to James. The vehemence of their nationalism was revealed when James, who landed in Ireland in March 1689, summoned a Parliament to meet in Dublin.

[1] II, 789 n. (vi).

[2] II, 806 (vi).

[3] III, 1430 (xii).

One question which has excited much controversy is the action of the Irish Parliament in repealing the Act of Settlement of 1662 and restoring the heirs of all owners whose land had been forfeited by the government since 1641 to the possession of their estates, and passing a general bill of attainder against the Protestant landowners who had fled to England. It was vindicated by T. O. Davis in a series of historical papers contributed to the Nation about 1843, and republished in 1893 under the title of The Patriot Parliament of 1689, edited by C. G. Duffy. Lecky[1] apologises to some extent for the repeal of the Act of Settlement and complains that Macaulay, while severely condemning the Act of Attainder passed by the Irish Parliament, omits to mention that a similar bill of attainder was passed by the English House of Commons. But the cases are different. The English bill never became a law, as it did not pass the House of Lords. Moreover, while the Irish act attainted more than 2,000 persons, the English bill proposed to attaint only a score.[2] A detailed answer to Davis's vindication of this Parliament is contained in an essay upon it by T. Dunbar Ingram, entitled Two Chapters of Irish History (1888).

On these two questions of the repeal of the Act of Settlement and the attainder bill, James was opposed to the policy adopted by the Irish Parliament. He knew that the alienation of English feeling would make his plan of using Ireland as a stepping-stone for the recovery of England impossible. He expressed his disapproval, but his feeble opposition was overborne by Tyrconnel and the Irish nationalists, who sought the separation of England and

[1] W. E. H. Lecky, History of Ireland in the Eighteenth Century (1892), i. 117-34.

[2] Manuscripts of the House of Lords, 1689-1690, x (1889), 227-43.

Ireland, and depended on France to effect it. To recover England reliance would have to be placed on Irish arms, and James could not afford to alienate his last supporters.

Jacobites in general seem to have thought this reconquest of England by Irish forces a possibility. Macaulay frequently quotes a manuscript Jacobite narrative of the war in Ireland, called A Light to the Blind. Since then the whole work, with a collection of illustrative documents, has been printed by J. T. Gilbert (in 1892) under the title of A Jacobite Narrative of the War in Ireland, 1688-91.[1] The author is said to be Nicholas Plunket, a Catholic lawyer. He makes Tyrconnel his hero. The Duke's death, he thought, 'pulled down a mighty edifice, videlicet, a considerable Catholic nation, for there was no other subject left able to support the national cause.'[2] Plunket's view is that the resources James possessed in Ireland were ample for the recovery of England. If James and his supporters were wise, consistent, diligent, and united, they might recover England by such means as were available in Ireland at the King's arrival. The army numbered at least sixty thousand men, a considerable proportion of them being veterans. Constant exercise would in two months make the rest skilful enough in the use of arms. The cavalry and dragoons were not to be contemned, because some regiments of horse and some of dragoons might vie with the best of Europe. There were battering cannon, and fieldpieces sufficient for their purpose in several towns of the realm. They had some store of small arms, and had iron and artificers to fashion enough in a short time, as also to cast mortars and bombs, pikes, half-pikes, scythes, spades,

[1] It is also to be found in Hist. MSS. Comm., Tenth Report, App., pt. v (1885), pp. 107-200.

[2] P. 155.

pickaxes, and other utensils of war. Horses and oxen for draught abounded. Merchant ships could have been collected out of several parts of the kingdom to transport the army into Scotland, whence it might have marched into England. 'To clothe and feed those forces there was an overflowing plenty in the country; for no land in Europe, for its extent, could show such flocks of sheep and so great stocks of black cattle. Corn was in redundancy.'

According to the same writer, James ought to have transported an army to Scotland in May 1689, before the Prince of Orange could send a fleet from England to stop it. From the army in Ireland there were then available for service in Scotland over twenty thousand chosen foot, and five thousand horse and dragoons, with provisions for three weeks. This force

> would make way for themselves through Scotland; would command the stores of the country, and would allure abundance of loyal subjects out of the Highlands to join them. They would have penetrated into the north of England by the middle of June, where infallibly they would receive a considerable augmentation of Catholicks and some Protestants from Northumberland, Westmoreland, Cumberland, Lancashire, Derbyshire and Yorkshire. They could not have been met with by the Prince of Orange and his army till they had come to York; at which time the King most certainly would be about fifty thousand strong, all resolute men. Now, I leave it to the judgment of any wise man whether the King was not in a condition to carry England before him at that juncture, wherein the Prince of Orange's throne was not settled.

Six causes are assigned for the failure to carry out this promising enterprise. The first was the King himself, because in this critical juncture he left the management of his affairs too much to the skill, care, and fidelity of others, and did not overlook their conduct of affairs. His Majesty was a sincere Christian, suspecting no evil of anybody whom he had not actually found to be bad, and believing that everyone he trusted would prove honest and diligent. Consequently he used to acquiesce often in the opinion of those who were commonly about his person; and this acquiescence proved his destruction, for those he trusted were either traitors or ignorant. The second cause was the want of wisdom or of fidelity in certain of his counsellors, of whatsoever nation they were. The third was the ignorance or treachery of some high officers and of some governors of garrisoned towns. The fourth was the dishonesty or neglect of particular commissaries of stores and provisions for the army. The fifth cause was in the government, that due care was not taken to see that the soil was tilled, just as in normal years, in those tracts of land spared the horrors of war. The sixth cause was that his Majesty, soon after his arrival at Dublin, did not transport an army into Scotland without waiting for the reduction of Londonderry.[1]

This narrative of Plunket's is more valuable for the opinions it expresses than the facts it contains. The resources of Ireland might be considerable but the administration was so bad that they could not be utilised. James might have sixty thousand men under arms, but they were too badly disciplined and drilled and officered to constitute a serious danger to England, although in Ireland they proved capable of offering a tolerably prolonged resistance. Captain John Stevens, an English Jacobite who fought at the battle of the Boyne, left a narrative of his adventures during the Irish war, a portion of which was printed in the appendix to Ranke's History of England, and all of which was edited for the Clarendon Press by R. H. Murray in

[1] A Jacobite Narrative, pp. 49-50.

1912. His opinion of the Irish army was less flattering than Plunket's. It is very hard, he complains, to give an account of the Irish army. The common computation was incredible, for it included the whole nation, 'every poor country fellow having armed himself with a skeine as they call it or dagger, or a ropery like a halfpike, weapons fit only to please themselves, or else to put them in a posture of robbing and plundering the whole country, under pretence of suppressing the rebellious Protestants.' These rapparees committed many outrages so that

> having overstocked themselves with other men's cattle they destroyed millions throughout the kingdom only for their hides or tallow, and sometimes only to exercise their malice, leaving the carcasses to rot in the fields. . . . Our muster rolls ran high, every officer being quartered near home the better to enable him to raise his men or rather to put it into his power to muster all the rabble of the country, which when he was to march towards the enemy either he had no right to command or else they deserted. I am an eye-witness that regiments that mustered 700 and upwards at home came not into the field or even to Dublin 400 strong. . . . Our men were newly brought from the mountains, used to live in slavery without the use of any weapon: the most of them had never fired a musket in their lives. A people used only to follow and converse with cows, so hard to be made sensible of the duty of a soldier or be brought to handle their arms aright, that it was difficult to make many of them understand the common words of command, much less to obey them. Besides their natural uncouthness, they are stubborn and conceited, to be governed with rigour and severity, not to be wrought upon with lenity and gentleness. . . . They will follow none but their own leaders, many of them men as rude, as ignorant, and as far from understanding any of the rules of discipline as themselves. This was the utter ruin of the army. . . . The commissioned officer could not punish his sergeant or corporal because he

was his cousin or foster brother, and they durst not correct the soldier, lest he should fly in their face or run away. These officers had seen and knew no more than their men, and consequently understood as little how to exercise or train them.[1]

Who these officers were is shown by John D'Alton's Illustrations, Historical and Genealogical, of King James's Irish Army List, published in 1861 in two parts (first edition, 1855). D'Alton takes every regiment and gives a biography of each commissioned officer, as far as materials for the purpose exist, and some account of the family to which the officer belonged.

On the policy pursued by James in Ireland and his conduct there Macaulay quoted largely from the despatches of Avaux, the French Ambassador. These despatches were then available in a privately printed volume ; recently, the Irish Manuscripts Commission has reproduced the volume under the title, Négociations de M. le Comte D'Avaux en Irlande, 1689-90 (1934). The French policy in Ireland was clearly set forth in one of the despatches of Louvois, a minister of Louis XIV, to Avaux :

In the position in which the King of England [James II] now is, he ought only to think how to maintain himself in Ireland and to realise that if he is driven thence he will never return to England. He ought then, forgetting that he has ever been King of England and of Scotland, only to think of what can improve Ireland and of the measures which can facilitate his stopping there.[2]

Another interesting passage is the character of Tyrconnel which Avaux draws :

He is not as able as could be wished, and he does not like trouble or work. But he does accomplish much good be-

[1] Journal of John Stevens, pp. 61-64. [2] Avaux, p. 277.

cause he acts on good principles, consults the people of the country, and gives them work to do which suits them. . . . He listens to reason and every time that I have told him that he ought to do such and such things, he has immediately ordered them to be done. Lord Melfort is exactly the opposite. . . . He is a man of insupportable vanity, of which you will be fully pursuaded when you learn that he tries to manage all the affairs of this kingdom, of which he has no knowledge, without consulting the leading Irishmen and without having taken any account of the finances or matters concerning the war and the police.[1]

In fact, while Tyrconnel was the leader of the faction that hoped to make Ireland independent of England if dependent upon France, Melfort represented Jacobitism rather than nationalism.

One of the causes which prevented the success of James was the defence of Londonderry. As he meant to transport his army from Ulster into the west of Scotland the possession of Derry was of importance to him. He could not afford, at all events, to leave a hostile garrison there, and the subjugation of Ulster in general was needful.

The siege lasted from April 18 to July 30, 1689. No new documents of great importance concerning it have come to light since Macaulay wrote. In the Manuscripts of the House of Lords, 1689-1690 (pp. 134-92), are papers laid before a committee appointed June 15, 1689, for enquiring into miscarriages in Ireland. Amongst others are records of the proceedings of the English Privy Council with regard to the relief of Londonderry, orders, letters from Ireland, and other documentary material of value, including Colonel Lundy's instructions as governor of Londonderry. The chief authorities Macaulay used are easily accessible. Walker's True Account of the Siege of Londonderry and

[1] Ibid. pp. 292-3.

some other pamphlets were reprinted and edited by the Reverend Philip Dwyer in 1894. Hamilton's True Relation and McCormick's Further Account of the Actions of the Enniskillen Men were similarly reprinted at Duncannon in 1896. J. Mackenzie's answer to Walker's account of the siege, entitled A Narrative of the Siege of Londonderry, was edited by W. D. Killen and published at Belfast in 1861.

One of Macaulay's authorities is the Life of Sir John Leake, by Stephen Martin-Leake, privately printed in 1750 and edited for the Navy Records Society by Geoffrey Callender (2 vols.; 1920). Now, though Macaulay cites this as one of the sources for his account of the relief of Londonderry, it is remarkable that in the most important point he sets aside the very definite story of the breaking of the boom given in this book and follows, instead, Walker's account. Walker says the boom was broken by the 'Mountjoy' and the 'Phoenix', the two merchant ships. According to Leake's narrative, it was cut by the boats of the 'Dartmouth'.

Leake describes the boom as 'a *Stoccado*, being a boom of timber, joined by iron chains, and strengthened by a cable of twelve inches thickness twisted round it. And at each end thereof were redoubts with heavy cannon; and they had likewise sunk several boats, etc.' Because the 'Swallow', the only man-of-war available, was too large to go up the river, Leake had to be content to borrow her longboat to cut the boom.

Having well concerted beforehand what was to be done, he agreed with the commanders of the two victuallers, upon the manner of the attack: that he leading the van, should engage the castle and batteries, whilst they, in the meantime, should pass by and run with full sail against the boom, in order to break it. And the boats being well manned and prepared for the work, were immediately to join them, and use their best endeavours to cut the boom asunder, and haul the ships through ; and the evening was judged most proper to make the attack.

About seven in the evening of the same day Captain Leake in the 'Dartmouth' sailed towards the river,

followed by the victuallers, viz. the Mountjoy of Derry and the Phoenix of Coleraine, but under the great disadvantage of having but little wind to enable them to pass the batteries, or carry them with any force against the boom.

When the ships had passed the castle, the slight wind they had had failed them, and a dead calm succeeded, so that the victuallers not having force to break the boom recoiled, and the 'Mountjoy' ran stern foremost on shore. By great Providence, the shock of firing her guns loosened her so that by the help of the rising tide she got clear, though with the loss of Mr. Browning, her commander, who was killed by the enemy's shot.

In the meantime, the cannon of the Dartmouth had done great execution against the batteries, . . . and whilst the enemy were exulting with joy for the success they seemed to have over the Mountjoy, the boats' crews got upon the boom, cut it asunder and hauled the Phoenix through ; and soon after the Mountjoy followed, Captain Leake continuing the fight till he saw they had both got in safety to the city.[1]

Various contemporary pieces of evidence confirm the story of the cutting of the boom. A newsletter dated August 12, 1689, reports that

[1] Life of Sir John Leake, i. 24-29.

Captain Brow[n]ing ship stoped at the bomb wher he was killed [and] the boat swayne and the boat swayne mate of the *Swallow* who commanded her long boat cutt the bombe soe that the wieght of the ship broke it and the ships went up but with soe little wind that the long boat towed the *Mountjoye* all the way to the towne.[1]

In one of William's conversations with the Marquis of Halifax, dated August 18, 1689, the King said 'he would remember Shelly, who cut the chain at Londonderry.'[2] Who Shelly was and what reward he obtained remain unknown, but this is evidence that the King and his minister believed the boom was cut. The only pension granted for breaking the boom was £60 a year to the widow of Micaiah Browning.

How did the story that the boom was broken by a ship's weight get into circulation? One reason certainly is that it was related in Parliament, as the following extract from Sir Robert Rich's speech proves.

What is said, gives me occasion to tell you something of my own knowledge. A captain who lived twenty or thirty miles from Londonderry, and who loved the place, had applied to the Council of Scotland for the relief of it: they loaded him with meal; he sailed by our fleet, and was brought aboard to give an account why he did go by the fleet without calling, and he must give an account to the general; he said, 'he knew no general.' They caused him to lie there five weeks; he asked them the reason: they told him, 'There was a prodigious boom cross the river, choaked up with sunk vessels, and a battery on the river, with small shot, on each side.' He asked, 'Whether, in five weeks, any long-boat was sent to view the boom?'—The boy he sent, who swam in, gave a dismal account of the condition of the town. He was ordered to go up the river,

[1] Hist. MSS. Comm., Le Fleming MSS., p. 255.

[2] Foxcroft, Halifax, ii. 231.

and if he could not get up to the town, to fire his ship, to be useless—The man of war, and two more, stopped short of the fort; the meal-ship was before. When he was near, he dropped anchor. The anchor drew, and the tide carried the ship's stern athwart the boom and this dismal boom, only with the weight of this ship broke in the middle, and no wind at all.[1]

This captain was clearly Andrew Douglas, commander of the 'Phoenix', who was recommended by the Earl of Shrewsbury to the Admiralty for employment in the navy for his service in the relief of Londonderry.[2]

A fortnight after the relief of Londonderry, Schomberg landed in Ulster with an army of about 12,000 men and, having taken Carrickfergus and Lisburn, established himself at Dundalk, where his army remained throughout the winter. Macaulay describes the sufferings of the army during the winter, and discusses the question of Schomberg's generalship. Was he right in maintaining a defensive attitude rather than accepting the battle which James offered? According to Burnet and Macaulay he was right. His own army was very much smaller than that of James, and was badly disciplined and imperfectly trained, as Schomberg's letters show. These letters, some of which were printed by Dalrymple, are calendared at length, with other documents bearing on the question, in the Calendar of State Papers, Domestic, 1689-1690, and fully bear out this conclusion. It is also confirmed by Ailesbury, who relates in his memoirs that Schomberg

took that important post of Dundalk, a low moist ground under great hills, and there he was entrenched the whole summer, losing a great part by far of his men by the bloody

[1] Grey, Debates of the House of Commons, ix. 481.

[2] Calendar of State Papers, Domestic, 1689-1690 (1895), p. 303.

flux &c., and the stench was insufferable; but he bore all this like an old crafty general. Sir Edward Deering, my Lord Hewit, and others, came to let him know they were not there to have their arms across. The Marechal was a man free from passion, but knew how to be obeyed, and told them with a soft voice 'Gentlemen, I observe you always come to me in the afternoon,' meaning by that they had been playing the good fellow; 'pray when you have anything to say to me, come fasting. But let me tell you that if you continue in this way of murmuring, I know what I have to do.' Mr. William Harbord, Commissary General and of the Privy Council, was with him generally and as a friend besides, and this I had from him. . . . Mr. Harbord added that the Marechal told him, 'Sir, you are under my orders as well as the rest, but I regard you as my friend, and you, having the honour to be one of the Prince's Council, I will reason with you. Pray take this perspective glass, and then give me your opinion.' That gentleman perceived King James with his blue ribbon riding about the ranks, and his army in all appearance numerous and in excellent order, and also the troopers well mounted. The Marechal went on, 'Now, Mr. Harbord, you see the reason I cannot quit my post, and we are in a manner but with a handful of men in comparison of the other army. Here I will stay. What hinders me besides advancing to the enemy hinders them the same from attacking of me, the defiles being lined with cannon; so here I will rest, and will surmount all difficulties. The great rains come in generally in this country about Bartholomew-tide, and then the Irish army must of necessity go into quarters, and then we shall have another year for it.' And for this great action he was reproached . . . but I was told then by men of experience that the Marechal, during the whole course of his service, never shewed himself so great a general as he did this summer by doing of nothing, that is by inaction; and what he foretold came to pass, and the armies went into quarters.[1]

[1] Memoirs, i. 252-3.

In June 1690 William III landed in Ireland, and on July 1 the battle of the Boyne took place. One of Macaulay's authorities for the history of the campaign is Dumont de Bostaquet, the Huguenot officer whose memoirs he saw in manuscript. These were published in Paris in 1864. Macaulay regretted the disappearance of the despatch on the battle of the Boyne which Lauzun, who commanded the French auxiliaries serving in James's army, must have written to Louvois.[1] That despatch and several other letters from Lauzun were discovered by Ranke and printed in the sixth volume of his History. According to the English Jacobite, John Stevens, the Irish infantry behaved extremely badly at the Boyne though some of the Irish horse fought extremely well, and this statement is confirmed by the evidence of various French officers quoted by Macaulay and by Lauzun's despatch. Another eyewitness of the battle was George Clarke, Judge Advocate General in William's army. Thirteen volumes of Clarke's official correspondence during the war are preserved in the library of Trinity College, Dublin, and Macaulay made some use of them, but he did not know the brief and extremely interesting autobiography of Clarke printed by the Historical Manuscripts Commission.[2] Clarke describes with singular vividness the opening of the battle.

Next morning, about eight or nine o'clock, our cannon began to fire upon two houses, with yards walled about, that stood on each side the road on the other side the Boyne just over against the ford where the Guards were to pass. The enemy had posted some foot in those houses, whose fire was silenced by our cannon, but as the Guards were got almost through the water they rose up from behind the walls and

[1] IV, 1881 (xvi).

[2] Leyborne-Popham MSS. (1899), pp. 259-89.

gave one fire upon them and ran away. Part of the troops marched directly on between these two houses up the hill, and there the Duke of Schonberg and Mr. Walker were killed, and news was brought of it to the King, who had not passed the river, but was looking upon the action and in great concern for his Blue Guards, who had marched to the left between the two houses and the river and were forming as fast as they could to receive a body of Irish horse that was coming towards them upon a full trot. The King was in a good deal of apprehension for them, there not being hedge nor ditch before them nor any of our horse to support them, and I was so near his Majesty as to hear him say softly to himself: 'My poor Guards, my poor Guards, my poor Guards,' as the enemy were coming down upon them, but when he saw them stand their ground and fire by platoons, so that the horse were forced to run away in great disorder, he breathed out, as people use to do after holding their breath upon a fright or suspense, and said he had seen his Guards do that which he had never seen foot do in his life.

Thanks to the resistance of the French and in part also to the Duke of Schomberg's death, the defeated army escaped with a loss of some 1,500 men. 'The loss of the conquerors', said Macaulay, 'did not exceed five hundred men: but among them was the first captain in Europe. To his corpse every honour was paid. . . . It was announced that the brave veteran would have a public funeral at Westminster.'[1] John Paget, in his Paradoxes and Puzzles (p. 182), pointed out that Schomberg was buried in St. Patrick's Cathedral, Dublin, and that no monument or inscription marked his last resting place until Dean Swift and the chapter erected a tablet.[2]

[1] IV, 1885 (xvi).

[2] The Correspondence of Jonathan Swift, ed. F. Elrington Ball (1913), iv. 213.

After the battle of the Boyne, James fled to France, and William, having occupied Dublin, laid siege to Limerick. The siege lasted most of August, but was then abandoned because Sarsfield intercepted and destroyed the convoy which was bringing William's siege train. Of this first siege, there is a French account printed by Gilbert in the appendix to his Jacobite Narrative. There is also a Life of Sarsfield (1895) by John Todhunter, written from a nationalist's point of view, which gives many details about Sarsfield and collects much information about the war in Ireland.

William returned to England after raising the siege of Limerick, but the campaign of 1690 was not yet over. An expedition set sail from England, under the command of Marlborough, which was joined by the Duke of Wurtemburg and some regiments of the army William had left in Ireland. After short sieges, Cork and Kinsale were captured, and Marlborough then came home. A detailed account, with plans, of this successful little expedition is to be found in Viscount Wolseley's Life of Marlborough (pp. 217-25). In the next campaign, in 1691, the subjugation of Ireland was completed by Ginkle. On June 30, 1691, he stormed Athlone; on July 12 he defeated the Irish at Aghrim; a month later he laid siege to Limerick, and on October 3 that town capitulated. Some of Ginkle's letters on the progress of this campaign are to be found in the Historical Manuscripts Commission, Eighth Report (pp. 317-25). Others are in the Calendar of State Papers, Domestic, for that year. A diary of the siege, by Colonel Richards, is printed in the Jacobite Narrative, which contains also a curious description of the battle of Aghrim, written in Latin verse. From all these various sources much may be gathered which supplements and in some particulars corrects the narrative in chapter xvii of Macaulay's History.

The end of the war brought to the front a marked difference of policy, which had existed between King William and the representatives of the English colony in Ireland ever since the battle of the Boyne. After his victory, William wished to offer a general pardon for their lives and estates to the Irish nobility and people. The English in Ireland opposed this. According to Burnet, they 'thought the present opportunity was not to be let go, of breaking the great Irish families, upon whom the inferior sort would always depend. And, in compliance with them, the indemnity now offered was so limited, that it had no effect.'[1] After the capitulation of Limerick, the differences between the King and the Anglo-Irish became evident to everyone.

The question of the treaty of Limerick and its observance or non-observance has been much discussed. The text itself is printed in full in an appendix to the Jacobite Narrative. Some new evidence on the course of the negotiations which led to it is in the autobiography of George Clarke, who was one of the negotiators. He explains the origin of the disputed clause, viz. some words added to Clause 2 which extended the benefits of the capitulation to a large number of persons not forming part of the garrison. When Sir Toby Butler, an Irish negotiator, asked what the preamble meant when it spoke of articles granted to all persons in the city of Limerick and in the Irish army in the counties of Clare, Kerry, Cork, and Mayo, and other garrisons in their possession, Clarke states that he answered

that we meant to capitulate with and grant terms to those who were in a condition to oppose us. Sir Toby replied

[1] Own Time, ii. 57. There is other evidence to confirm the Bishop's statement. See Onno Klopp, Der Fall des Hauses Stuart und die Succession des Hauses Hannover in Gross-Britannien und Irland im Zusammenhange der europäischen Angelegenheiten von 1660-1714 (14 vols.; 1875-88), v. 167, 214, 303, 306.

that if we meant to go no further there must be an end of the treaty, and Sarsfield added that he would lay his bones in those old walls rather than not take care of those who stuck by them all along, so the second article was explained to extend to *all such as are under their protection in the said counties*, which I mention the more particularly because those words, though first agreed to, were omitted by mistake in transcribing that copy of the articles which was signed and the mistake not found out till next day, when Mons. Ginckle's son was actually gone towards England with the original or a copy to be laid before their Majesties. This occasioned a great deal of trouble.[1]

It is certain that William III and his government did their utmost to carry out the terms of the treaty but were frustrated by the Parliaments of both England and Ireland. The English Parliament in 1691 passed an act to compel all members of the Irish Parliament to take an oath of supremacy and to subscribe to a declaration against transubstantiation. This exclusion of Catholics from Parliament in Dublin was contrary to the spirit, at least, of the treaty, which promised that they should enjoy such privileges in the exercise of their religion as they had possessed in the reign of Charles II. Furthermore, the Irish Parliament in 1695 passed a large number of acts against the Catholics and they two years later, when nominally confirming the articles of Limerick, limited their confirmation expressly to so much of them as consisted with the safety and welfare of his Majesty's subjects in Ireland. Mr. T. D. Ingram, in Two Chapters of Irish History (1888), argues at length that the Irish Parliament was neither legally nor morally bound to ratify the treaty. On the other hand Mr. Robert Dunlop concludes : ' Whether in doing as it did Parliament acted within its constitutional rights or not, is a moot point ; but

[1] Leyborne-Popham MSS., p. 280.

there can be no doubt that its repudiation of the treaty was as politically unwise as it was morally unjustifiable.' [1]

During the last ten years of William's reign the civil government of Ireland was in various hands. First there were two Lords Justices, Coningsby and Porter.[2] When Coningsby was removed for embezzlement and extortion in 1692,[3] Henry, Viscount Sydney, was named Lord Lieutenant. In 1695 Henry, Lord Capel, became Lord Deputy and in 1701 Lawrence Hyde, Earl of Rochester, was appointed Lord Lieutenant. During the whole period, whoever the nominal Lord Lieutenant or Lord Deputy might be, the conduct of the government was in the hands of the Lords Justices, of whom, until his death at the end of 1696, the most important was Sir Charles Porter, and then probably Narcissus Marsh, Archbishop of Dublin. The correspondence of these various officials is included in the Calendar of State Papers, Domestic, published down to the end of 1698. Among the papers of the Duke of Buccleuch at Montagu House, calendared by the Historical Manuscripts Commission (1903), are many letters addressed to the Duke of Shrewsbury when Secretary of State, by Capel, Galway, and others, between about 1694 and 1700. On church matters during the same period, the papers of William King, successively Bishop of Derry and Archbishop of Dublin, shed new light.[4]

Another thorny question concerns the restriction imposed by England upon the export of woollen goods from Ireland. Macaulay states that the act imposing the restric-

[1] Cambridge Modern History, v (1908), 322.

[2] Macaulay, IV, 1922 (xvi). [3] Ibid. V, 2309-10 (xix).

[4] Hist. MSS. Comm., Second Report (1871), pp. 231-56. Sir C. S. King's A Great Archbishop of Dublin (1906) is mainly autobiography and correspondence.

tions was altogether indefensible in principle. 'Practically it was altogether unimportant.'[1] The origin and result of the commercial restrictions have led to much controversy. In 1779 John Hely-Hutchinson, in the second of his letters on The Commercial Restraints of Ireland, had set forth the grievances of Ireland on this point. These letters were edited in 1882 by W. G. Carroll, with a number of useful notes. Lecky has restated the case against the act in his History of Ireland. On the other hand, William Cunningham, in an article on The Repression of the Woollen Manufacture in Ireland,[2] minimises the damage done by the acts and exalts the motives underlying them. His conclusion is that 'there was little if any positive damage done to the native Irish, though a hindrance was imposed on their subsequent progress. . . . The real grounds for the introduction and enforcement of the repressive measures' were 'a short-sighted, but public-spirited regard for the political interests of the realm as a whole.' This paradox, however, is not proved. Miss A. E. Murray in her History of the Commerical and Financial Relations between England and Ireland (1903) demonstrates that the consequence of these restrictions on the woollen trade was serious and far-reaching. In fact the traditional view, with some small emendations, is the correct one.

At the time, far more interest was excited in England by the question of the resumption of William III's grants of confiscated lands in Ireland than by the restrictions imposed on trade there. A clause added to the land-tax bill by the Commons in 1699 ordered seven commissioners selected by the House to take account of the property forfeited during the late war. The Lords protested against

[1] VI, 2772 (xxiii).

[2] English Historical Review, i. 277-94.

this tacking, but afterwards yielded.[1] In 1700, the report of the committee was read before the two Houses. The Commons brought in a bill for annulling William's grants and vesting the forfeited property in trustees, to be divided according to the will of Parliament. There followed a long and bitter conflict between the two Houses, when a final rupture was avoided only by the withdrawal of the bishops, which secured the passing of the bill. On these questions there is a considerable amount of new evidence printed in the Calendar of the Manuscripts of the House of Lords.

The fear of the Anglo-Irish that the native Irish had been granted too favourable terms at Limerick, interference in the Irish administration by the English Parliament and Privy Council, and the commercial jealousy felt in England against possible rivalry from across St. George's Channel—these sentiments combined to foster the desire for a union. As early as November 1691 James Bonnell, Accountant General of Ireland, urged that a united England and Ireland, as it was in Cromwell's time, would be much better than a Parliament in Dublin. Such a union 'would take this kingdom out of the hands of the Irish and would take away all jealousy of it from the English, since it would seem then but to be a part of themselves as much as Wales.'[2] Statesmen like Sir Richard Cox argued with Englishmen

that it is your interest to unite and incorporate us with Englishmen for by that meanes the English interest will be always prevalent here, and the kingdome as secure to you as Wales or any county in England. Your taxes will be lessened when we beare part of the burden. Your forces will be augmented, especially at sea. . . . All our money will still center at London, and our trade and communica-

[1] Macaulay, VI, 2958-76 (xxv).

[2] Portland MSS., iii. 480.

tion with England will be soe considerable that we shall think ourselves at home when there; and where one goes thither now, ten will goe when all our business is transacted in your Parliament.[1]

Early in Anne's reign both houses of the legislature in Dublin addressed Queen Anne in favour of a more strict union with England, and the conclusion of the union of England and Scotland caused the Irish Commons to pray that the Queen would add to the strength and lustre of her crown by a yet more comprehensive union. The later stages of this movement are outside Macaulay's field, but it is strange that he should have ignored its early manifestations.

[1] Ibid. p. 610.

CHAPTER X

COLONIAL AND FOREIGN AFFAIRS

ANYONE who habitually refers to Macaulay's History as a collection of facts about the period it covers will find in the end that there are some subjects upon which it supplies ample and exact information and others upon which it is neither full nor accurate. This is natural since every historian must form his own conception of the relative importance of the different episodes included in his narrative and treat them at greater or less length accordingly. But often this selection is influenced by accidental or purely personal reasons. Some subjects may be briefly treated because the information accessible at the moment is insufficient. Others may be treated in a perfunctory fashion because the author has little interest in a particular class of questions. So it is with Macaulay. It is clear that constitutional, social, and economic questions attracted him most. Nothing which happened inside the British Isles was without interest for him or unfamiliar to him; but he took less trouble to understand events which happened outside them, even when they greatly influenced the development of the British state, and the future of the British race. Often he failed to appreciate the connection of European or extra-European affairs with British affairs, and the limitation of his horizon affects the perspective of the story.

One result is very remarkable. Macaulay practically omits the history of the British colonies during the whole period he treats. He devotes many long passages to the small beginnings of British power in India, and narrates in detail the quarrels of the two East India companies, but finds hardly anything to say about the new empire rising across the Atlantic. It is easy to understand the prominent place Indian affairs fill in his pages; one reason is his four years' service in India as Member of the Council, and another is the extent to which the dispute between the two companies influenced the party politics of William's reign. But these facts do not explain his neglect of the West Indies and America. Even if he decided to ignore the internal history of the plantations, at least their trade with England should have received attention.[1] We know from Macaulay's essay on Chatham that the story of the loss of the American colonies had the greatest interest for him. Why was he so little interested in their acquisition? Contemporary events too might have been expected to direct Macaulay's attention to the colonial problems of the seventeenth century. He had seen how similar problems were solved in the nineteenth century; the Canadian rebellion, Lord Durham's mission to Canada, the concession of self-government to the Australian colonies, all took place under his eyes. Yet there is hardly any reference to these events in his diary or his letters or his speeches, and his views on colonial policy must be gathered from passages in the History dealing with the government of Ireland, which, as he observes, 'Our jurists then regarded as a mere colony.'

[1] 'In this growing commerce, the trade with the American plantations—the colonial trade proper—was assuming an ever-increasing importance. During the first decade of the Restoration, it amounted to only about one-tenth of the whole. Twenty years later this trade had increased from roughly £800,000 to £1,300,000, and towards the end of the century it had considerably more than doubled itself. It then amounted to £1,750,000 and constituted one-seventh of England's total foreign commerce.' Beer, Old Colonial System, i. 15. On the trade with India, see W. W. Hunter, History of British India, ii (1900), 278.

Incidentally, while discussing the famous book of William Molyneux—The Case of Ireland's Being Bound by Acts of Parliament in England Stated—he sets forth his opinion on colonial self-government.

> The doctrine that the parent state has supreme power over the colonies is not only borne out by authority and by precedent, but will appear, when examined, to be in entire accordance with justice and with policy. During the feeble infancy of colonies independence would be pernicious, or rather fatal, to them. Undoubtedly, as they grow stronger and stronger, it will be wise in the home government to be more and more indulgent. No sensible parent deals with a son of twenty in the same way as with a son of ten. Nor will any government not infatuated treat such a province as Canada or Victoria in the way in which it might be proper to treat a little band of emigrants who have just begun to build their huts on a barbarous shore, and to whom the protection of the flag of a great nation is indispensably necessary. Nevertheless, there cannot really be more than one supreme power in a society. If, therefore, a time comes at which the mother country finds it expedient altogether to abdicate her paramount authority over a colony, one of two courses ought to be taken. There ought to be complete incorporation, if such incorporation be possible. If not, there ought to be complete separation. Very few propositions in politics can be so perfectly demonstrated as this, that parliamentary government cannot be carried on by two really equal and independent parliaments in one empire.[1]

This was Macaulay's theory of the relations of the mother country and the colonies and of those of England and Ireland. It is evident that he had no conception of the possibility of a federal system, or of an empire bound together by traditions and feelings and interests rather than by constitutional machinery. For him an incorporating union

[1] VI, 2773 (xxiii).

like that between England and Scotland or between England and Ireland was one possible alternative; the other possible alternative was complete independence: there was no intermediate solution. Probably, like most Whigs, he looked forward to the peaceful parting of Great Britain and her colonies when the colonies were strong enough to shift for themselves. Thinking thus, it is less surprising that he paid so little attention to the history of the American colonies of England during the seventeenth century. There are indeed passing references to them. The forfeiture of the Massachusetts charter is mentioned in order to illustrate the attachment of Halifax to representative government,[1] and the system of contract labour, or, as it is often termed, the 'white slavery' of Virginia, is noted in order to show the causes of Bristol's commercial prosperity.[2] A paragraph is devoted to the earthquake in Jamaica, in 1692, which completely destroyed Port Royal, but it is mentioned merely as an example of the calamities which 'increased the public ill humour' and made William's government unpopular.[3] The story of Captain Kidd leads Macaulay to explain that New York and the New England colonies connived at piracy, but it is told for the sake of its effect on the fate of an English ministry, not as an episode in colonial history.[4] On the other hand nearly thirty pages are devoted to an account of the attempt of the Scots to found a colony at Darien.[5] In that connection we hear that the governors of the West Indian colonies prohibited communication with the Darien colony[6] and that the surviving settlers made their way to New York.[7] But the

[1] I, 262 (ii).
[2] I, 324 (iii).
[3] V, 2250 (xix).
[4] VI, 2945-8 (xxv).
[5] VI, 2907-34 (xxiv).
[6] VI, 2927.
[7] VI, 2930.

Darien incident is introduced solely to explain the relations of England and Scotland. Thus, throughout, whenever colonial matters are mentioned they are subordinated altogether to English politics.

Even when the events which happened in the colonies were closely connected with the English events Macaulay related, he was not tempted to narrate them. The struggle between the Stuarts and representative government was not confined to England. Speaking of the reaction which followed the triumph of Charles II over the Whigs Macaulay says:

> The Court of King's Bench pronounced that the franchises of the City of London were forfeited to the crown. Flushed with this great victory, the government proceeded to attack the constitutions of other corporations which were governed by Whig officers, and which had been in the habit of returning Whig members to Parliament. Borough after borough was compelled to surrender its privileges; and new charters were granted which gave the ascendency everywhere to the Tories.[1]

A similar attack on the rights of the English colonies in America followed, but Macaulay omits it, though it was part of the same movement. The government of Charles II had long cherished the design of bringing the colonies directly under the control of the Crown. When the Council of Trade and Plantations was established in 1671 the first question which came before the commissioners concerned New England. 'For the condition of that colony', says Evelyn, 'was such that they were able to contest with all other plantations about them and there was fear of their breaking from all dependence on this nation; his Majesty, therefore, commanded this affair more expressly.' In

[1] I, 257 (ii).

another passage he says, 'We understood they were a people almost upon the very brink of renouncing any dependence on the Crown.'[1] The chief complaint of the King's government against the colonists was their persistent non-observance of the Navigation Act. They carried on a constant and a direct trade with foreign countries and exported thither commodities which the Act prohibited them from exporting. Massachusetts was the worst offender, and the Lords of Trade reported to the King that its government was conducted without the least regard to his authority or the least concern for his revenue. To the government of Charles II political reasons seemed to require the annulment of the Massachusetts charter and commercial reasons to supply a legal justification for it. Hence on June 13, 1683, the day after judgement was recorded against the charter of London, the Privy Council ordered the Attorney-General to bring a writ against the Massachusetts company. Fifteen months later, on October 23, 1684, the charter was annulled by a judgement in the Court of Chancery. The King was free to erect in its place whatever sort of government he thought fit. Macaulay mentions the forfeiture of the Massachusetts charter, to illustrate the character of Halifax, not as part of the King's anti-democratic policy.

At one of the last councils which Charles held a remarkable scene took place. The charter of Massachusetts had been forfeited. A question arose how, for the future, the colony should be governed. The general opinion of the board was that the whole power, legislative as well as executive, should abide in the crown. Halifax took the opposite side, and argued with great energy against absolute monarchy, and in favour of representative government. It was vain, he said, to think that a population, sprung from the English stock, and animated by English feelings,

[1] Diary, May 26, June 6, 1671.

would long bear to be deprived of English institutions. Life, he exclaimed, would not be worth having in a country where liberty and property were at the mercy of one despotic master. The Duke of York was greatly incensed by this language, and represented to his brother the danger of retaining in office a man who appeared to be infected with all the worst notions of Marvell and Sidney.[1]

The scheme which Charles II had in his mind and which James II carried out was the formation of a 'Dominion of New England' by the union of all the New England colonies under one government.[2] A governor-general and a council were to be appointed by the Crown; no representative assembly was to exist, taxes were to be imposed by the Crown, and the occupiers of land were to take out new patents. During the reign of James II this scheme was put into effect. Writs of quo warranto were issued against Connecticut and Rhode Island. Rhode Island submitted in July 1686, Connecticut in October 1687 (though it never gave up the original of its charter); Plymouth, which had no charter, submitted at the same time as Rhode Island; New Hampshire and Maine had been crown colonies since 1679; New York and the Jerseys were annexed to the dominion in August 1688. With the exception of Pennsylvania and Delaware all the territory from forty degrees north latitude to the boundaries of Canada was brought by this process under one rule. The governor-general originally selected for this dominion was the notorious Colonel Percy Kirke, but since James had other work for him to do in England, Sir Edmund Andros, a major in the army, who had been for some time governor of the province of New York, was appointed in Kirke's place, and arrived at Boston

[1] I, 262 (ii).

[2] See Beer, Old Colonial System, chap. 12.

December 1686. Personally Andros was not a bad governor despite the evil reputation which he possesses in American history ; he was not brutal, or oppressive, or unjust.[1] But the policy he was instructed to carry out was arbitrary and unconstitutional. The main grievance of the New Englanders against the government he directed was set forth in the protest with which the General Court of Massachusetts accompanied its submission. 'The subjects', they complained, 'are abridged of their liberty as Englishmen both in the matters of legislation and the laying of taxes' ; and though Andros gave New England a better administration than either Maryland or Virginia possessed, it could not reconcile the colonists to the loss of their liberties. In April 1689, when the news of the revolution in England reached America, the inhabitants of Boston rose against the government, imprisoned Andros, seized the forts which dominated the town, and captured a frigate which lay in the harbour. 'We have been quiet, hitherto,' they declared, 'but now [that] the Lord has prospered the undertaking of the Prince of Orange, we think we should follow such an example. We, therefore, seize the vile persons who oppressed us.'[2] There were similar revolutions in Connecticut and Rhode Island, and more violent ones in Maryland and New York. Before the close of 1689 William and Mary were accepted and proclaimed all through the American colonies.

The policy of James in the colonies was the counterpart of his policy at home, in so far as it was an attempt to substitute personal government for self-government. But in so far as it was an attempt to strengthen the control of the mother country over the colonies it was a national rather

[1] See C. M. Andrews, Colonial Self-Government (1904).

[2] Ibid. p. 277.

than a personal policy. Hence the constitutional settlement which followed the Revolution did not simply restore the old state of things in America. Connecticut and Rhode Island, but not Massachusetts, got back their forfeited charters. Massachusetts received, instead, a new constitution which vested in the Crown the appointment of its governor and in the governor a veto over the appointment of the Council and the laws passed by the Assembly. The King took the government of Maryland into his own hands and for the next generation it was a royal province instead of a proprietary colony. In New York, though representative government was restored, the act in which the Assembly defined the rights of the colony was annulled by William on the ground that it granted 'too great and unreasonable privileges.'[1] In short, while the result of the Revolution was to restore representative government, it strengthened the authority of the Crown and tightened the bonds between the colonies and England.

In another way too the history of the American colonies is closely connected with that of England. The struggle between France and England, which began in Europe after the accession of William III, was beginning in America during the reign of James. In 1686 three forts of the Hudson's Bay Company were captured by an expedition from Canada under d'Iberville, while Denonville, the governor of Canada, attacked the Iroquois, and Dongan, the governor of New York, allied himself with them.[2] Long before the War of the Austrian Succession, 'Red men scalped each other by the Great Lakes of North America'[3] to serve

[1] Ibid. p. 287; J. A. Doyle, The Middle Colonies (1907), p. 286.

[2] See Doyle, Middle Colonies, pp. 222-34; and, above all, Francis Parkman's Frontenac and New France.

[3] Macaulay, Essay on Frederic the Great, in Essays, iii. 196.

the ends of European sovereigns. After the Revolution, when the Marquis de Frontenac had succeeded Denonville as governor of Canada, open war broke out between the French and the English colonies along the whole length of the frontier. In 1690 one mixed party of Indians and Frenchmen captured the Dutch settlement of Schenectady in New York and massacred its inhabitants, another destroyed a village in New Hampshire, a third a fort in Maine. The same year seven hundred men from Boston led by William Phipps captured Port Royal and other French settlements in Acadia, and a larger expedition also under his leadership made an unsuccessful attack on Quebec. More raids and massacres followed in subsequent years, for the English colonists proved incapable of combining either for attack or defence, and the brunt of the war fell on New York and Massachusetts. Meanwhile the forts and factories on Hudson's Bay changed hands time after time, and at the peace of Ryswick only Fort Albany was left in the possession of the company. There was also continual fighting in the West Indies. Every other year a fleet sailed from England to assist in the capture of the French islands. St. Kitts was taken in 1690; Guadaloupe was unsuccessfully attacked in 1691, Martinique in 1693, and the French settlement in San Domingo in 1695. More than once, too, English and French squadrons met and fought with varying fortune in West Indian waters. All these minor military and naval operations, subsidiary to the main contest in Europe, give the War of the Grand Alliance its distinguishing character in British history. It marks the beginning of the world-wide struggle with France which Seeley speaks of as a second Hundred Years War,[1]

[1] Cf. Seeley, Expansion of England (1883), p. 21; idem, Growth of British Policy, ii. 315.

and to narrow its extent as Macaulay does obscures its significance.

Macaulay's account of the War of the Grand Alliance is defective in another way. It is evident that his knowledge of European history was somewhat superficial, and hence his representation of William's position and William's policy is open to a good deal of criticism. When the third and fourth volumes of the History appeared its shortcomings in this respect were pointed out by J. M. Kemble in an article which is still worth reading.[1]

After praising Macaulay's account of English affairs given in the History, the critic observes :

We feel anxious to call attention to the large field of action which he leaves well-nigh untouched. We mean, of course, the foreign policy of William. Mr. Macaulay tells us more than once that the King was his own Foreign Secretary : he justifies this, not only upon the acquiescence of the wisest politicians of the time, but upon grounds which are in themselves amply sufficient. Now, if William's true greatness lay in the manner in which he framed and upheld the coalition against Lewis ; if this was pre-eminently his own work, one in which a share of honour could not be claimed by any Englishman ; has not Mr. Macaulay done injustice to his hero in letting us know so little of the difficulties which were to be overcome, and the means by which success was attained? Must we not naturally be anxious to know what obstacles were to be removed, what conflicting interests reconciled, by the man who took upon himself to consolidate and wield so vast a power? Here, however, Mr. Macaulay leaves us nearly in the dark, contenting himself with a few sentences here and there, of a very indefinite

[1] Published in Fraser's Magazine for Feb. 1856, pp. 147-66. Kemble's State Papers and Correspondence Illustrative of the Social and Political State of Europe from the Revolution to the Accession of the House of Hanover (1857) contains 250 pages of documents relating to the period dealt with by Macaulay.

and general character, laudatory of William, abusive of his allies, particularly the Princes of the Empire, but conveying either no clear impression at all, or a very unfair one.

Kemble goes on to say that Macaulay too much neglected German archives and German histories. He then takes as his text a long passage at the beginning of Macaulay's nineteenth chapter, in which the author endeavours to set forth William's foreign policy, dealing in particular with the affairs of the year 1692 and the difficulties experienced by William in keeping the coalition against France together. 'Two of the allied powers, and two only, were hearty in the common cause,' England and Holland, both of which, though 'torn by internal factions' and

separated from each other by mutual jealousies and antipathies . . . were fully resolved not to submit to French domination. . . . With those two communities, unhappily, other states had little sympathy. Indeed those two communities were regarded by other states as rich, plain-dealing, generous dupes are regarded by needy sharpers. England and Holland were wealthy; and they were zealous. Their wealth excited the cupidity of the whole alliance; and to that wealth their zeal was the key. They were persecuted with sordid importunity by all their confederates, from Cæsar, who, in the pride of his solitary dignity, would not honour King William with the title of Majesty, down to the smallest Margrave who could see his whole principality from the cracked windows of the mean and ruinous old house which he called his palace. It was not enough that England and Holland furnished much more than their contingents to the war by land, and bore unassisted the whole charge of the war by sea. They were beset by a crowd of illustrious mendicants, some rude, some obsequious, but all indefatigable and insatiable. One prince came mumping to them annually with a lamentable story about his distresses. A more sturdy beggar threatened to join the

Third Party, and to make a separate peace with France, if his demands were not granted. Every Sovereign too had his ministers and favourites; and these ministers and favourites were perpetually hinting that France was willing to pay them for detaching their masters from the coalition, and that it would be prudent in England and Holland to outbid France.[1]

After challenging this description of the part taken by the German princes in the war and pointing out some serious errors in Macaulay's statements about Saxony, Hanover,[2] and Brandenburg, Kemble concludes by regretting that one error pervades the whole book, 'viz. the striving to exalt William at the expense of everyone with whom he is brought into contact', and by protesting against 'the distortion of view which presents our foreign relations in so untrue a light, and for the sake of displaying one giant, peoples all Europe with pigmies.'

These criticisms were brought to the notice of Macaulay but he dismissed them very lightly. In his diary, he says of the article:

Very laudatory. The author evidently John Kemble. He is quite right in saying that I have passed lightly over continental politics. But was this wrong? . . . I am writing a History of England; and as to grubbing, as he recommends, in Saxon and Hessian archives for the purpose of ascertaining all the details of the continental negotiations of that time, I should have doubled my labour, already severe enough. That I have not given a generally correct view of our continental relations he certainly has not shown.[3]

[1] V, 2210-12 (xix).

[2] For instance, he says, 'For the Duke of Brunswick Lunenburg, William not without difficulty procured the long desired title of Elector of Hanover.' William's intervention had but a small share in the achievement of this result. See A. W. Ward, The Electress Sophia (1909), pp. 226-39.

[3] Trevelyan, ii. 442.

This is not a satisfactory answer. No doubt Macaulay lacked time to search the German archives, but he might have made much more use of German printed books. And he ought certainly to have corrected those statements of fact which Kemble showed to be erroneous, but he left the text unaltered and the errors remain there to this day.

Kemble proves clearly that one part of Macaulay's account of our continental relations contained errors of fact and produced in consequence an erroneous impression. If he had examined other parts of it in equal detail he might have added further proofs. For instance Macaulay's hostility to Austria is hardly concealed. It seems to be inspired by the political feelings of the time when he wrote rather than by historical facts. The Emperor Leopold is continually accused of lukewarmness and slackness in the struggle against Louis XIV, and blamed for leaving the whole burden of the war to fall upon England and Holland. Nowhere is the position of Austria fairly stated. Holland and England had to carry on the war against one enemy only, France; Austria had to wage war against two, France and Turkey. Leopold therefore was obliged to provide an army for the Danube as well as one for the Rhine or the Low Countries. Furthermore, France and Turkey were acting in conjunction; it was in order to keep Austria occupied and prevent it from employing its forces against France that Louis XIV had instigated the Turks to attack Austria in 1682 and obstructed all negotiations for peace ever since.

Macaulay knew these facts. In chapter xix, where he describes the weakness of the coalition, he complains that Austria did not put forth all its strength against the House of Bourbon, and adds: 'To the Emperor indeed the war against France was a secondary object. His first object was the war against Turkey.'[1] That is true. But the explanation of the Emperor's conduct which follows is absolutely unfair.

He was dull and bigoted. His mind misgave him that the war against France was, in some sense, a war against the Catholic religion; and the war against Turkey was a crusade. His recent campaign on the Danube had been successful. He might easily have concluded an honourable peace with the Porte, and have turned his arms westward. But he had conceived the hope that he might extend his hereditary dominions at the expense of the Infidels. Visions of a triumphant entry into Constantinople and of a Te Deum in Saint Sophia's had risen in his brain. He not only employed in the East a force more than sufficient to have defended Piedmont and reconquered Lorraine; but he seemed to think that England and Holland were bound to reward him largely for neglecting their interests and pursuing his own.[2]

Macaulay writes as if Austrian interests alone were involved in the war against Turkey; as if the defeat of the Turks was not a European interest just as much as the defeat of Louis XIV; as if Turkey was a weak, decaying power which aggressive neighbours were plotting to partition. The impression which he produces is that the Turkey of 1692 was something like the Turkey of 1854. On the contrary, during the seventeenth century the Ottoman Empire was still an aggressive, barbarous power, making a waste wherever its armies trod, the deadly foe of civilisation and Christianity, and strong enough seriously to endanger both. The Turks were still gaining ground at the expense of the Christians. Ever since the sixteenth century Turkish pashas had ruled at Buda, and all Hungary had been in their hands, excepting a strip on the north.

[1] V, 2213 (xix). [2] V, 2213-14.

Throughout the country, Turkish fleets plundered the coasts of Italy and carried off captives to their galleys. From 1644 to 1669 the Turks had waged war against the Venetians for the possession of Crete, which they finally wrested from them in 1669. In 1661 a new war began between the Emperor and the Sultan, in which, though Montecuculi won the battle of St. Gotthard in 1664, the Turks obtained two new conquests, the fortresses of Waradin and Neuhausel in Hungary. In 1672 the Turks invaded Poland, took the fortress of Kaminiec, and added the Ukraine to their dominions (1676). In 1682 the Turks once more attacked Austria, and next year they besieged Vienna. Macaulay states that 'the great Austrian monarchy . . . seemed to be on the point of destruction.'[1] But Vienna was rescued by Sobieski and the Poles, and the Turks were driven back into Hungary. By 1686, says Macaulay, 'the House of Austria had, by a succession of victories, been secured from danger on the side of Turkey.'[2] The zeal of Innocent XI brought about a triple alliance between Austria, Poland, and Venice in 1684, which Russia joined in 1686. For several years one success after another crowned the arms of the allies. In 1686 the Duke of Lorraine captured Buda from the Turks; in 1687 he defeated them in a great battle at Mohacz. In 1688 Belgrade fell into the hands of the Austrians. Meanwhile the Venetians conquered the Morea and Dalmatia.

Louis XIV's attack on Germany in 1688 saved the Turks. The Emperor had to recall half his troops to face this new enemy, and in 1690 the Turks retook Belgrade and re-entered Hungary. But the Margrave of Baden in 1691 defeated the Turks at Salankamen and drove them once more out of Hungary. It was certainly possible for the

[1] II, 841 (vii). [2] II, 842.

Emperor to make peace with the Turks, but not unless he abandoned the territories he had conquered and the Christian peoples he had freed from the Turkish yoke. Nor could he honourably make peace without his allies.

England and Holland continually tried to mediate and bring about a peace, while France as incessantly sought to frustrate the efforts of the English and Dutch ambassadors. It was not till Prince Eugene had inflicted another crushing defeat on the Turks at Zenta, in 1697, that they were willing to listen to the advice of the mediators and recognise the necessity of yielding. By the peace of Carlowitz in 1699 the Turks gave up Hungary and Transylvania to Austria, ceded the Peloponnesus and half Dalmatia to Venice, and restored to Poland all she had lost in 1676. The advance of Turkey was permanently checked, and it cannot be doubted that this was as necessary to Europe as it was to check the aggressions of Louis XIV.

Here again it is not a question of errors of fact which can be set right in a footnote; by emphasising certain facts and omitting others, Macaulay produces a false impression which it would take pages of explanation to remove. Look into his accounts of the attitude of the northern powers during the struggle and of the part which Savoy played in it; both are equally unsatisfactory. In short the view of our continental relations presented is so far from being 'generally correct' that it requires rewriting rather than revision.

This defect is not due to the insufficiency of the materials then available to historians, though that accounts for some of the mistakes. Macaulay did not make the best use of the authorities which were accessible. He did not put himself back into the seventeenth century, and endeavour to understand the position and the interests of the various states concerned in the struggle. He judged European politics purely from the standpoint of a nineteenth-century Englishman.

For these reasons every student of the reigns of James II and William III is obliged to seek an account of their foreign policy in the pages of other historians. There are many monographs by foreign writers dealing with particular parts of the subject, though few Englishmen have done anything to elucidate it. There are also some general histories of the period. Onno Klopp's Fall of the House of Stuart[1] contains a detailed exposition of the negotiations and diplomatic intrigues of the time, based on English as well as foreign archives. But the best introduction to the subject is Leopold von Ranke's History of England,[2] and it is also the best corrective of Macaulay.

It has been well said that Ranke would scarcely have devoted over a volume to the period treated by Macaulay, merely to add a little new information here and there or correct some errors in the details. He must have believed that there were faults in Macaulay's representation of events which made it worth while to tell the story over again. There is a closer connection between the two works than a casual reader suspects. Though Ranke hardly ever mentions Macaulay, there are many indirect references to his book. Sometimes they are unmistakable. For instance, in commenting upon the attacks of James II on the constitution Ranke says: 'We do not consider ourselves authorised to adopt the tone which English historians have borrowed

[1] Vols. iii and iv deal with the reign of James; vols. v-ix with that of William. Klopp is as strongly pro-Austrian as Macaulay is the opposite.

[2] Englische Geschichte, vornehmlich im sechzehnten und siebzehnten Jahrhundert (7 vols.; 1859-68). The English translation in six volumes was published at Oxford in 1875. It is divided into 22 books, of which books xvii to xxi deal with the reigns of James and William.

from the proceedings of criminal courts; we have only to do with the contemplation of the historical event.'[1] Throughout he strives to preserve this philosophical attitude, unmoved by the passions of contemporaries, but seeking to understand and explain them. Sometimes Ranke dismisses an episode with surprising brevity; the reason often seems to be that the particular episode had been adequately treated by Macaulay and that he had little to add. At other times he narrates an event or series of events in considerable detail because he has much to add.

The difference between Macaulay's and Ranke's general view is more important than any difference in their judgements of particular men or their accounts of particular incidents. In the prefaces which stand before the various books into which Ranke divides his History, his point of view is stated and emphasised. To him the reign of James II is not so much an episode in the history of England as a chapter in the history of Europe. Two questions, he says in the introduction to the seventeenth book, had to be determined in that reign: the relation of the monarchy and the people of England, and the relation between England and France. Louis XIV was aiming at universal monarchy, and the independence of the states of Europe could not be maintained any longer, unless Louis found somewhere or other an energetic resistance. 'To offer such resistance seemed the natural vocation of England.... But if it was to fulfil this task, it must not again be crippled by internal disorders.' All depended on the question whether a Catholic king and a Protestant nation could work together. If they could, a vigorous foreign policy was possible. If they could not, religious and political dissensions would render a

[1] iv. 364.

vigorous foreign policy impossible, and France would extend its power unopposed. 'It might be doubted which was of the greater importance for the life of Europe, the decision of the internal English, or of the external continental, questions.'[1]

In book xvii Ranke confines himself to the internal question, showing by which acts James II proved that the combination of a Catholic king and a Protestant nation was impossible in England.

In the introduction to book xviii, Ranke insists on the international aspect of the revolution which this incompatibility produced. The states of Europe, he says, are often held to be more independent of each other than they really are. They are a general community of peoples closely connected with each other and possessing a kind of common life. 'Even insular England' feels the effect of tendencies generally prevailing in Europe and influences them in turn. The proceedings of James II which aimed at the reintroduction of Catholicism into England were but a part of the general struggle between Catholicism and Protestantism in Europe. The fact that Louis XIV was the great champion of the Catholic interest and that James II relied upon his aid made the struggle in England of European importance. 'The strife which awaited its decision in England thus lost its insular character; it entered into connexion with the great religous and political conflict which then . . . divided Europe, and appears as an essential part of it.'[2]

In the first chapter of book xviii, Ranke shows that James, who felt the aid of Louis XIV to be a necessity, took the side of Louis in his quarrel with the House of Austria and came to an understanding with France for operations against Holland and the German Empire. 'No prince',

[1] iv. 210. [2] iv. 370.

Ranke says, 'has ever had less thought for the balance of power in Europe than James II.'[1] The result was that Europe became as indifferent to the fate of James II as James II was to the fate of Europe. Another chapter, the third, is headed Preparations and German Alliances of the Prince of Orange. Ranke shows that the pro-French policy of James II and the dangers with which it threatened Holland and Germany led the Dutch republicans and the German princes to further William's enterprise, and traces the steps by which William secured their aid. The next book, xix, is almost entirely given up to English affairs; that is, to the Revolution settlement, to the struggle carried on by the supporters of James II in Scotland and Ireland, with the assistance of France, and the final defeat, at the battle of the Boyne, of the efforts of France to restore James. At the beginning of book xx Ranke returns to the relations of England and Europe.

> The wish to throw the resources of England into the balance against the overwhelming power of Louis XIV was undoubtedly the original cause of the attack which William of Orange made on the throne of James. Resistance to Louis XIV had now become a European necessity; but it never could have been successful without the adhesion of Great Britain. . . . When William III came to England, he was leagued with the States-General and some few German princes for this one object; but in order to give the undertaking the desired direction, and to turn it against the preponderance of France, a far more comprehensive union had to be arranged.[2]

The result was the formation of the Grand Alliance, which is the subject of the first chapter of book xx. In a few pages

[1] P. 384. This is what S. R. Gardiner says of Charles I.

[2] v. 3-4.

Ranke states the reasons which brought Catholic powers like Spain and Austria into a close alliance with Protestant powers like England and Holland, and explains how Savoy was brought in and why Denmark was left out. Compare this passage with Macaulay's account of the origin of the Grand Alliance in his fourteenth chapter and you perceive that, while the one makes clear the causes of events, the other gives only a rhetorical summary of them.[1] Again, compare Macaulay's account of the congress at The Hague in 1691, given in his seventeenth chapter, with Ranke's treatment of the same gathering, and you perceive that one historian tries to bring out the essence of things while the other dwells on their externals.[2] Macaulay's battle pieces are elaborately finished works of art. Ranke in his narrative of the war of the Grand Alliance pays little attention to the battles; he relates Steinkirk in eight lines and Neerwinde in two; the effects of the war on the relations of the European powers attract him more than its most picturesque episodes. The moving incident was not his trade. Read Macaulay's and Ranke's accounts of the Peace of Ryswick, side by side.[3] Both relate the negotiations, but while Ranke shows clearly why William was obliged to make peace Macaulay does not furnish the true explanation. The real cause was the defection of Savoy from the Grand Alliance by the treaty of Turin in August 1696. This secured Louis on the side of Italy, and enabled him to use against the allies 30,000 excellent soldiers hitherto employed in Italy. The allies had to give up the idea of overcoming Louis and reducing France to the position it had occupied in 1659, at the time of the treaty of the Pyrenees. They had to lower their terms. Since Louis XIV was obliged to make con-

[1] v. 4-14; IV, 1698-1700 (xiv).

[2] IV, 1974-6 (xvii); v. 22.

[3] VI, 2702-20 (xxii); v. 132-49.

cessions too it was possible to arrive at the compromise known as the treaty of Ryswick. Macaulay casually mentions the defection of the Duke of Savoy, but does not realise its importance or appreciate its bearing on the contest.[1] Hence he represents the concessions as entirely on the side of Louis [2] and so makes the treaty more of a triumph for William than it really was.

To the period which elapsed between the treaty of Ryswick in August 1697 and William's death in March 1702 Ranke devotes the whole of his twenty-first book. Macaulay's narrative practically ends in April 1700. It is possible to compare the accounts of the two partition treaties given by the two historians, but on the preparations for the war of the Spanish Succession, which Ranke terms William's 'political masterpiece', Macaulay's unfinished history is silent. Anyone who studies the estimate of William's character and his place in history with which Ranke concludes his narrative of the reign will find William's greatness explained and demonstrated as generously as any disciple of Macaulay could desire. The man is judged sympathetically, without extenuating his faults, the statesman justly praised because both his difficulties and his achievements are exactly appreciated.[3] But Ranke's portrait of William is cold beside Macaulay's. The two historians once met. Macaulay had reviewed Ranke's Popes in 1840, and three years later, when Ranke visited England, Macaulay was asked to meet him. Charles Greville described the meeting in his Diary.

I went prepared to listen to some first-rate literary talk between such luminaries as Ranke and Macaulay, but there never was a greater failure. The professor, a vivacious

[1] VI, 2637-8 (xxii). [2] VI, 2712-16 (xxii).
[3] v. 298.

little man, not distinguished in appearance, could talk no English, and his French, though spoken fluently, was quite unintelligible. On the other hand, Macaulay could not speak German, and he spoke French without any facility, and with a very vile accent. It was comical to see the abundance of his matter struggling with his embarrassment in giving utterance to it, to hear the torrent of knowledge trying to force its way through the impediment of a limited acquaintance with the French language and the want of habit of conversing in it. But the struggle was of short duration. He began in French, but very soon could bear the restraint no longer, and broke into English, pouring forth his stores to the utterly unconscious and uncomprehending professor. This babel of a breakfast, at which it was impossible for seven people to converse in any common language, soon came to an end, and Ranke was evidently glad to go off to the State Paper Office, where he was working every day.[1]

One naturally wonders whether William III was the subject which they had discussed.

The comparison between the histories of Macaulay and Ranke, suggested above, has often been made before.[2] Carl von Noorden gave a series of lectures on the subject at Leipzig. He also published an article on the subject in

[1] Greville, Memoirs, Pt. II, vol. ii, p. 203.

[2] Professor Paul Frédéricq describes in The Study of History in Germany and France (Johns Hopkins University Studies, 8th Ser., v-vi; 1890), pp. 20-21, a seminar by Delbrück, at the University of Berlin, which he attended in 1881. In it Macaulay's introductory chapter was compared with the first chapter of Ranke's History of England. The lecturer, 'an enthusiastic admirer of Ranke, pointed out, with malicious satisfaction, the faults of his English rival. I was reminded of the curious articles by Prof. A. Pierson, of Amsterdam, which appeared in the Dutch review, De Gids, where the author, comparing Ranke's work with Macaulay's, clearly brings out the superior impartiality and good judgment of the German historian.' Professor Frédéricq mentioned these articles to Ranke. 'He was unacquainted with them and seemed flattered by the judgment passed upon his History of England, but he took up with spirit the defense of Macaulay.'

Sybel's Historische Zeitschrift for 1867.[1] His verdict is that Macaulay had but a superficial knowledge of the European events of the period he treated: it seldom extended beyond the facts to be found in any good general history. He rarely contributed any new information about foreign affairs, and when he did his researches went but a little way, not to the bottom of the matter. Von Noorden goes on to say that French and English historians alike were mostly too prone to neglect European history. They considered events which happened in other countries too exclusively in their effect on their own countries. Hence they did not judge either men or events with sufficient independence, nor carry their researches far enough to form a really impartial judgement.

Nowadays this criticism would not be true, but it certainly applied to Macaulay. He did not devote a tithe of the attention to foreign affairs which he devoted to English affairs. What happened abroad, however important, interested him much less than some relatively trivial incident at home. His comparative neglect of European affairs and his complete neglect of colonial affairs arose from the same cause, insufficient breadth of view—in a word, from insularity.

Insularity is a failing which English historians naturally find it difficult to avoid. In Macaulay's case it was aggravated by conditions under which he grew up and by his surroundings. The Whig party as a whole has usually been inclined to concentrate its attention and its energies on internal questions, and during the period which followed the Battle of Waterloo this tendency was accentuated. Considering the debt which the great war had imposed and the distress which prevailed in the country after the peace, it is not surprising that there was some feeling that England had

[1] xvii. 87; see also p. 107.

concerned herself overmuch with European interests, and ought to consider her own first. The lines which Dryden wrote after the treaty of Ryswick expressed the feelings of the Whigs during the period which followed 1815 as truly as they expressed those of the Tories at the time when they were written.

> Enough for Europe has our Albion fought;
> Let us enjoy the peace our blood has bought.[1]

So the peace which lasted for the next forty years was employed in domestic reforms, and schemes for domestic reforms. What Disraeli termed 'the condition of England question' engrossed the minds of Macaulay's contemporaries, and the affairs of Europe were almost forgotten. As little did most men think of the new colonies which were growing up to replace those lost in the previous century. In short, between 1815 and 1850 England was very self-centred, and Macaulay, like other historians, was influenced by the tendencies of his time.

It may be said that the position of Germany was similar to that of England; the Germans too were slowly recovering from the results of a whole generation of great wars, and chiefly concerned with their domestic affairs. Yet Ranke, born only five years before Macaulay, was the most cosmopolitan of historians. On the other hand a politician was naturally more influenced by the conditions of his time than a man who gave up his whole life to historical studies, and aimed at founding a school of scientific historians. Macaulay admitted, with his usual frankness, the narrowness of his standpoint, and was surprised at the success of his History outside England. 'I am almost as much puzzled as pleased; for the book is quite insular in spirit. There is nothing cosmopolitan about it.'[2]

[1] Epistle the Fifteenth. To John Driden. Written in 1699.

[2] Trevelyan, ii. 390.

CHAPTER XI

MACAULAY'S ERRORS

THE complaint has often been made that in his History Macaulay displays strong prejudices. Certainly he was himself a man of firm convictions and he had a robust faith in their correctness. He naturally took a partisan attitude and scorned neutrality. He was not troubled by intellectual doubts and was frequently unfair to those who were. He was liable to judge men and events once for all and to label them good or bad without much discrimination. His sympathies, though warm, were rather limited, and he could rarely appreciate the good points in anyone or anything unpleasing to him personally. As Leslie Stephen said, 'his likes and dislikes indicate a certain rigidity and narrowness of nature.'[1] Consequently, though he sometimes stated both sides of a question fairly, his own preference is evident. He hardly ever adopted a strictly objective attitude, but at least he is generally consistent in his bias.

Some of Macaulay's prejudices were inherited and others may have been derived from his early environment or reading, but a main source was unquestionably his political career. As a Whig he had taken a leading part in the bitterest political struggle of the nineteenth century, that over the first Reform Bill, and the passions aroused by that struggle remained strong enough to cloud his view of the past. In a speech made at the Edinburgh election in

[1] Hours in a Library (1892), ii. 347.

1839 he recounted in glowing periods the history of the Whigs.

> I entered public life a Whig; and a Whig I am determined to remain. I use that word, and I wish you to understand that I use it, in no narrow sense. I mean by a Whig, not one who subscribes implicitly to the contents of any book, though that book may have been written by Locke; not one who approves the whole conduct of any statesman, though that statesman may have been Fox; not one who adopts the opinions in fashion in any circle, though that circle may be composed of the finest and noblest spirits of the age. But it seems to me that, when I look back on our history, I can discern a great party which has, through many generations, preserved its identity; a party often depressed, never extinguished; a party which, though often tainted with the faults of the age, has always been in advance of the age; a party which, though guilty of many errors and some crimes, has the glory of having established our civil and religious liberties on a firm foundation; and of that party I am proud to be a member. It was that party which, on the great question of monopolies, stood up against Elizabeth. It was that party which, in the reign of James the First, organized the earliest parliamentary opposition, which steadily asserted the privileges of the people, and wrested prerogative after prerogative from the Crown. It was that party which forced Charles the First to relinquish the ship money. It was that party which destroyed the Star Chamber and the High Commission Court. It was that party which, under Charles the Second, carried the Habeas Corpus Act, which effected the Revolution, which passed the Toleration Act, which broke the yoke of a foreign church in your country, and which saved Scotland from the fate of unhappy Ireland. It was that party which reared and maintained the constitutional throne of Hanover against the hostility of the Church and of the landed aristocracy of England. It was that party which opposed the war with America and the war with the

French Republic ; which imparted the blessings of our free Constitution to the Dissenters ; and which, at a later period, by unparalleled sacrifices and exertions, extended the same blessings to the Roman Catholics. To the Whigs of the seventeenth century we owe it that we have a House of Commons. To the Whigs of the nineteenth century we owe it that the House of Commons has been purified. The abolition of the slave trade, the abolition of colonial slavery, the extension of popular education, the mitigation of the rigour of the penal code, all, all were effected by that party ; and of that party, I repeat, I am a member.[1]

One can imagine a Tory's answer to this which would bring out the errors of the Whigs as well as their merits. Admitting that the Whigs were on the whole the progressive party, a Tory might argue that the progress of the Whigs was not always in the right direction. It was that party, he might say, which by attempting in 1640 to overthrow the existing government of the Church of England and to substitute a Presbyterian form of government caused the first Civil War ; and by its aggressive intolerance to all who were not Presbyterians caused the second Civil War, in 1648. It was that party which by its intolerance rendered a settlement in Ireland impossible and which by its fanatical and exaggerated dread of Catholicism and its attempt to place a pretender on the English throne caused the futile political struggle over the exclusion bills and the still more futile Monmouth Rebellion (1678-85). And going to the later history of the Whigs he might point out that their wiser and more liberal policy towards America was offset by the blindness and foolishness of their views on foreign policy during the revolutionary and Napoleonic wars, and remind the Whigs that if they had had their way, Wellington's army would have been withdrawn from the

[1] The Works of Lord Macaulay (1875), viii. 158-9.

Peninsula and Napoleon would not have been defeated at Waterloo.

Macaulay's Whiggism affected his judgement of classes and personages alike. His treatment of the clergy and the country gentry are discussed in chapter vi. Other objects of his antipathy are the Scottish Covenanters and the English non-jurors. Macaulay managed to shatter both with one barrel. The Jacobite non-jurors and the Cameronian non-jurors, he said, 'were perhaps the most remarkable specimens that the world could show of perverse absurdity. Each of them considered his darling form of ecclesiastical polity, not as a means, but as an end, as the one thing needful, as the quintessence of the Christian religion. Each of them childishly fancied that he had found a theory of civil government in his Bible. Neither shrank from the frightful consequences to which his theory led. To all objections, both had one answer—Thus saith the Lord.'[1] Rhetoric like this is a poor substitute for plain statement of the peculiar tenets of the two kinds of non-jurors. In fact the reader has the feeling that Macaulay's contempt for them was not of the kind that familiarity breeds.

When dealing with persons instead of classes or parties Macaulay's political bias again proves a stumbling-block. It prevents him from judging men fairly. Things which are crimes in James II become venial errors in William III. Compare for instance the tone in which Macaulay speaks of James II's connection with Catherine Sedley and William III's connection with Elizabeth Villiers. His perception of moral defects is much keener in the case of a Tory than in that of a Whig.

But this is not the only reason which led Macaulay seriously to misrepresent certain historical figures. Mr.

[1] IV, 1945 (xvi).

Gardiner, quoting a passage from Macaulay's essay on Hallam, incidentally observes that his 'judgement of a political situation was as superb, as his judgement of personal character was weak'; and the observation is very true.[1] Macaulay had little insight into men's motives and very little sympathy or imagination. He made no serious attempt to appreciate the beliefs and ideas of men from whom he differed—to put himself in their place. Though he describes characters at great length the hardness of the lines and the crudeness of the colouring give most of his portraits the air of caricatures. As Leslie Stephen says, 'He likes to represent a man as a bundle of contradictions because it enables him to obtain startling contrasts. He heightens a vice in one place, a virtue in another and piles them together in a heap without troubling himself to ask whether nature can make such monsters or preserve them if made. To anyone given to analysis these contrasts are actually painful.'[2]

It is curious that in one of Macaulay's essays there is a passage which illustrates his own error. He is comparing the drawing of a character (Sardanapalus) in one of Byron's plays, with a similar character (Otho) drawn by Juvenal. After quoting Juvenal, Macaulay proceeds:

> These are excellent lines in a satire. But it is not the business of the dramatist to exhibit characters in this sharp antithetical way. It is not thus that Shakspeare makes Prince Hal rise from the rake of Eastcheap into the hero of Shrewsbury, and sink again into the rake of Eastcheap. It is not thus that Shakspeare has exhibited the union of effeminacy and valour in Antony. A dramatist cannot commit a greater error than that of following those pointed

[1] Cromwell's Place in History (1902), p. 17.

[2] Op. cit. ii. 365.

descriptions of character in which satirists and historians indulge so much. It is by rejecting what is natural that satirists and historians produce these striking characters. Their great object generally is to ascribe to every man as many contradictory qualities as possible: and this is an object easily attained. By judicious selection and judicious exaggeration, the intellect and the disposition of any human being might be described as being made up of nothing but startling contrasts. If the dramatist attempts to create a being answering to one of these descriptions, he fails because he reverses an imperfect analytical process. He produces, not a man, but a personified epigram. Very eminent writers have fallen into this snare.[1]

Macaulay here couples together historians and satirists, as if it were natural and correct that historians should use the same method as satirists. But the truth is that in drawing characters the historian ought to endeavour to imitate the method of the dramatist. He should note externals but pierce through them. He should not heighten contradictions, but should try to discover their cause and explain them.

Political prejudice, exaggeration, and want of real insight combine to produce the misrepresentations of certain historical characters to be found in Macaulay's pages. Three cases are chosen here to exhibit his failings. All three have been exhaustively treated in Paget's New Examen.[2]

Macaulay styles Dundee 'a soldier of distinguished courage and professional skill, but rapacious and profane, of violent temper and of obdurate heart.'[3] Another passage refers to his 'seared conscience and adamantine heart.'[4] Then are recapitulated the crimes by which he and others

[1] Essays, i. 334.

[2] Included in Paradoxes and Puzzles.

[3] I, 492 (iv). [4] I, 493.

'goaded the peasantry of the Western Lowlands into madness.'[1] In a third passage, he is described as 'haunted by that consciousness of inexpiable guilt, and by that dread of a terrible retribution, which the ancient polytheists personified under the awful name of the Furies.'[2] However, it is certain that Dundee was not profane or rapacious or merciless, and that the crimes attributed to him were mainly fables. The Scottish Whigs of the next generation put down to 'bloody Clavers' most of the acts of cruelty committed during the period of repression. Of the crimes to which Macaulay refers he gives five examples, but in three of them Claverhouse had no share whatever; in the fourth he protested against the execution of the victim and endeavoured to save his life; in the fifth case Macaulay misrepresents the statements of the authorities.

This fifth case is that of John Brown, 'commonly called the Christian Carrier,' whom Macaulay represents Claverhouse as arresting and sentencing to death on the sole ground of nonconformity, and not only condemning him, but in a fury shooting him dead with his own hand.

Macaulay's story is based on the narrative of Wodrow,[3] which appeared in 1722, thirty-seven years after the event referred to. Some of the statements it contains are so absurd that Macaulay silently omitted or altered them. There are two other accounts extant, both of which contradict the assertion that Claverhouse shot John Brown, and say that he had him shot by a file of soldiers, as he naturally would have done. Further it is quite clear, first, that Brown was not shot for nonconformity alone, inasmuch as, a year before, he had been summoned to give himself up as a

[1] I, 492-8. [2] IV, 1564 (xiii).

[3] Robert Wodrow, The History of the Sufferings of the Church of Scotland (1830), iv. 244-5.

fugitive rebel and to stand his trial. Secondly, arms were found concealed about his premises. Lastly, he refused to take the oath disowning the declaration of war against the King issued by the Covenanters, or to swear not to rise in arms against the King. To sum up, his execution was strictly legal, implied no special barbarity in the officer who ordered it, and would not have taken place if he had been willing to pledge himself to keep the peace.[1] The omission of a number of material facts by Macaulay, the selection of the least trustworthy authority as the basis of his story, and the alteration of the statement made by that authority in order to make the story more probable, deserve severe censure.

Take another case, that of Marlborough. In chapter iv it has been shown that Macaulay uses against Marlborough evidence drawn from lampoons and pamphlets which he must have known to be untrustworthy. He accepted it because he had formed from the beginning an unfavourable estimate of Marlborough's character and swallowed any kind of testimony which seemed to confirm it. Marlborough's 'public life', he states, 'to those who can look steadily through the dazzling blaze of genius and glory, will appear a prodigy of turpitude.'[2] It is obviously not because he deserted the cause of James II for that of William that Macaulay comes to this conclusion, though he puts forward the statement when he is discussing that particular incident. It can hardly be because in 1691, when he was in disgrace with William, Marlborough entered into communication with James and promised to return to his allegiance. That was nothing exceptional; many another

[1] For a careful account of Brown's execution, see Terry, John Graham of Claverhouse, pp. 197-203.

[2] II, 900 (vii).

nobleman, equally concerned in bringing about the Revolution, made similar promises. In this way, they sought to hedge and to provide against the possibility of a restoration. The thing was so common that it does not place Marlborough on a sort of pinnacle of infamy. It shows he was not high-minded and had no objection to deceit. By it, he obtained a free pardon from James, and James got nothing but words in return. In a conversation about Marlborough with Charles Greville, the Duke of Wellington sums up the matter with his usual good sense. 'As to his character, we must not judge of it according to the maxims by which men in our time were governed; besides that they were less strict in his day; the condition of affairs itself produced a laxity; and though it was true he communicated with the Pretender, and acted a double part, that was no more than many in France did in Napoleon's reign, and he told a curious anecdote of Talleyrand.'[1]

Macaulay's antipathy must have arisen from the alleged plot of Marlborough to overthrow William and put Anne on the throne in his place, in order to become himself chief director of the civil and military government. But of such a plot there is no evidence save conjecture. What Marlborough really aimed at seems to have been security in case of a counter-revolution. The facts do not warrant us in saying more than that. But Macaulay will not hear of this simple and natural interpretation of the facts. 'His

[1] Greville's Diary, 2d Ser., ii. 193. Referring to Marlborough and Sunderland, the Duke of Wellington once said: 'I never rightly understood the characters at that period or made due allowances for them until I observed the effects which the Revolution in France had produced upon the minds of their statesmen. After such movements the principles of men become relaxed. They are not then so much attached to dynasties or to principles as their successors become afterwards even to parties.' Philip Henry, 5th Earl Stanhope, Notes of Conversations with the Duke of Wellington (1888), p. 157.

treason was not that of a fainthearted man desirous to keep a retreat open for himself in every event, but that of a man of dauntless courage, profound policy, and measureless ambition.'[1]

It is unusual for a historian of sober and well-balanced judgement to claim such omniscience about men's motives. What Macaulay does is to state his conjecture as if it were a fact; the conjecture is perhaps plausible, but the evidence on which it is based is so slight that it ought to be clearly stated and its validity questioned.

The account of the unsuccessful expedition against Brest in 1694 supplies another example of the same prejudice. It is certain that Marlborough sent information to James II, about the beginning of May, telling him that the expedition then being prepared in England was directed against Brest. But it is certain also that, some time previously, similar information had reached Louis XIV from Godolphin and Lord Arran, and that before the receipt of Marlborough's information Louis XIV had ordered Vauban to go to Brest and erect batteries and gather troops to frustrate the intended attack. Furthermore, William III and his government were aware that their design upon Brest was well known to the French and that active preparations had been made to meet it. Macaulay omits these facts: he represents Marlborough as the sole source of the information possessed by Louis XIV, and the preparations of the French as the immediate consequence of Marlborough's warning. He supplements these material misstatements by a purely conjectural explanation of Marlborough's motives, and gives this conjecture as a certain fact. Marlborough wished, he asserts, to get rid of his rival, Talmash, the general who commanded the expedition. Talmash was

[1] V, 2124 (xviii).

'lured into a snare' by Marlborough's treachery; he 'perished by the basest of all the hundred villanies of Marlborough.'[1] 'Yet never', Macaulay continues,

> had Marlborough been less a Jacobite than at the moment when he rendered this wicked and shameful service to the Jacobite cause. It may be confidently affirmed that to serve the banished family was not his object, and that to ingratiate himself with the banished family was only his secondary object. His primary object was to force himself into the service of the existing government, and to regain possession of those important and lucrative places from which he had been dismissed more than two years before. He knew that the country and the Parliament would not patiently bear to see the English army commanded by foreign generals. Two Englishmen only had shown themselves fit for high military posts, himself and Talmash. If Talmash were defeated and disgraced, William would scarcely have a choice.[2]

Here again omniscience intervenes to supply the want of evidence. Macaulay has formed beforehand a clear conception of Marlborough's character; he is therefore absolutely convinced that he knows motives, though there is no record which reveals them, and suppresses facts and evidence which tell against his theory. The account of the Brest expedition is a good example of the way in which history should not be written.

In the case of Dundee and Marlborough there were circumstances forming the basis of Macaulay's charges against their characters. Claverhouse did execute John

[1] V, 2450 (xx).

[2] E. M. Lloyd, Marlborough and the Brest Expedition, 1694, in English Historical Review, ix. 130-2. Cf. Arthur Parnell, James Macpherson and the Nairne Papers, ibid. xii. 254-84; Godfrey Davies, Macpherson and the Nairne Papers, ibid. xxxv. 367-76; Winston S. Churchill, Marlborough, ii (1933), chap. 7.

Brown and he did handle the Scottish Whigs with great severity; Marlborough did enter into treasonable communications with James II. Under Macaulay's distortion of the evidence and his misstatements of the facts there was a substratum of fact. The case of Penn is much worse because there is no real foundation for the charges Macaulay brings against him. 'To speak the whole truth concerning Penn', he states, 'is a task which requires some courage: for he is rather a mythical than a historical person.' He goes on to say that Penn, under the reign of James II, became 'a courtier and almost a favourite', that he was 'without doubt a man of eminent virtue' but that 'his rectitude was not altogether proof against the temptations to which it was exposed', and that consequently 'he bore a chief part in some transactions condemned . . . by the general sense of honest men'.[1]

As a proof, he alleges that Penn helped to extort money from the young women threatened with punishment for taking part in Monmouth's reception at Taunton. Their relations had to pay a fine which was fixed at £7,000 and was to go into the pockets of the Queen's maids of honour. They asked a local gentleman to extort the money for them, but he 'excused himself from taking any part in a transaction so scandalous'. Penn, however, according to Macaulay, accepted the task.

The maids of honour then requested William Penn to act for them; and Penn accepted the commission. Yet it should seem that a little of the pertinacious scrupulosity which he had often shown about taking off his hat would not have been altogether out of place on this occasion. He probably silenced the remonstrances of his conscience by repeating to himself that none of the money which he ex-

[1] I, 502-4 (iv).

torted would go into his own pocket; that if he refused to be the agent of the ladies they would find agents less humane; that by complying he should increase his influence at the court, and that his influence at the court had already enabled him, and might still enable him, to render great services to his oppressed brethren.[1]

The charge is false. It rests on a confusion between William Penn and a certain George Penn, who had no connection with the great Quaker. Finding a document which mentions Mr. Penn as employed in this matter, Macaulay followed Mackintosh[2] in assuming that Mr. Penn necessarily meant William Penn, though there is no further evidence of any kind against William Penn and there is good evidence that George Penn was employed in other cases to extort similar ransoms from persons concerned in Monmouth's rebellion.

The next important charge is that Penn was employed by James II in 1687 to induce the Fellows of Magdalen College to give way to his demands. According to Macaulay, after the Fellows had refused to yield to the King's threats, James employed the agency of Penn in the hope that the college 'might still be terrified, caressed, or bribed into submission'. He goes on to relate Penn's interview with the Fellows and his attempt to 'seduce the college from the path of right'.[3] An examination of the evidence shows that Penn was concerned in the affair as the agent of the college rather than of the King. He interceded with the King on behalf of the college, and that not once but twice over. Far from trying to persuade the Fellows to give way he wrote to James that 'in their circumstances, they

[1] II, 645 (v).

[2] History of the Revolution (1834), i. 202.

[3] II, 948 (viii).

could not yield obedience without a breach of their oaths.'[1] Macaulay misrepresents the whole position and makes his view seem plausible by a number of small perversions of the facts.

Curiously enough, there is another instance of a similar nature. King James was anxious to persuade William Kiffin, a leader amongst the Baptists, to accept the post of alderman of London, and according to Macaulay employed Penn to persuade him.[2] On the contrary, Kiffin says that he used all the means at his disposal to be excused, and amongst others' sought Penn's assistance.[3]

Further charges against Penn are that he conspired against William III, sent information to James II in France, and urged him to invade England. The evidence adduced is very slight, and of very little value, but instead of being simply stated for what it is worth, it is rhetorically exaggerated and supported by many misstatements of minor facts.

Macaulay's original conception of Penn's character prevents him from soberly appreciating the value of evidence or correctly stating it. Having come to the conclusion that Penn was the accomplice of James in a design against the liberties of England during 1686-1687, he was incapable of seeing any facts which told against his view. Penn's attitude to toleration and his sympathy with any attempt to promote it is fully explained in a letter written from Philadelphia to the Duke of Ormonde in January 1683.

Of all that falls under thy administration, in the love of God and the sincere affection of a friend, lett me prevale with the to avoide troubling conscientious and quiet liveing

[1] Thomas Clarkson, Memoirs of William Penn (1849), p. 182.

[2] II, 878-80 (vii).

[3] Remarkable Passages in the Life of William Kiffin (1823), p. 85.

dissenters. . . . I cannot think that God will damn any man for the errors of his judgement. . . . 'Tis what I ever told both the King and Duke, and that at parting; if God should suffer men to be so farr infatuated as to raise commotions in the kingdom, he would never find any of that party [1] among them, at least of note or credit. . . . I am for the just and mercifull thing, whoever getts or looses by itt, as ought all men of truth, honour and conscience to be.[2]

Penn's real position with regard to James II is very well stated by Ranke,[3] who devotes nearly a whole chapter to the subject. Macaulay's charges were refuted, almost as soon as made, by W. E. Forster in the preface to a new edition of Clarkson's Life of Penn in 1849, and by Hepworth Dixon in a life of Penn published in 1851. But though Macaulay's charges were completely disproved, he was unwilling to withdraw a single one of them or, rather, mentally unable to see that they were disproved. A deputation from the Society of Friends came to see him in order to state the case for Penn. His account of the interview is a fine example of complacent infallibility.

Lord Shelburne, Charles Austin, and Milman to breakfast. A pleasant meal. Then the Quakers, five in number. Never was there such a rout. They had absolutely nothing to say. Every charge against Penn came out as clear as any case at the Old Bailey. They had nothing to urge but what was true enough, that he looked worse in my History than he would have looked on a general survey of his whole life. But that is not my fault. I wrote the History of four years during which he was exposed to great temptations; during which he was the favourite of a bad king, and an active solicitor in a most corrupt court. His character was

[1] Quakers.

[2] From the Carte Papers in the Bodleian Library, vol. xl, fols. 212 et seq. Printed by C. E. Doble in the Academy of Jan. 4, 1896, pp. 36-7.

[3] Bk. xvii, chap. 5.

injured by his associations. Ten years before, or ten years later, he would have made a much better figure. But was I to begin my book ten years earlier or ten years later for William Penn's sake? The Quakers were extremely civil. So was I. They complimented me on my courtesy and candour.[1]

It is likely that the Quakers did not do much of the talking, and that if they had 'absolutely nothing to say' it was because they were not allowed to speak. When Macaulay's mind was made up he was never given to listening to the arguments of the other side.[2]

Whether it was a question of measures or men, we see always in Macaulay this same lack of open-mindedness and accessibility to new ideas or new information. The defect was a permanent source of weakness to him as a historian. He formed an opinion about the character of a man from only part of the evidence, and having formed it he was unaffected by further evidence. Instead of revising his opinion as he ought to have done, he made the new evidence square with the preconceived opinion by any device which occurred to him. There is a story told about Carlyle and Macaulay which illustrates Macaulay's way of forming his conceptions of historical personages.

Almost the only occasion on which I remember to have heard Carlyle engaged in an elaborate defence of his opinions or assertions was at a breakfast-party in London, against an opponent no less formidable than Lord Macaulay. The subject of dispute was the character of Henry Cromwell, whom Lord Macaulay described, in words quoted from Mrs. Hutchinson's Memoirs, as 'a deboshed

[1] Journal, Feb. 5, 1849. Trevelyan, ii. 251-2.

[2] Cf. the experience of Max Müller, who was asked to discuss new regulations for the civil service with Macaulay, and who was totally unable to get a word in edgeways. Auld Lang Syne, ser. i (1898), pp. 161-2.

cavalier'. Carlyle maintained not only that the charge was unjust, but that Henry Cromwell was an able and upright statesman. Both disputants were equally vigorous and voluble; but, not pretending to have any independent opinion on the question, I observed that Carlyle referred to many contemporary authorities, while Lord Macaulay, at the end of every rhetorical period, invariably reverted to Mrs. Hutchinson and her deboshed cavalier. 'I have read', Carlyle once answered, not without impatience, 'all that that shrill female ever wrote, and I can assert that she knew nothing of Henry Cromwell. I have read every existing letter which he wrote, and all that is written about him, and know that he was not a deboshed cavalier.' The only other speaker who intervened was Sir George Lewis, whose sceptical instinct never failed him. In answer to Carlyle's argument from the letters he suggested that Henry Cromwell, when he was Lord Deputy in Ireland, probably saved himself the trouble of writing, by merely signing letters written by his secretary. I forget whether Lord Macaulay accepted the aid of his unexpected ally.[1]

In this case Carlyle was absolutely right and Macaulay absolutely wrong; the latter had formed a positive opinion on imperfect data, and adhered to it with as much tenacity as if it had been formed after a study of all the evidence.

Why did Macaulay do this? A historian can make no greater mistake than forming his opinions too soon. When he begins to study a subject his opinions are bound to be more or less provisional, to be altered and modified as he obtains more evidence and larger light. Does not Milton in Areopagitica say that opinion in good men is but knowledge in the making?

A historian is not bound to make up his mind in a hurry: he can wait till he knows or has good reason for thinking he

[1] G. S. Venables, Carlyle in Society and at Home, in Fortnightly Review, xxxix. 632.

knows. On the other hand a politician, having to act, or to pronounce an opinion at a moment's notice, must make up his mind with rapidity and must have a very definite opinion too. Macaulay had the mental habits of the politician, not those of a historian. His political opinions were fully formed at an extremely early date; they never altered; there is no sign of any gradual development or growth about them. He was a politician of the kind people praise as 'singularly consistent'. His historical opinions were mostly formed just as early as his political opinions, and he clung to them with the same constancy. For his peculiar intellectual gift was one which tended to produce tenacity rather than open-mindedness. One of his critics has pointed this out. James Spedding 'was in the habit of suggesting a conjectural excuse for Macaulay's occasional inaccuracies and for his obstinacy in refusing to correct his mistakes. Both peculiarities were with much probability ascribed to habitual reliance on a marvellous memory. The errors which could not always be avoided during his youthful accumulation of various knowledge became stereotyped in a recollection which probably reproduced with unfailing fidelity the original impression.' [1]

Macaulay's mental habits increased this reliance on his memory. His impressions and his recollections were singularly vivid and concrete; they became as real to him as if they were palpable external things. His sister once said to him that she was surprised at the great accuracy of his information, considering how desultory his reading had been. 'My accuracy as to facts', he said, 'I owe to a cause which many men would not confess. It is due to my love of castle-building. The past is in my mind soon constructed into a romance.' He then went on to describe the way in

[1] Spedding, Evenings with a Reviewer (1881), i, p. xxiv.

which from his childhood his imagination had been filled by the study of history. 'With a person of my turn', he said,

the minute touches are of as great interest, and perhaps greater, than the most important events. Spending so much time as I do in solitude, my mind would have rusted by gazing vacantly at the shop windows. As it is, I am no sooner in the streets than I am in Greece, in Rome, in the midst of the French Revolution. Precision in dates, the day or hour in which a man was born or died, becomes absolutely necessary. A slight fact, a sentence, a word, are of importance in my romance. Pepys' Diary formed almost inexhaustible food for my fancy. I seem to know every inch of Whitehall. I go in at Hans Holbein's gate, and come out through the matted gallery. The conversations which I compose between great people of the time are long, and sufficiently animated: in the style, if not with the merits of Sir Walter Scott's. The old parts of London, which you are sometimes surprised at my knowing so well, those old gates and houses down by the river, have all played their part in my stories.[1]

The 'castle-building', as Macaulay called it, is the source of some of his inaccuracies and errors. Before he began to write the history of the reigns of James and William he had formed his conceptions of the chief figures in his story—conceptions so vivid and so clear that they had become realities to him, and he did not remember that they were his own creatures. And he had constructed these figures, not after a systematic examination of all the accessible evidence, but on the basis of his wide and desultory reading. Amongst these familiar figures were no doubt the barbarous Claverhouse with his 'seared conscience and adamantine heart', that 'prodigy of turpitude', Marlborough, and the eminently virtuous William Penn who was always being seduced from the path of rectitude.

[1] Margaret Macaulay's Journal, Mar. 30, 1831. Trevelyan, i. 183-4.

CHAPTER XII

MACAULAY'S CHARACTER OF JAMES II

READERS of Macaulay's History must often have wondered whether James was as black as he is painted there. James is not given a full-length portrait. When he is first mentioned his character is summed up in two lines: 'Though a libertine, James was diligent, methodical, and fond of authority and business. His understanding was singularly slow and narrow, and his temper obstinate, harsh, and unforgiving.'[1] After this preliminary estimate Macaulay dwells at length, first on one feature of James's character and then on another, as opportunity offers, leaving the reader to collect from these partial glimpses and from the acts recorded his own estimate of the King's character. The acts are generally discreditable and the comments unfavourable.

To begin with, it is certain that Macaulay underrates the ability of James II—that is, his administrative, not his political ability. He made a good Lord High Admiral, and the navy was better administered by him than by the commissioners who took his place after the passing of the Test Act in 1673. During his short reign he did much to restore the fleet which Charles II had allowed to fall into a state of disorganisation and decay. On this point the evidence of Pepys is consistent and conclusive.

Another favourable witness is the Duke of Wellington. In one of his conversations with Lord Stanhope he said:

[1] I, 151 (ii).

'The most curious book ever written perhaps is the Memoirs of James II. . . . By his own showing he was a very weak fellow; but he had great skill nevertheless, for the head of a department. His arrangements at the Ordnance were excellent. When I was Master-General I brought it back very much to what he had made it.'[1] Therefore, for Macaulay to assert that James 'would have made a respectable clerk in the dockyard at Chatham'[2] is to be unjust to the King.

On the other hand all the new evidence available confirms Macaulay's verdict that James's 'understanding was singularly slow and narrow'. His character is perhaps best revealed in the letters written to his friends before he became king.[3] He expressed himself with freedom, both to the Prince of Orange and to George Legge, afterwards Lord Dartmouth. Portions of his correspondence with them were accessible to Macaulay.[4]

These letters throw no new light on the character of James, but they make his attitude clearer and more certain. They show the reality of his attachment to his religion, and the firmness with which he refused to abandon it for any worldly advantage. He wrote to Legge: 'You are a man of conscience, as well as honnor, do but thinke what a base

[1] Stanhope, Notes of Conversations with the Duke of Wellington, p. 66.

[2] I, 440 (iv).

[3] The letters of James to the Prince of Orange from October 1678 to November 1679 were printed by the Hist. MSS. Comm. in the Report on the Savile Foljambe MSS. (1897); the majority of these were, however, printed by Dalrymple from the originals among the domestic State Papers and now calendared. For the years 1677-84, there are the letters printed in Groen van Prinsterer's Archives . . . de la Maison d'Orange-Nassau, Ser. II, vol. v. James's letters to George Legge, Earl of Dartmouth, covering the period 1679-82 and 1688, are in volume i of the Dartmouth MSS.; those addressed to the Duke of Queensberry (1682-85) are in the Buccleuch MSS. at Drumlanrig Castle, i. 168-215.

[4] Dalrymple, Memoirs of Great Britain and Ireland.

meane thing it would be in me, besids the sin of it, to dissemble, and deny my religion, I have [?resolved] by God's grace never to do so damnable a thing.'[1] That he would hear of no compromise on this question is greatly to his credit.

These letters prove that James was despotic and a firm believer in the theory of the divine right of kings. He was evidently unable to understand any of the conditions of constitutional government, or to appreciate the necessity of the smallest concession. His father had yielded to the demands of the Parliamentarians and had been beheaded;[2] he meant to crush discontent, not to try to remove its causes. The exclusion bill, wrote James, 'was against law, and destroys the very being of the monarky, which, I thanke God, yett has had no dependency on Parliments nor on nothing but God alone, nor never can, and be a monarky; and I hope his Majesty will be of this mind, and never lett this House of Commons sitt againe. If he dos, he is ruined for ever.'[3]

James expressed these autocratic ideas of kingship with monotonous regularity in his correspondence, and regarded all who did not accept them as traitors. In every line, his inferiority to Charles II in political ability and worldly wisdom is apparent. Charles weathered the storm raised by the Popish Plot by giving his opponents rope enough: James thought his brother was surrendering the essence of monarchy. After the dissolution of the Oxford Parliament and the arrest of Shaftesbury the Whigs were paralysed, and James urged his brother 'to follow the blow now that they were stunn'd, as the only way to master a faction which

[1] Dec. 11, 1680. Dartmouth MSS., i. 40; cf. The Life of James the Second, ed. J. S. Clarke (2 vols.; 1816), i. 560.

[2] Macaulay, II, 718-9 (vi); cf. II, 1019 (viii).

[3] July 6, 1679. Savile Foljambe MSS., pp. 133-4; Dalrymple, ii. 224.

by long experience he had found was never to be gain'd by concessions nor indulgence, that the hand of God was visibly in it not only in bringing their villanies to light, but by turning their own malicious designes upon themselves, and had cast them into the pit they had dug for others.' [1]

The reign of James II and the revolution which ended it can be predicted from the letters of the Duke of York. There is, however, one startling change. Nothing indicates that James was likely to pose as the champion of toleration, as he did during the last two years of his reign. On the contrary, in the spring of 1680 James writes exultantly to the Prince of Orange that there had been the greatest alteration for the better that could be imagined, and attributes this to the purging of the commissions of the peace of all disaffected people, thus encouraging the old friends of the monarchy, the cavalier or church party. If the King would continue steady on the course he has now laid down, he will be more master and in a better condition then he has been these many a yeare.' [2]

A more favourable view of James's character can be gathered from the Memoirs of the Earl of Ailesbury. Participation in Jacobite plots against William forced Ailesbury to go into exile, where he wrote his Memoirs forty years after the Revolution. They are naturally full of inaccuracies and rambling digressions, but nevertheless reproduce the impressions of a loyal adherent of James, who witnessed what he recorded and had both a memory for picturesque incidents and the power to describe them in vigorous language. If Macaulay had known of their existence they would have supplied him with many striking touches.

[1] Life of James, i. 690.

[2] Groen van Prinsterer, v. 393.

Ailesbury's opinion was that James was a good but not a clever man. Himself a high Tory, he thought the King's political principles were very sound. 'The King had a true English spirit.' 'His heart and soul were set on the flourishing condition of the navy, with this English expression, "Our fleet is our bulwarks, and therefore each true patriot ought to wish the prosperity of it." . . . Trade he had much at heart, and his topic was, liberty of conscience and many hands at work in trade.' For this reason he aided the Huguenot refugees,[1] who repaid his kindness by welcoming his downfall.

According to the same writer the King after an amorous youth became very moral and religious, and unduly neglected temporal affairs.

> God forbid that I should have anything to say against devotion, or serving our Creator, but a king who hath three kingdoms to govern, cannot have all those leisure hours that subjects enjoy, and too much of his time was taken up at holy exercises, all which, as I said, was praiseworthy before God, but took up so great a part of his time, that public affairs of the Crown and nation suffered greatly, and gave too much occasion for crafty statesmen to accomplish their villanous projects.

Had the King 'been less devout it had been better for us, and, I may add, had he not been too credulous . . . He lost his crown by the means of a fool and a knave.' The fool was the King's religious adviser, the Jesuit Father Petre—a man 'filled with vanity and great passions, and as to state affairs a perfect novice and resembled little most of his order, where there are generally many crafty, and wise, and intriguing men.' The knave was the King's political adviser, Sunderland, 'the Prime Minister and Secretary . . .

[1] Cf. Macaulay, II, 678-80 (vi).

Pen cannot describe worse of him than he deserved.' After the Revolution Sunderland was asked 'how it was possible for a person of his great parts and experience for to have given his master, King James, such pernicious counsels, and the executing of which brought on the King all his misfortunes. . . . He replied with a sneer, that but for those counsels the Prince of Orange had never landed and succeeded.' [1]

Unluckily the King's trusting nature led him to repose all his confidence in this knave instead of playing off one minister against another as Charles II had done. 'The King had a good judgement, but was diffident of it, which made him to resort to a minister's advice (I wish it had been in the plural) and the King his brother knew his humour but too well, and told me once that he [Charles II] would follow his brother of France's politics, to make use of more than one as he [Louis XIV] did by Colbert and Louvois, who were like fire and water; adding, "Gods fish! when rogues fall out, the master is like then to know the truth."' [2]

In all these remarks about Petre and Sunderland, Ailesbury followed the Jacobite tradition. Macaulay accepts it as far as Petre was concerned. 'He was weak and vain, covetous and ambitious. Of all the evil counsellors who had access to the royal ear, he bore, perhaps, the largest part in the ruin of the House of Stuart.' [3] But he rejects the Jacobite theory about Sunderland. 'This idle story has been repeated down to our own day by ignorant writers. . . . His conduct is to be ascribed to the alternate influence of cupidity and fear on a mind highly susceptible of both those passions, and quicksighted rather than farsighted.' [4]

[1] Ailesbury, i. 102-3, 131-2, 127-8, 218.
[2] Ibid. p. 104.
[3] II, 718 (vi).
[4] II, 721 (vi), 1086, 1094 (ix), 2387-8 (xx).

The reign of James began on February 6, 1685; on June 11 Monmouth landed at Lyme. When Macaulay wrote, the chief modern authority on the career of Monmouth and his expedition to England was the Life by George Roberts published in 1844—a work of considerable research and still worth consulting. A new biography entitled King Monmouth (1902), by Allan Fea, brings together many new details, and contains some additional documents. But this new evidence in no way alters the old conception of Monmouth's character. His weakness and vanity made his misfortunes inevitable.

On the other hand much light upon the origin of the expedition is afforded by the deposition of a certain Robert Cragg,[1] an agent employed by Monmouth's friends in England in March 1685 to persuade him to go with Argyle to Scotland instead of coming to England. This narrative reveals very clearly the dissensions amongst Monmouth's partisans. It also to some extent implicates Lord Delamere, who was subsequently tried but acquitted.[2]

Monmouth was accompanied on the expedition by Robert Ferguson the Plotter, whom Macaulay describes as Monmouth's 'evil angel'.[3] He is said to have written Monmouth's declaration and to have persuaded him to assume the title of king. A life of Ferguson by James Ferguson, published in 1887, refutes some of Macaulay's statements. Ferguson himself said that he thought it inexpedient for Monmouth to take the title at that juncture and wished him to confine himself to asserting a claim to the crown, leaving Parliament to decide upon its validity later.

On the military measures against Monmouth there is also new evidence. The local militia which was at first

[1] It is printed in Manuscripts of the House of Lords, 1689-1690.

[2] II, 697-700 (vi).

[3] II, 526-7, 564, 576-8, 650 (v).

charged with the suppression of the rising was commanded by Christopher Monck, second Duke of Albemarle. He was not much of a soldier at best, and as the three or four thousand Devonshire militia under his command were disaffected,[1] he was probably not to blame for his failure to beat the rebels at once. Louis de Duras, Earl of Feversham, the French soldier who commanded James's forces, had, at all events, military experience, though he is generally described, on the strength of contemporary satires, as lazy and incompetent. Five long letters of his are now available, together with a detailed narrative of his marches during the campaign, and of the battle of Sedgemoor.[2] According to Macaulay, Feversham was in bed when the attack began, but as it took place at one in the morning the fact is not so criminal as it may seem. Moreover it is admitted, even by Macaulay, that he did not remain there. 'Feversham had been awakened by the firing, had got out of bed, had adjusted his cravat, had looked at himself well in the glass, and had come to see what his men were doing.'[3] In the letters above mentioned there is a full account of his movements during the fight and of the orders he gave.

The best account of the campaign, from a military point of view, is to be found in the two chapters devoted to the subject in Wolseley's Life of Marlborough. Wolseley's book contains also a contemporary plan of the battle drawn by Edward Dummer and reproduced from the original in the Pepysian Library at Cambridge. A second plan, drawn by Andrew Paschall, rector of Chedzoy, is reproduced in Fea's King Monmouth. A third, also attributed

[1] II, 570 (v); Estelle Frances Ward, Christopher Monck, Duke of Albemarle (1915), bk. v.

[2] Hist. MSS. Comm., Stopford Sackville MSS., i (1904), 2-29.

[3] II, 600 (v). For Feversham's dandyism, see The Battle of Sedgmoor, a farce by the second Duke of Buckingham (in Works [1775], vol. ii).

to Paschall, is in the Bodleian, and is reproduced in volume iii of the Collectanea of the Oxford Historical Society. There it serves to illustrate a number of letters addressed by the Earl of Clarendon to the Earl of Abingdon to inform him of the progress of the rebellion. Abingdon, who was Lord Lieutenant of Oxfordshire, was busy raising volunteers in the county and university, and arresting nonconformist ministers and other suspected persons. Further details of the zeal of Oxford for the royal cause may be found in the third volume of Anthony Wood's Diary.

On the savage punishment of the rebels which followed the suppression of the rising, new evidence is collected in F. A. Inderwick's Side Lights on the Stuarts (1891). He succeeds in showing that the number of sufferers has been exaggerated.

Those who have read Macaulay—and who has not?—must have had their blood run cold over his graphic descriptions of the brutality and the butchery of the Bloody Assize. Having passed through this preliminary stage, one's natural inclination is to consider whether after all the story may not have been somewhat exaggerated; whether Jeffreys was the bloodthirsty and lawless tyrant there described, and whether those hecatombs of victims existed in fact or in imagination. Circumstances recently put into my hands the gaol books of the Western Circuit, containing a complete record of the prisoners and of the convictions during this remarkable period, and I am bound to admit that I do not find the record to be altogether in accordance with the statement of Lord Macaulay and of others who put the number of the slain at this assize at figures varying from three hundred and twenty to seven hundred. This gaol-book is, as far as I am aware, the only original and authentic record of the proceedings at this assize. The entries are made regularly day by day, recording the name of, and the charge against, the accused, together with his plea of guilty or not guilty, and his sentence if convicted.[1]

According to the gaol book, at Winchester, Salisbury, Dorchester, Exeter, Taunton, and Wells, 1,388 persons were indicted for high treason, of whom 1,381 were found guilty or pleaded guilty, and 65 were executed. These were the figures in September 1685, when the assize ended. Another official return, dated November 1685, shows an increase in the number; 74 had by that time been executed for high treason in Dorset and 11 in Devon. Over a thousand persons were still in prison. Of these some 235 were under sentence of death, and 843 had been made over to various persons for transportation. It is likely that all these 235 were not executed, that many of them were eventually transported instead, and that some of those who were sentenced to transportation were allowed to ransom themselves. Mr. Inderwick comes to the conclusion that not more than 150 persons—less than half the figure given by Macaulay—were actually executed by process of law. As to the number transported he holds it impossible to give an exact estimate. Judging from the Calendar of Colonial State Papers there were certainly several hundreds, though not, apparently, so many as 843. No figures are available about the number of rebels summarily executed by the soldiery after the battle of Sedgemoor.

What transportation meant can be gathered from the narratives of some of the sufferers. Macaulay refers to the manuscript narrative of John Coad.[2] This was printed in 1849 under the title of A Memorandum of the Wonderful Providences of God to a Poor Unworthy Creature. Coad

[1] Pp. 370-1. [2] II, 640 (v).

was transported to Jamaica, and suffered much on the voyage thither, during which twenty-two out of the ninety-nine prisoners on board his ship died. But he was well treated when he reached Jamaica, save for the hardship of being obliged to work without pay for a planter. Another narrative, one not quoted by Macaulay, is A Relation of the Great Sufferings and Strange Adventures of Henry Pitman.[1] Pitman was sent to Barbados; nine out of his company of a hundred died on the way. He was beaten and set in the stocks by his master and otherwise ill-treated, but managed to get a boat and escape with half a dozen prisoners whose adventures he tells.

The question whether James or Jeffreys was responsible for these severities has been much discussed. According to Macaulay 'no English sovereign has ever given stronger proofs of a cruel nature than James II. . . . Jeffreys was a judge after his master's own heart'. The King watched 'what he facetiously called his Lord Chief Justice's campaign in the West' with 'interest and delight'. Macaulay continues:

At a later period, when men of all parties spoke with horror of the Bloody Assizes, the wicked Judge and the wicked King attempted to vindicate themselves by throwing the blame on each other. Jeffreys, in the Tower, protested that, in his utmost cruelty, he had not gone beyond his master's express orders, nay, that he had fallen short of them. James, at Saint Germain's, would willingly have had it believed that his own inclinations had been on the side of clemency, and that unmerited obloquy had been brought on him by the violence of his minister. But neither of these hardhearted men must be absolved at the expense of the other. The plea set up for James can be

[1] Published in 1689; reprinted in vol. vii of Arber's English Garner (8 vols.; 1877-96) and in Stuart Tracts (1903).

proved under his own hand to be false in fact. The plea of Jeffreys, even if it be true in fact, is utterly worthless.[1]

Mr. H. B. Irving's Life of Judge Jeffreys (1898) attempts a vindication, but it is not very thoroughgoing. He represents Jeffreys as executing over three hundred persons on his western circuit. But Mr. Irving argues at some length that the Judge acted under direct and strict instructions from the King. As a new witness on the point he brings forward Ailesbury, whom he represents as saying that he protested to the King himself against Jeffrey's severity, that the King said he abhorred it, and that he said to James, 'Your Majesty ought to turn out the Justice and Mr. Percy Kirke, and that will show the world your true abhorrence.'[2] Unluckily for Mr. Irving's argument Ailesbury does not say that he made the remark to James but that he would have liked to make it. 'I knew the King's temper too well for to give my advice but it was at my tongue's end'[3] to say . . . Ailesbury's own view is that Jeffreys was 'a man of great and fiery passion, and did more ill things out of his natural temper, which was insufferable, than out of a design to render the King odious.'

Ailesbury was very anxious to prove that James was a merciful man, much maligned by rumour. He quotes the cases of Lord Gerard of Brandon and Lord Delamere.[4] The first was convicted of treason for his share in the Rye House Plot, but was pardoned, and remained loyal to James even though his father, the Earl of Macclesfield, came over with William of Orange.[5] Delamere was tried for complicity in Monmouth's rebellion, but was acquitted by his peers. Ailesbury argues that James intended the trial to

[1] II, 652-4 (v).

[2] Irving, p. 306.

[3] Memoirs, i. 121.

[4] Ibid. pp. 132-3, 133-6.

[5] Cf. Macaulay, II, 696 (vi).

exhibit his love of justice, and that he rejoiced in the result.[1] Even so, two instances of this kind cannot weigh in the balance against the Bloody Assizes. The special pleadings of Ailesbury and other apologists must be rejected : James was callous, vindictive, and cruel. It is impossible to show that he was ignorant of the severities in the west, or that he disapproved of the conduct of Jeffreys.

Immediately after the suppression of Monmouth's rebellion the King's intention to suspend the action of the laws against the Catholics became apparent. At the opening of the session, November 9, 1685, the King's speech announced that the standing army was to be permanently increased and that officers were to retain their commissions although they had not taken the Test. The Commons replied by a respectful protest, and the Lords were about to follow suit, when on November 20 James prorogued Parliament to prevent them. The two Houses never met again during the King's reign.

As Macaulay points out, the leaders of the Catholic aristocracy disapproved of the King's policy. They would have welcomed a discreet attempt to persuade Parliament to repeal the penal laws, but they feared the results of an effort to set aside the Test Act by the exercise of the prerogative or by force.[2] Ailesbury, after mentioning the King's speech and saying that its policy was ' contrary to the sense of the old and landed Roman Catholics ', adds :

> The two Houses were in a deep melancholy. That very evening, according to custom, I went to visit my worthy friend and kinsman the Lord Bellasis, who seldom stirred out, being so infirm in his limbs. My Lord Bellasis, who

[1] Macaulay's account (II, 697-700 [vi]) is as different as possible to that of Ailesbury.

[2] Klopp, Der Fall des Hauses Stuart, iii. 203, 306, 328.

was in a great chair, took me by the hand saying, 'My dear Lord, who could be the framer of this speech? I date my ruin and that of all my persuasion from this day.' This is true on my honour; and from that time downwards, he expressed all grief and sorrow.[1]

Exactly in the same way, the agents of the House of Austria, the Pope, and other Catholic sovereigns predicted that the headstrong zeal of the King would be detrimental to Catholicism. Since Macaulay wrote, there has been printed a series of despatches of Terriesi, the agent of the Grand Duke of Tuscany. In one after another he speaks with disapproval of the King's measures, and expresses his fears of their consequences. As early as November 1685 he prophesied that the soldiers James had raised might in the end turn their arms against him. By May 1686 he was already discussing the possibility of a general rising against the government.[2]

Even more full and explicit are the warnings contained in the despatches of the agents and ambassadors of the Emperor. In September 1686 the Emperor Leopold sent a new ambassador, Kaunitz, to England. His instructions ordered him, after explaining the ambitious designs of the French king against Europe and the Empire, to represent to James that his untimely religious zeal would create discontent amongst his people and would be detrimental both to the spread of Catholicism and to the development of the King's influence abroad in the interests of peace. The ambassador was instructed to say that this was the opinion of the Pope as well as of the Emperor. If the King showed that he demanded nothing contrary to the laws or against

[1] Memoirs, i. 126; cf. Macaulay, II, 704-6 (vi).

[2] La Marquise de Campana de Cavelli, Les derniers Stuarts à Saint-Germain en Laye (2 vols.; 1871), ii. 84, 108. Klopp quotes other evidence to support this view.

the established religion, but took part decisively with other powers against French domination, his people would be entirely at his disposal. He would not only establish his own house and the Catholic religion on a firm foundation, but be praised everywhere as the protector and preserver of the peace of Europe.[1]

No warnings had any effect on James. His idea of coming to an agreement with his people and settling the question of the penal laws in a constitutional way was to pack a Parliament for the purpose. On December 11, 1687, he announced in the London Gazette that the list of deputy lieutenants and justices of the peace was to be revised, and only those were to be retained in office who supported the King's policy.

In the counties the Lord Lieutenants were to examine the deputy lieutenants and justices, make them answer certain test questions, and report these answers to the government. Those whose answers were unacceptable were to be turned out. A similar operation was to be applied to the municipal corporations. Aldermen and others who did not give satisfactory promises were to be reported to the government. Boroughs were to be bullied into resigning their charters, or their charters were to be annulled on some legal pretext and new ones granted, whose members were to be nominated by the King. As in many municipal boroughs the election of Members of Parliament was entirely in the hands of the corporations, this would guarantee the return of pliable representatives.

Macaulay describes the operation of this scheme and gives some account of its results.[2] Amongst the Rawlinson Manuscripts in the Bodleian Library are returns made by Lord Lieutenants and other agents, reporting the answers made by the justices and others in a number of counties, and

[1] Klopp, iii. 256.

[2] II (viii).

there are also reports on a few boroughs. These were privately printed in 1883 by Sir George Duckett under the title, Penal Laws and Test Act (2 vols.). The three questions to be asked each of the justices were: (1) whether in case he should be chosen knight of the shire or burgess of a town, when the King should think fit to call a Parliament, he would be for taking off the penal laws and the Tests; (2) whether he would assist and contribute to the election of such members as should be for taking off the Penal Laws and Tests; and (3) whether he would support the King's Declaration for Liberty of Conscience by living friendly with those of all persuasions as Christians and subjects of the same prince ought to do.

Ailesbury, who was Lord Lieutenant of Bedfordshire and Huntingdon, called together a meeting of the deputy lieutenants and justices of the peace. He found that 'not one agreed to the first and second questions, and to the third Pocklington only dissented '.[1] Many others declined to pledge themselves. Sir G. Blundell, a Bedfordshire deputy lieutenant, answered to the first question, 'That as a private person he does not apprehend that he has any legal power to preingage himselfe against the acts of parlament established, before they have undergone another Parlamentary debate.' As to the second he said, 'he submissively answers, ye occurrances are so variable in future contingancies by ye order of Divine Providence, that he cannot pretend to a capacity of determining beforehand, what his thoughts and actions shall be in progress of time, as to affairs of this nature.' A Huntingdonshire deputy lieutenant replied to the first question that 'he thinks it a great presumption in any person to promise or engage the making or abrogating laws, because when he comes into

[1] Memoirs, i. 163.

the House of Commons, (where every man hath free liberty of speech) he may hear such reasons as he coulld never imagine for or against the same.'[1]

Naturally these answers did not satisfy the King any more than they would modern electors. Accordingly it rained dismissals. But even when corporations had been filled with dissenters, wherever there was any semblance of a popular vote at all the Church party was too strong for them, and it became clear that the royal nominees had very little chance. 'The Dissenters are firm for us,' reported the government candidate for Bedford in December 1687, 'but the Churchmen are implacable against us.'[2]

Nowhere can the change in public opinion be better traced than in the University of Oxford, thanks to Anthony Wood's diary. Macaulay had before him only an abridged version. In The Life and Times of Anthony Wood[3] are many additional facts illustrating the process by which loyalty was transformed into rebellion. At the beginning of James's reign, Oxford was all exuberant loyalty. The proclamation and his coronation were celebrated with bonfires, illuminations, and, as Wood says, 'great extraordinaries in eating and drinking in each college.'[4] Early in 1686 came the first signs of a change of heart. In March Obadiah Walker, the Master of University College, declared his conversion to Roman Catholicism, and in August opened his chapel for public mass. Rioting began almost at once, and Walker became a byword to all—'Obadiah Ave Maria.' In January 1687 Wood noted that 'he hath the curses of all, both great and small.' There was similar dis-

[1] Duckett, ii. 48, 68. [2] Ibid. p. 61.

[3] Edited for the Oxford Historical Society by Andrew Clark (5 vols.; 1891).

[4] iii. 144.

order at Christ Church when John Massey, the popish dean, said vespers in the chapel in Canterbury Quadrangle. When the High Commission expelled twenty-five fellows of Magdalen, Charnock, the new vice-president, gave notice that mass would be said in the chapel, whereupon, according to Wood, 'people resorted to that place more than ordinary to fill up the chappel.'[1] Moreover the new Roman Catholic fellows appointed were jeered at whenever they appeared in the streets, and even in their own grounds, so that they had to close all the gates leading to the walks. Thus by the beginning of 1688 the excitement and resentment at Oxford had risen higher than elsewhere. On June 3, 1688, the day appointed for the second reading of the Declaration of Indulgence, only one minister in Oxford obeyed the royal order. On June 10, the birthday of the Prince of Wales, there were no celebrations at Oxford except by papists or officers. It is significant of the temper of Oxford that James, like Cromwell before him, found it necessary to quarter troops there.

The spirit which James had aroused at Oxford was gradually diffused over the country. He made it difficult for a Tory to be both a churchman and a royalist, and, apparently much to the King's surprise, loyalty to the monarchy yielded to loyalty to the Church. The diaries of Tories like John Evelyn and Sir John Reresby revealed the progress from criticism to disapproval and from disapproval of the King's policy to acceptance of a new king. Macaulay used both works, but he scarcely extracted the full value from either, and anyone wishing to trace the development of public opinion would find them admirable supplements to Wood.

There was a group of moderate opponents of James,

[1] Ibid. pp. 209, 254.

headed by the Marquis of Halifax, to whom Macaulay does less than justice. In October 1685 Halifax was dismissed from the position he held as Lord President of the Council, for refusing to countenance the employment of Catholic officers in the army and for opposing the repeal of the Test Act. New evidence proves that Halifax offered a more determined resistance to James's measures than Macaulay suggests. Halifax wrote to Compton, Bishop of London, advising him to stand firm against the sentence of the High Commission Court and not to submit or petition for restoration to his ecclesiastical functions.[1] He also drew up a petition and offered it to the seven bishops when they were in the Tower. They were to sign it and present it to the King, and Halifax probably intended to get it printed as an appeal to the people.[2]

Further, after the landing of William of Orange, a certain number of peers endeavoured to promote an accommodation between William and James on the basis of calling a free Parliament, and at a meeting they drew up a petition for the purpose. Halifax and some others refused to sign, and stood aloof from any association with the court. The reasons for this opposition are more explicitly explained in a letter[3] from Lord Nottingham which was unknown to Macaulay. There is another still more important document. After James and his army retired from Salisbury the King returned to London and held a meeting of the peers there on November 27. At their instigation he now opened negotiations with William, appointing Halifax, Nottingham, and Godolphin to treat. The official report of their mission, made by these negotiators to the Secretary of State, is

[1] Foxcroft, Halifax, i. 448-53. [2] Ibid. pp. 472, 505.

[3] Ibid. ii. 12; cf. Hatton Correspondence, ed. E. M. Thompson (1878), ii. 103.

U

printed by Miss Foxcroft.[1] Its unfavourable nature was one of the reasons which led to the flight of James on December 10.

Halifax, like Nottingham, represented the moderate section of the opposition among the peerage. Neither of them signed the famous letter of June 30, 1688, inviting William to England and promising him assistance. On this particular point little additional information has appeared since Dalrymple published his Memoirs in 1773. On the other hand local and family records of every kind show the universality of the disaffection to the King's government and the progress of the general rising against James II which followed the landing of the Prince of Orange. Many papers published in the reports of the Historical Manuscripts Commission elucidate the different incidents in the rebellion. One of its leaders was Danby, who seized York on November 22 and Scarborough six days later. At the beginning of December the officers of the garrison of Hull revolted and declared for the Prince of Orange. Letters from Danby to his wife give an account of these proceedings, and the correspondence also contains a letter from Danby to the Prince of Orange, dated December 10, in which he promises to join the Prince with six hundred horse.[2]

The rising of the north took place during the latter half of November. The Prince of Orange, having landed at Torbay on November 5, had established his headquarters at Exeter on November 9, remained there until the twenty-first, and then advanced to Axminster. James set out from London to meet him on November 17 and arrived at

[1] Halifax, ii. 24.

[2] Lindsey MSS. (1895). Other letters of the same period are in the Leeds MSS. (1888), but are described too briefly to be of much use.

Salisbury on Monday, the nineteenth. A battle seemed imminent. Most of the regiments in the royal army were at Warminster, where it was arranged that the King should review them on the twenty-first, as a preliminary to advancing against William. Macaulay[1] relates how at the moment when James was about to set out for Warminster he was prevented from starting by a violent attack of bleeding at the nose, and that three days elapsed before the hemorrhage was entirely stopped. According to the Jacobite legend this bleeding was providential. Churchill and his accomplices had arranged to seize the King when he got to Warminster and to hand him over to William. The story of the plot is probably a simple invention based on the fact that Churchill deserted to William. James apparently believed it, however, and Ailesbury is certain about its existence.

New authorities help us to correct Macaulay's account of events at Salisbury. There seems to be no good authority for the picturesque detail that the bleeding came on just when James was setting out for Warminster. The Life of James distinctly says that the bleeding began 'the evening before his Majesty designed to go '.[2] This is confirmed by Ailesbury, who arrived at Salisbury on November 20 to attend the King as a Gentleman of the Bedchamber. He went to Court soon after his arrival: 'The King was in his bedchamber in a great chair, his nose having bled for some time, and the moment I arrived they put a cold key on the back of his neck, and all was over.'[3] Nevertheless the bleeding continued the next day, and prevented the journey

[1] III, 1159 (ix).

[2] ii. 222. Abel Boyer's Reign of James II (in his History of King William the Third) explains the origin of the error.

[3] Memoirs, i. 188.

to Warminster. On Thursday the King held the Council of War which Macaulay describes, but wrongly places on the Saturday. On Friday night (November 23-24) Churchill and Grafton deserted,[1] and on Saturday James began his retreat. George Clarke, who, as judge advocate, was summoned to the headquarters of the army and had set out from London in company with Dr. Radcliffe, met the King and the army marching back:

> We went with the King to Andover and waited upon him at his quarters, with the Prince of Denmark and the Duke of Ormond. I can never forget the confusion the court was in; the Lord Churchill had gone over to the Prince of Orange from Salisbury the night before, and the Duke of Grafton that morning; the King knew not whom to trust, and the fright was so great that they were apt to believe an impossible report just then brought in that the Prince of Orange was come with twelve thousand horse between Warminster and Salisbury. Upon hearing it the Lord Feversham, the general, never questioned the truth, but cried out: Zounce, then Kirk be asleep. This I was an ear witness of. Everybody in this hurly-burly was thinking of himself, and nobody minded the King, who came up to Dr. Radcliffe and asked him what was good for the bleeding of his nose: it was the last time that ever I saw him.[2]

The same night the Prince of Denmark and the Duke of Ormond deserted and went back to Salisbury to join the Prince of Orange. News of Prince George's desertion and of the impending return of James to London reached the Princess Anne on the following day. Afraid to face her father, she fled from Whitehall late that night, took shelter with the Bishop of London in Aldersgate Street, and set on next day to Epping Forest on her way to Nottingham.

[1] Macaulay's dates are clearly wrong here.

[2] Leyborne-Popham MSS., p. 267.

Macaulay[1] gives a very picturesque description of her flight. Since he wrote, there has appeared an excellent letter from Pepys to Dartmouth, written the night of November 26 by the King's special direction, which explains the reason for the flight, and gives an account of its discovery, which took place about eight o'clock on the morning of November 26.[2]

All these desertions and the evident untrustworthiness of the army, and the progress of the rising in the north and Midlands, obliged James to treat. But he had no intention of waiting for the return of his commissioners. He had made up his mind to seek safety in flight. Ailesbury vainly urged the King to abandon this fatal resolution and to march, instead, against the rebels in the north. 'But in a manner he begged the question, viz: "If I should go, who can wonder after the treatment I have found? My daughter hath deserted me, my army also, and him that I raised from nothing the same, on whom I heaped all favours; and if such betrays me, what can I expect from those I have done so little for? I knew not who to speak to or who to trust; some would have persuaded me that you was confederate with them, but I could not believe it."'[3]

Every reader of Macaulay knows his description of the King's flight and of his seizure by the Kentish fishermen somewhere near the island of Sheppey on December 12, and of the indignities which he suffered from his captors. He remained a prisoner for some days, first at Faversham and then at Rochester. A narrative of what happened there, written by a Kentish gentleman named Sir John Knatchbull, was printed in Notes and Queries as an illustra-

[1] III, 1162-6 (ix).

[2] Dartmouth MSS., i. 214. Ailesbury (i. 191) also describes the flight.

[3] Memoirs, i. 195.

tion of Macaulay's History.[1] When the news of the King's arrest reached London the council of peers who had assumed authority for the purpose of preserving order sent Ailesbury to Faversham to take charge of the King and to persuade him to return to London. He found him in a lawyer's house at Faversham, with a sort of guard of sailors round him, and some of the deputy lieutenants of the county acting as head gaolers.

The King was sitting in a great chair, his hat on, and his beard being much grown, and resembled the picture of his royal father at the pretended High Court of Justice. He rose up to meet me ; I bent my knee, not being able to kneel by reason of my jack-boots. He took me to the window with an air of displeasure, indeed quite contrary to what I expected, and said, 'You were all Kings when I left London.' I could not dissemble, but spoke my mind in these terms. 'Sir, I expected another sort of welcome after the great dangers I ran last night by repairing to you.' 'I know', said the King, 'you meant well as to your particular.' I replied, 'It is certainly so, and give me leave to tell your Majesty that by your going away without leaving a Commission of Regency, but for our care and vigilance the City of London might have been in ashes ; but the Lord Mayor and City respecting us, all was kept in a calm.' His countenance became more serene, and he then told me he was glad to see me, and sorry for the danger I had run, and then told me that the deputy lieutenants were so saucy that morning as to ask him reason why he had sent letters sealed to London. The room was filled with men, women and children, and talking as if they had been at a market, but I silenced them. . . . Dinner being ready, I asked him if he would be served with ceremony. He said, yes, if I could hold it out, for fatigued I was very much. . . . I observed his shoulders moved much : I asked him if he was indisposed. He told me, 'No ; but I hope you can give

[1] 3rd Ser., vi (1864), 1, 21, 41, 81 ; cf. v (1864), 391.

me a clean shirt'; for they had left him nothing but what was on his back when they seized him, and neither night-gown, cap, or slippers. About the middle of dinner, Mr. Tomlinson, the yeoman of the Robes, and others under him appeared.

I know not who were more rejoiced, the King or them, and the latter gushed out their tears for joy to see their King and master. He told me smilingly, 'I can now give *you* a shirt.' As soon as dinner was ended he ordered me to go and eat, and empty I was to the last degree, but my appetite was lost. During the short time I was at dinner, the King went into the hall to take leave of those faithful seamen that had lain there night and day. 'Honest friends,' said the King, 'You will not know me presently.' And indeed after shaving and dressing, and with a good periwig, he had not the same countenance. I asked those trusty sailors for what reason they had been so diligent. Their answer was, 'My lord, that no one should touch so much as a hair of the King's head'; and those wicked deputy lieutenants would have every one believe that the King was their prisoner.[1]

The King returned to London on Sunday, December 16, and the applause with which he was received in the streets appeared to some to prove that there was a reaction in his favour. In reality it seems to have been merely relief at the prospect of the cessation of the anarchy which had prevailed since his flight. Meanwhile the Prince of Orange, called to London by the Lords forming the provisional government, was approaching the capital. James was told that he must leave Whitehall, and elected to go to Rochester, because he had returned to his resolution of fleeing to France. On the morning of December 18, the King embarked in his barge at Whitehall stairs and set out for Gravesend. Ailesbury describes the voyage down the Thames.

[1] Memoirs, i. 209-10.

At eleven the King was in his barge with twelve oars, and others of eight attended, and on the Dutch side oars were provided for eighty of the foot guards, four in a boat, and for the officers. The shooting of the bridge was hideous, and to myself I offered up many prayers to God Almighty, and with this consolation only, that if I perished it was for a righteous cause, and not forsaking my king and sovereign in his bitter afflictions.[1]

That night the King slept at Gravesend. Next morning he went on to Rochester. James preferred to ride, and Ailesbury went in the King's coach. It was a melancholy journey, for the King's servants were well aware that their master's chance of retaining his throne had completely vanished, and were anxious about both his future and their own.

The King ordered me to go in his body coach, and being all alone and drowsy, I endeavoured to sleep, but was soon awakened by the King's coachman's bloody oaths ; and I told him that if he continued I would go in the second coach. He begged my pardon and promised fair, but very soon after I was awakened again out of a little slumber by that man's repeated oaths, and whipping his horses, crying out 'God damn Father Petres!' I said to him, 'Dixie, what harm hath he done you?' 'Damn him!' he replied again, 'but for him we had not been here.' He spoke so much truth that I had not the force to chide him, only praying him to forbear his oaths.[2]

James stayed at Rochester from December 20 to 22. After dinner on the twenty-second the King sent for Ailesbury and said to him :

'If I do not retire, I shall certainly be sent to the Tower, and no king ever went out of that place but to his grave. It is a cruel thing for a subject to be driven out of his native

[1] Ibid. pp. 218-9. [2] Ibid. pp. 219-20.

country,' (my case 10 years after) 'much more for a king to be driven out of his three kingdoms. I call God to witness I had no design of retiring. For your own sake I do not tell to what place I go, but you, more than another, may guess where. . . . I declare to you that I retire for the security of my person, and I shall always be in a readiness to return, when my subjects eyes may be opened. . . . And my Roman Catholic officers, etc., I have directed them to retire and live quietly.' After a small pause, he looking steadfastly on me, 'Can you advise me to stay?'

No doubt he had in mind my former persuasions when he retired some few days before, after my parting from him. I told him, 'Sir, this is a matter of the most nice nature, that I will not take on me to give you any advice, nor be so presumptuous.' After which I kissed his hand, and weeping, he was pleased to embrace me tenderly, as in French A Dieu, and he ordered me to let in the company, as at a couchee as usual.[1]

James's second flight took place on the night of December 22-23; he landed at Ambleteuse on Christmas morning. A French narrative[2] of his flight describes his landing. James had with him a French valet, and his son the Duke of Berwick. They had embarked on a little smack employed in fishing for mackerel. As the smack approached Ambleteuse a boat from a French frigate hailed it, and asked for news of the King of Great Britain, for it was known that James had fled from Rochester and he was expected all along the coast of France. There was only one man on the deck of the fishing smack, and he answered the question of the lieutenant in command of the French boat by saying, 'I am the King of England.'

[1] Ibid. pp. 224-5.

[2] Campana de Cavelli, ii. 400.

CHAPTER XIII

MACAULAY'S CHARACTER OF MARY

MACAULAY draws Mary's character very favourably and very fairly. He appreciated the difficulties she had to face when her husband and her father were the leaders of opposing parties, shows a keen insight into her actions and sentiments both as a sovereign and as a woman, and displays more sympathy towards her than for most of his characters.

The least satisfactory part of Macaulay's account of Mary is that which deals with her career before the Revolution. To begin with he is wrong about the motives which led Charles II to consent to her marriage. 'Charles sometimes from levity and indolence, suffered Danby to take steps which Lewis resented as mortal injuries. . . . The King was brought to consent to a marriage between the Lady Mary, eldest daughter and presumptive heiress of the Duke of York, and William of Orange, the deadly enemy of France and the hereditary champion of the Reformation.'[1]

On the contrary, the marriage was deliberately arranged by Charles for political purposes. 'I judge this marriage', he told the French ambassador,

> to be very advantageous to my interests. . . . It will put a stop to the suspicions cherished by my subjects that the connection I keep up with France is based on a change of religion. . . . Since the Duke of York declared himself a Catholic all England is alarmed and has come to apprehend that I

[1] I, 214 (ii).

have the same designs, too, and that all my measures were directed towards a change in the government and religion of the country. . . . I am assured that the marriage of the Prince of Orange and my niece will dissipate some of these suspicions, and will greatly serve to show that I have no design not in accordance with the laws of England and the religion therein established. This destroys the cabals which might be made, and puts my nephew in my interest. I thereby confound the hopes of those seeking a pretext for rising against me and trying to get the Prince of Orange on their side by making him conceive pretensions which he can only found now upon my friendship for him and his real attachment to my interests.[1]

Apart from a brief mention of Mary's kindness to Monmouth during his exile in Holland, Macaulay has no further occasion to mention her until 1687, when the growing discontent with the arbitrary policy of her father turned the eyes of most Englishmen towards her husband as their deliverer. Then a short account of the first ten years of her married life is given. William's marriage, Macaulay wrote,

had not at first promised much domestic happiness. His choice had been determined chiefly by political considerations: nor did it seem likely that any strong affection would grow up between a handsome girl of sixteen, well disposed indeed, and naturally intelligent, but ignorant and simple, and a bridegroom who, though he had not completed his twenty-eighth year, was in constitution older than her father, whose manner was chilling, and whose head was constantly occupied by public business or by field sports. For a time William was a negligent husband. He was indeed drawn away from his wife by other women, particularly by one of her ladies, Elizabeth Villiers, who, though destitute of personal attractions, and disfigured by a hideous squint, possessed talents which well fitted her to

[1] Campana de Cavelli, Les derniers Stuarts, i. 201. Cf. Burnet, i. 408-11.

partake his cares. He was indeed ashamed of his errors, and spared no pains to conceal them : but in spite of all his precautions, Mary well knew that he was not strictly faithful to her. . . . She, however, bore her injuries with a meekness and patience which deserved, and gradually obtained, William's esteem and gratitude. Yet there still remained one cause of estrangement.

This was that, in the event of Mary's becoming Queen of England, William would ' hold power only from her bounty and during her pleasure '. Through the agency of Gilbert Burnet a complete explanation was effected. When Mary understood what was amiss she told her husband that she had only recently learnt

' that there was such a difference between the laws of England and the laws of God. But I now promise you that you shall always bear rule ; and, in return, I ask only this, that, as I shall observe the precept which enjoins wives to obey their husbands, you will observe that which enjoins husbands to love their wives.' [1] Her generous affection completely gained the heart of William. From that time till the sad day when he was carried away in fits from her dying bed, there was entire friendship and confidence between them. Many of her letters to him are extant ; and they contain abundant evidence that this man, unamiable as he was in the eyes of the multitude, had succeeded in inspiring a beautiful and virtuous woman, born his superior, with a passion fond even to idolatry.[2]

Consequently in 1688, when William was preparing to intervene in England, he had no opposition to apprehend from his wife. ' Her understanding had been entirely subjugated by his ; and, what is more extraordinary, he had won her entire affection. . . . His empire over her heart was

[1] Macaulay has rendered his authority, Burnet (i. 693), extremely freely.

[2] II, 822-4, 830-1 (vii).

divided only with her God.' Furthermore, James was seeking to impose upon England a form of worship she regarded as sinful and idolatrous, while William was the champion of her beloved Protestantism. Therefore, to her his enterprise seemed ' not only just, but holy '.[1]

On her arrival in England she soon became very popular, and her affability to some extent compensated for William's unsociability.

> She was English by birth, and English also in her tastes and feelings. Her face was handsome, her port majestic, her temper sweet and lively, her manners affable and graceful. Her understanding, though very imperfectly cultivated, was quick. There was no want of feminine wit and shrewdness in her conversation; and her letters were so well expressed that they deserved to be well spelt. She took much pleasure in the lighter kinds of literature, and did something towards bringing books into fashion among ladies of quality. The stainless purity of her private life and the strict attention which she paid to her religious duties were the more respectable, because she was singularly free from censoriousness, and discouraged scandal as much as vice. . . . Mary had a way of interrupting tattle about elopements, duels, and playdebts, by asking the tattlers, very quietly yet significantly, whether they had ever read her favourite sermon, Doctor Tillotson's on Evil Speaking.[2]

It is clear that Macaulay drew from Burnet most of his materials for his account of the Queen. Burnet gives three

[1] III, 1054-6 (ix).

[2] III, 1356-8 (xi). Cf. Burnet, An Essay on the Memory of the Late Queen (1695). ' She thought it a cruel and barbarous thing, to be merry on other peoples cost; or, to make the misfortunes or follies of others the matter of their diversion. She scarce ever expressed a more entire satisfaction in any sermon that she had heard, than in our late Primates against *Evil Speaking*. When she thought some were guilty of it, she would ask them, if they had read that sermon. This was understood to be a reprimand, tho' in the softest manner.' Pp. 86-7.

distinct characters of Mary, all written at different times: his original narrative,[1] the versions in his History,[2] and his Essay on the Memory of the Late Queen. All are highly eulogistic, as the writer himself recognised: 'I am sensible I have not set faults or defects enough in opposition to all the Princess's virtues; but I protest I have taken all the pains I could to seek for them.'[3]

Burnet's description of her attainments and manner of living is based on personal knowledge. In his Essay he gives particulars, not found in the History, that relate mainly to the period after her accession. After stating that she gave 'the most of her hours to the study of the Scriptures, and of books relating to them,' he proceeds:

Next to the best subjects, she bestowed most of her time on books of history, chiefly of the later ages, particularly those of her own kingdoms, as being the most proper to give her useful instruction. Lively books, where wit and reason gave the mind a true entertainment, had much of her time. She was a good judge as well as a great lover of poetry: she loved it best when it dwelt on the best subjects. So tender she was of poetry, tho' much more of vertue, that she had a particular concern in the defilement or rather the prostitution of the muses among us. She made some steps to the understanding philosophy and mathematicks, but she stopp'd soon; only she went far in natural history and perspective, as she was very exact in geography. She thought sublime things were too high flights for the sex; which she oft talked of, with a liberty, that was very lively: but she might well be familiar with it, after she had given so effectual a demonstration of the improvements it was capable of. Upon the whole matter, she studied and read

[1] Supplement, ed. Foxcroft, pp. 194-6. This section was written in 1686-7 (p. 190, n. 1).

[2] i. 690; ii. 133-4, 137-8. Revised 1702-4.

[3] Supplement, p. 195.

more than could be imagined, by any, who had not known, how many of her hours were spent in her closet.[1]

When her eyes were endangered by reading too much, she found out the amusement of work: and in all those hours that were not given to better imployments, she wrought with her own hands; and that sometimes with so constant a diligence, as if she had been to earn her bread by it. It was a new thing, and looked like a sight, to see a queen work so many hours a day. . . . Her example soon wrought on, not only those that belonged to her, but the whole town to follow it: so that it was become as much the fashion to work, as it had been formerly to be idle. In this, which seemed a nothing, and was turned by some to be the subject of railery, a greater step was made, than perhaps every one was aware of, to the bettering of the age. While she diverted her self thus with work, she took care to give an entertainment to her own mind, as well as to those who were admitted to the honour of working with her: one was appointed to read to the rest, the choice was suited to the time of the day, and to the employment: some book or poem that was lively, as well as instructive. Few of her sex, not to say of her rank, gave ever less time to dressing, or seemed less curious about it.[2]

Other clerical writers also throw light on Mary's character. Lake gives a few details of her grief at leaving England on her marriage,[3] and her first chaplain in Holland, Hooper, has stated that 'in the time he attended her, which was about a year and a half, he never saw her do, nor heard her say a thing, that he could have wished she had

[1] Essay, pp. 73, 79-81. In her journal for 1691 Mary says, 'I got a book of the Bishop of Sarum which I pleased my self much with.' She adds, 'I continued constant in reading the Scripture and for other matters set my self to the reading our English history with attention.' Memoirs of Mary, Queen of England, ed. R. Doebner (1886), pp. 43-4.

[2] Burnet, Essay, pp. 82-5.

[3] Diary of Dr. Edward Lake, printed in Camden Miscellany, vol. i (1847).

not.'[1] The few letters of Hooper's successor, Ken, contain no information of any value about her,[2] but there is other evidence that he was 'horribly unsatisfied with the Prince, and thinks that he is not kind to his wife.'[3] Covel's opinion was the same as Ken's, and he was dismissed because he informed James's ambassador at The Hague of William's infidelity. He also testifies to Mary's 'being a very duty-full daughter (as she may be in time as kind a mother) of our Church of England'.[4] The next chaplain was Stanley, who retained his position until the Revolution. Two of his letters to Sancroft are printed,[5] and seven others to Compton are in the Bodleian Library.[6] All praise the Princess highly: 'one of the best temper'd persons in the world and everyone must needs be happy in serving her.'[7]

Macaulay had at his disposal the printed evidence mentioned, except Ken's letters, but very few of Mary's own letters before the Revolution. A considerable number of these letters have since been found, and, with other miscellaneous historical materials, enable the modern biographer to amplify and correct the narrative of the earlier historian.

A point to be noticed is that Macaulay seems to have deliberately understated William's harshness to Mary. As late as 1685 her chaplain wrote that 'it is too true the Princess's heart is ready to break; and yet she . . . counterfeits the greatest joy. . . . The Prince hath infallibly made

[1] App. i to A. H. Trevor's William III, vol. ii (1836).

[2] E. H. Plumptre, Life of Thomas Ken (1888), i, chap. x.

[3] Henry Sidney, Diary of the Times of Charles II, ed. R. W. Blencowe (1843), i. 19.

[4] Covel to Compton, Aug. 14-24, 1683. Bodleian Library, MS. Rawl. C. 983, fol. 97. Other correspondence of Covel's is in the British Museum.

[5] John Gutch, Collectanea Curiosa (1781), i. 302-8.

[6] MS. Rawl. C. 983, fols. 99-111.

[7] Ibid. fol. 107.

her his absolute slave.'[1] Macaulay implies too that after about 1687 Elizabeth Villiers ceased to have more intimate relations with William than those of intellectual companionship.[2] It is difficult to be positive on such a question, but it is reasonably certain that her husband's infidelity was a cross Mary bore until her death. One of her last acts was to ask the Archbishop of Canterbury 'to look carefully for a small scrutoir that she made use of, and to deliver it to the King.'[3] There is little doubt that the scrutoire contained 'a strong but decent admonition to the King, for some irregularity in his conduct,'[4] and that his resolution, recorded by Burnet, 'of breaking off all bad practices whatsoever,'[5] was the result of remorse. Macaulay ignores these incidents, possibly because they conflicted with his opinion that Mary's self-abnegation 'completely gained the heart of William'. Moreover no new evidence has been discovered to confirm Burnet's account of his intervention which led Mary to declare that, in the event of her becoming Queen of England, William should direct the government.[6] Stanley, in an unpublished letter to Compton, states that Mary was 'pleased also to send for me to inform her of the affairs of England as to its constitution and government, both in Church and State, which is very fit for her to know, and yet which is but little known here.'[7] It

[1] Diary and Correspondence of Henry, Earl of Clarendon, ed. S. W. Singer (1828), i. 165.

[2] V, 2414 (xx); VI, 2962 (xxv).

[3] Burnet, ii. 137-8.

[4] Ibid. Hardwicke's note.

[5] Supplement to Burnet's Own Time, p. 406. Cf. Own Time, ii. 138: William 'entered upon solemn and serious resolutions of becoming, in all things, an exact and an exemplary Christian'. Mary refers to Elizabeth Villiers in her meditation for 1691. Doebner, pp. 42-3.

[6] Clarke and Foxcroft, Burnet, pp. 217-8.

[7] Mar. 21-31, 1687. MS. Rawl. C. 983, fol. 111.

is therefore probable that Burnet exaggerated the effect of his interference, and that Macaulay followed him too implicitly.

On the other hand it is curious that Macaulay neglects the epistolary controversy between James and his daughter in 1687, for although the letters were not published until 1880, Burnet gives a full summary of them.[1] James explained his reasons for becoming a Catholic with a view to converting Mary, and sent her a book to study. She replied in a couple of letters which show a very sound knowledge of the points at issue and furnish a convincing proof of her firm attachment to the Protestant faith. She criticises the book with great keenness, and the vigour and clearness of her arguments contrast very remarkably with those of her father, who seems to have thought her incurable. The interest of this little controversy lies in the light it throws on the characters of the two disputants.

A more important matter Macaulay had perforce to leave untouched, through lack of material, was the gradual development and elevation of Mary's character. In the possession of the Earl Bathurst at Cirencester Park are nearly a hundred letters of Mary's, a few of which were written to Lady Apsley but most to her daughter Frances, who married Sir Benjamin Bathurst. About a third were written before Mary's marriage and all before the Revolution.[2] The Princess styled herself Mary Clorine and pretended to be the wife of her friend Aurelia, as Frances Apsley was called— and the pretence was kept up after she

[1] Lettres et mémoires de Marie, Reine d'Angleterre, ed. Countess Bentinck (1880). Cf. Burnet, Own Time, i. 720-6; Supplement, pp. 266-7. Stanley also saw the correspondence. Gutch, op. cit. i. 302-6.

[2] A. B. Bathurst published a few of these letters in the History of the Apsley and Bathurst Families (1903); a larger number in the Quarterly Review, Jan. 1911, and all of them in Letters of Two Queens (*ca.* 1924).

had a real husband. Mary writes about plays and scandal, and uses the endearing and coarse language which characterised the drama of the day. Some of her letters seem to indicate that she was a jolly, rather vulgar-minded girl: she refers to her pregnancy in 1678 in terms as immodest as some of the repartees attributed to Nell Gwyn. Others reveal that intense longing for sympathy and love which is so marked a feature of her letters to William during his absence in Ireland in 1690. But it is clear that Mary soon came to love her husband in spite of his unkindness to her. A letter dated March 3, 1678, is conclusive on this point:

> I supose you know the Prince is gone to the army but I am sure you can geuse at the troble I am in I am sure I coud never have thought it half so much I thought coming out of my own contry parting with my friands and relations the greatest that ever coud as long as thay lived hapen to me but I am to be mistaken that now I find till this time I never knew sorow for what can be more cruall in the world then parting with what on loves and nott ondly comon parting but parting so as may be never to meet again to be perpetually in fear for God knows when I may see him or wethere he is nott now at this instant in a batell I recon him now never in safety ever in danger oh miserable live that I lead now.[1]

Of even greater interest are Mary's meditations and other writings printed in Lettres et mémoires de Marie, edited by the Countess Bentinck, and Memoirs of Queen Mary, edited by R. Doebner. In the former are an account of the events of the year 1688 and some short pieces for 1690 and 1691, all written in French; in the latter are reflections in English for 1689-1693, which seem to have been compiled at the end of each year from fuller diaries which Mary pro-

[1] Letters of Two Queens, pp. 88-9.

bably destroyed just before her death.[1] These narratives enable a modern writer to set forth her ideas and feelings much more plainly than was possible before their appearance.

Mary's attitude towards the Revolution was clear and consistent. She believed from the first that James's son, born on June 10, 1688, was a supposititious infant. This belief was encouraged by the letters her sister Anne wrote to her before and after the birth of the child, and was strengthened by the rumours which reached her from England. Anne told Mary on March 3, 1688, that because the Queen was so positive she would give birth to a son and because the principles of the Romanists were such that they would stick at nothing, however wicked, there was 'some cause to fear there may be foul play intended'. A week later she declared that no one would believe it really to be the Queen's child, 'except it prove a daughter.' Eight days after the birth she was still doubtful: 'It may be it is our brother, but God only knows . . . 'Tis possible it may be her child; but where one believes it, a thousand do not.'[2]

It is not surprising, therefore, that Mary imagined that she was being robbed of her right to the English crown by an imposture. She tells us in her narrative she was by no means anxious for the crown:

but whilst I was thus indifferent for myself, I found I could not long remain so, since the interest of the Protestant religion depends on it, so that whoever wishes it well (as it is the duty of every member of it to do) ought necessarily to be alarmed at the thought of a Popish successor. That drew

[1] Burnet, ii. 136. 'The journals I had kept, I put in a bag and tyed by my side resolving if anything happend to have them ready to burn,' wrote Mary in 1691. Doebner, p. 39.

[2] Dalrymple, Memoirs, ii, App., pt. i. 300, 301, 303; Bentinck, pp. 32, 34, 42-3.

me then from the sweet and satisfactory calmness I was enjoying and made me see how I was obliged to wish I could succeed to the crown. Apart from the interest of the Church, the love I have for the Prince influences me to wish him all he deserves. And whilst I regret that I have only three crowns to bring him, it is not my love which blinds me : no, I can see his faults, but I say that because I also recognise his virtues.[1]

Mary threw herself heart and soul into William's design, and had no doubt either of its justice or its necessity. In her narrative she describes her last interview with William before he set sail.

The 25th [of October] the Prince . . . told me again that in case it was God's will that I should never see him any more (words which cut me to the heart, and gave me such a shiver that at the hour at which I write it has scarcely passed off)—if that happened, he said, you must marry again. If the first word hurt me so cruelly, the latter surprised and gripped me so strongly and put me into such a state that I felt as if my heart had burst. There is no need, he continued, for me to tell you it must not be a papist. He could not pronounce these words without shedding tears, and during the whole interview he displayed as much tenderness for me as I could desire, so that I shall never forget it all my life. But I was so astounded by this suggestion that I could not reply for a long time. He protested that the anxiety he had for the religion was the sole cause of his speaking thus. I do not remember at all what I said. My agitation made me reply in a confused way, but I assured him that I had never loved anyone but him, and could never love another. In addition, having been married for so many years without its being God's will to bless me with a child, I believe that was enough to prevent my thinking of what he had suggested. I told him I hoped God would not suffer me to survive him ; if however I did survive him,

[1] Bentinck, pp. 62-3.

since it had not pleased God to give me a son by him, I should not wish to have one by an angel.[1]

Despite Mary's submission and obedience to all his wishes William seems to have purposely delayed her arrival in England, lest she should in one way or another be set above him. William landed November 5 but did not send for Mary till February 1. According to Burnet, Danby sent a messenger to the Princess, saying

> he did not doubt but he should be able to carry it for setting her alone on the throne [i.e. without William]. She made him a very sharp answer: she said, she was the Prince's wife, and would never be other than what she should be in conjunction with him and under him; and that she would take it extremely unkindly, if any, under a pretence of their care of her, would set up a divided interest between her and the Prince. And, not content with this, she sent both Lord Danby's letter and her answer to the Prince.[2]

In the original draft of his History Burnet calls this a piece of secret history of which he had only recently learnt, and did not know at the time.[3] Macaulay[4] accepts the story, but there is no reference to it in Mary's own narrative and the letters have never come to light. Burnet is the only authority for the story, and it is not confirmed or probable in itself. Ranke justly doubts it.[5] On the other hand the knowledge of her resolution to surrender her power to her husband if she became queen had been the decisive argument for offering the crown to William. 'Those to whom I gave the account of that matter were indeed amazed at it,' says Burnet, 'and concluded, that the Princess was either

[1] Ibid. pp. 80-1.
[2] Own Time, i. 819.
[3] Supplement, p. 310.
[4] III, 1290-2 (x).
[5] iv. 517, n. 1.

a very good or a very weak woman. An indifferency for power and rule seemed so extraordinary a thing, that it was thought a certain character of an excess of goodness or simplicity.' [1]

Mary arrived at Whitehall on February 12. She thus describes her feelings on her return :

When I saw England, my native country, which long absence had made me a stranger to, I felt a secret joy, which doubtless proceeded from a naturall simpathy, but that was soon checked with the consideration of my fathers misfortunes which came immediatly into my mind. The joy of seeing the Prince again, strove against that melancolly, and the thoughts that I should my husband see owned as the deliverer of my country, made me vain ; but alas, poor mortal! thought I then, from who has he deliverd it but from thy father. . . . I had a joy greater then can be expresd to come to the Prince, but I found him in a very ill condition as to his health, he had a violent cough upon him and was grown extreamly lean. He could not restrain as soon as we were alone we both shed tears of joy to meet, and of sorrow for meeting in England, both wishing it might have been in Holland, both bewailing the loss of the liberty we had left behind and were sensible we should never enjoy here ; and in that moment we found a beginning of the constraint we were to endure here after, for we durst not let owr selves go on with those reflections, but dryed up owr tears lest it should be perceived when we went out. And here I was guilty of a great sin, I let my self go on too much and the devil immediatly toock his advantage, the world filled my mind and left but litle room for good thoughts. The next day after I came, we were proclaimed, and the goverment put wholy in the Princes hand. This pleased me extreamly, but many would not believe it, so that I was fain to force my self to more mirth then became me at that time, and was by many interpreted as ill nature,

[1] Own Time, i. 821.

pride, and the great delight I had to be a queen. But alas, they did litle know me, who thought me guilty of that; I had been only for a regency, and wisht for nothing else; I had never[1] dreaded being queen, liking my condition much better (and indeed I was not deceived); but the good of the public was to be preferd and I protest, God knows my heart, that what I say is true, that I have had more trouble to b[r]ing my self to bear this so envyed estate then I should have had to have been reduced to the lowest condition in the world.[2]

The comments of Evelyn, unaware of the motives which governed Mary, show that contemporary observers thought that

the Princess, would have showed some (seeming) reluctance at least, of assuming her father's crown, and made some apology, testifying her regret that he should by his mismanagement necessitate the nation to so extraordinary a proceeding, which would have showed very handsomely to the world, and according to the character given of her piety; . . . but nothing of all this appeared; she came into Whitehall laughing and jolly, as to a wedding, so as to seem quite transported. She rose early the next morning, and in her undress, as it was reported, before her women were up, went about from room to room to see the convenience of Whitehall; lay in the same bed and apartment where the late Queen lay, and within a night or two sat down to play at basset, as the Queen her predecessor used to do. She smiled upon and talked to everybody, so that no change seemed to have taken place at court since her last going away, save that infinite crowds of people thronged to see her, and that she went to our prayers. This carriage was censured by many.[3]

[1] *Sic* in Doebner, but probably ' ever ' is correct.

[2] Doebner, pp. 10-11.

[3] Diary, Feb. 21, 1689.

During 1689 William remained in England, but every succeeding year his absences compelled Mary to take a prominent, though reluctant, part in the administration. She thus explained her attitude :

And my opinion having ever been that women should not medle in government, I have never given my self to be inquisitive into those kind of matters. I have ever used my self not to trouble the King about bussiness, since I was married to him ; for I saw him so full of it that I thought, and he has told me so himself, that when he could get from it, he was glad to come to me and have his thoughts diverted by other discourse ; and I found this so reasonnable, and seing it pleased him, I who desired nothing else, have continued still to live so with him ; which has made me very ignorant in all kind of bussiness, and I have this notion fully fixt in my mind that, all wisedom being the gift of God, he does impart it where he sees it necessary, and since it has pleased him to take all of my hands by giving me such a husband, I thinck I ought only to make it my bussiness to serve God, and do all the good I can in the world. And tho' there does not want those that would make me medle, in hopes to do mischief that way, and some times tell me, that I may come to govern alone, yet I am so persuaded, that if ever it pleased God to send that great misfortune, he would then time enough direct me how to behave my self.[1]

At the beginning of 1690 William made up his mind to conduct the war in Ireland in person and asked Mary what form of arrangement she would prefer. Finding that her mind was very open, he

told me, he would put it to my choice, whether in his absence all should be governd in my name or if it should be left to the Privy Council with order to them to acquaint me with all things. I only desired he would take care I should not make a foolish figure in the world. I told him that the

[1] Doebner, pp. 22-3.

thing in effect was the same, for I being wholy a stranger to bussiness, it must be the Privy Council must do all things. I did not say this as mistrusting him in the matter (for I really left the thing to him and would make no choice), but because I was in real fear of it; for I am sensible, a person in my station can not make an indifferent one, for if one does not make a very good, I am sure one must make a very bad figure.[1]

On June 4, 1690, William set out for Ireland, leaving nine Privy Councillors to act as the Queen's advisers in all affairs of state. She describes her position and the character of her councillors with great clearness and good sense.

> I found my self now at White Hall as in a new world, deprived of all that was dear to me in the person of my husband, left among those that were perfect strangers to me; my sister of a humour so reserved, I could have litle comfort from her; the great Council of a strange composition, the Cabinet Council not much better.

The Marquis of Caermarthen (the former Earl of Danby), the Lord President, had been particularly recommended by the King, and he was one to whom she must 'ever own great obligations, yet of a temper I can never like'. William told her Dorset was to be trusted, although vain, but she found him weak and obstinate, and a vehement partisan. Devonshire was too lazy to trouble about business, and Pembroke was as mad as most of his family, though very good-natured, and honourable, if unstable. Nottingham, the Secretary of State, was suspected by most as disaffected to the government, and generally distrusted, though all business went through his office. The King believed him an honest man, but too violent a Tory. Lord Monmouth

[1] Ibid. p. 22. Cf. Burnet, ii. 46-7, for William's anxiety for Mary during his absence.

was mad, and governed by his wife, who was madder. Marlborough could never deserve either trust or esteem. Sir John Lowther, honest but weak, was chief of the Treasury, and Russell, most recommended for sincerity, had his faults.

This was the Council I was to follow in all things. The Treasury was in a bad condition, there was no money, the fleet under the command of Lord Torrington, who lay drincking and treating his friends, till the French came upon the coast and had like to have surprised him. In this condition I was left with this powerfull fleet on the coast, many ennemies and discontented persons in the kingdom, and not above 5 or 6000 men to defend it; not secure of these at home, great reasons to apprehend dangers from abroad: so I believe never any person was left in greater streights of all kinds.[1]

Mary's letters to William during the three months' campaign in Ireland are printed at length in Dalrymple,[2] and so are frequently quoted by Macaulay. For one moment, namely during July 1690, after the battle of Beachy Head and while Tourville and the French fleet had the command of the Channel, Mary had to meet a double danger. There was the possibility of a French landing and the possibility of a Jacobite rising. Mary met both with equal intrepidity and calmness.

I never wanted those who put me perpetually in fear, Lord President himself once asking me the question the King had put to me before he went, what I would do in case of any rising or disturbance in the City, which they both thought likely to happen, I gave them both the same answer, which was that I could not tell how much frightened I might be, but I would promise not to be governd by my own or others fears, but follow the advise of those I believed

[1] Doebner, pp. 29-31.

[2] Memoirs, ii, App., bk. v.

had most courage and judgment. And indeed that was my private resolution, and was resolved in my self, let what would happen, I would never go from White Hall.[1]

Her attitude certainly gave confidence both to her council and to the people, and increased her popularity. 'I had no small addition to my vanity in the applause I had from most,' but, she adds, she was not puffed up by it. 'The only thing that pleased me was that my husband was satisfied and told me he was very much pleased with my behaviour.'[2]

Although during William's absences from England in 1690 and the following summers Mary proved herself equal to the conduct of affairs of state, she was far less concerned with them than with ecclesiastical questions. Her absorption in the latter was due to her extremely devotional nature and to her very definite views on moral and religious subjects. She assured Sancroft in 1687 that she took more interest in the affairs of the Church of England than in herself.[3] As Burnet says, 'She had a generous and a sublime idea of the Christian religion, and a particular affection to the Church of England: but an affection that was neither blind nor partial.'[4] Her Memoirs show that she thought that England, and the English court in particular, needed a moral reformation as well as a political revolution. 'The first thing that surprised me at my coming over', she wrote in 1689, 'was to see so litle devotion in a people so lately in such eminent danger.'[5]

In 1693 she observed on all sides 'so universal a corruption . . . that we seem only prepard for vengeance.'[6]

In the first place, the Queen was shocked by the for-

[1] Doebner, p. 31. [2] Ibid. p. 33.
[3] Oct. 1, 1687. N. S. Gutch, op. cit. i. 299.
[4] Essay, p. 74. [5] Doebner, p. 11.
[6] Ibid. p. 59.

mality and lack of devotion in all the public religious functions at court.

I did resolve to do what I could towards macking devotion loockt on as it ought, and would fain have it more serious. The first step I got made towards it was having of singing the prayers in the chapel, but I could not make people mind the Sunday more; that was counted an idle day and indeed it was made so to me by the company which came continually on those days to me.[1]

One of my grievances was the pomp and stir was observed at receiving the Sacrament. There was an old custom left since the time of P[o]pery, that the kings should receive almost alone; this had been alwais observed, this I could not resolve to do, but told the Bishop of London, who I found unreasonable upon that, and would keep up the foolery, but at last I got the better, and the King being of my mind, we resolved to make it a matter of as litle state as possible, yet there is to much left.[2]

At Christmas I had the satisfaction to receive the Sacrament at White Hall with the King and as many Lords and others as would. For I had with much ado gaind that point to have others receive with us at all times, and not make it no communion by the foolish formality that had been observed before.[3]

Another innovation which pleased her 'and most sober people' was afternoon sermons at Whitehall. She used to write down the text so that she could remember and examine herself upon it.[4]

In April 1691, while William was in England for about three weeks before returning to the campaign in Flanders, Mary notes:

The only thing of bussiness I concerned my self in, was the filling the bishoppricks which was now done; and I am

[1] Ibid. p. 12.
[2] Ibid. p. 13.
[3] Ibid. p. 19.
[4] Ibid. p. 16.

sure the King made it a point of conscience to do it well, which I thinck he has.[1]

Burnet has recorded a curious anecdote about her when he waited on her after his appointment as Bishop of Salisbury.

> She told me she hoped I would set a pattern to others, and would put in practice those notions with which I had taken the liberty sometimes to entertain her. She also recommended to me the making my wife an example to other clergymen's wives, both in the simplicity and plainness of her clothes and in the humility of her deportment.[2]

The same writer asserts that William left church matters wholly in her hands.

> She declared openly against the preferring of those who put in for themselves ; and took care to inform herself particularly of the merits of such of the clergy as were not so much as known at court, nor using any methods to get themselves recommended . . . She consulted chiefly with the Archbishop of Canterbury, whom she favoured and supported in a most particular manner.[3]

When Tillotson died Mary wished Stillingfleet to be his successor, but 'the Whigs did generally apprehend, that both his notions and his temper were too high', so Tenison, a strong Whig and latitudinarian, was nominated.[4]

[1] Ibid. p. 37.

[2] Supplement, pp. 326-7, 497-8.

[3] Own Time, ii. 117. Cf. p. 119 for an instance of Mary's refusing to allow a bad appointment to an Irish bishopric ; also Essay, pp. 103-4 : 'The raising the reputation and authority of the clergy, as the chief instrument for advancing religion was that to which she intended to apply her utmost diligence. She knew that the only true way to compass this, was to engage them to be exemplary in their lives, and eminent in their labours : to watch over their flocks, and to edifie them by good preaching and diligent catechising. She was resolved to have the whole nation understand, that by these ways, and by these only, divines were to be recommended to favour and preferment.'

[4] Own Time, ii. 136 ; Macaulay, V, 2464 (xx).

The instances mentioned above seem to prove that Mary exercised a steady influence upon ecclesiastical affairs in what may be called a Low Church direction, and that rather more importance should be assigned to this personal factor in the histories of the period.

Mary's purity and gentleness won her the affection of her subjects. Macaulay truly states that in the Jacobite lampoons of the day she was not often mentioned with severity. She herself said that God knew her weakness, and that, as she was not able to bear some imputations, He did not try her beyond her strength.[1] Occasionally, however, her attitude towards her father was the subject of spiteful prose or verse. An example is a satire comparing William and Mary to Tarquin and Tullia. Tullia, having instigated her husband Tarquinius to kill her father Servius Tullius, king of the Romans, in order to obtain his throne, caused her chariot to be driven over his body. This satire, entitled Tarquin and Tullia, was attributed to Dryden,[2] but was written in reality by Arthur Mainwaring.[3] The poem, after praising the virtuous Tullius at great length, adds :

This king removed, the assembled states thought fit,
That Tarquin in the vacant throne should sit ;
Voted him regent in their senate-house,
And with an empty name endowed his spouse.
The elder Tullia, who, some authors feign,
Drove o'er her father's corse a rumbling wain :

[1] III, 1358 (xi).

[2] In Sir W. Scott's edition of Dryden's Works, xv. 257-62. The parallel appears to have been in part suggested by an incident. A newsletter dated Sept. 2, 1690, says : 'Yesterday the Queen dined at Kensington. Her coach and horses stood in the square at Whitehall and upon a sudden fright the horses rushed upon the late King's effigy and defaced it. The harness of the horses was so entangled about the statue that one of them was killed by struggling.' Le Fleming MSS., p. 288.

[3] See his Life (1725), pp. 11-12.

But she, more guilty, numerous wains did drive,
To crush her father and her king alive;
And in remembrance of his hastened fall,
Resolved to institute a weekly ball.
The jolly glutton grew in bulk and chin,
Feasted on rapine and enjoyed her sin;
With luxury she did weak reason force,
Debauched good-nature, and cram'd down remorse;
Yet when she drank cold tea in liberal sups,
The sobbing dame was maudling in her cups.
But Brutal Tarquin never did relent,
Too hard to melt, too wicked to repent;
Cruel in deeds, more merciless in will,
And blest with natural delight in ill.[1]

More honourable Jacobites judged Mary with greater fairness. Ailesbury furnishes a conspicuous example of her generosity to him, a political opponent. When he was bailed he said he sent his wife to the Countess of Derby to beg her to thank Mary and to express his regrets that he could not pay his duty in person. The Queen answered: 'Tell my Lady of Ailesbury that I love to do good to all persons as far as I can, but more especially to her husband and his family, whom I knew so well in my youngest years.' The Queen sent for him and asked him to play at basset (though he excused himself), and enquired about his family. Her generosity gained her a strenuous defender. On one occasion after her death he had an argument with Nottingham about her character. When the former Tory minister suggested she had behaved badly towards her father, Ailesbury 'warmly replied, "My Lord, I esteemed her as a princess that had no fault. . . . She as a good wife (whether she had suitable returns I question much) submitted patiently, but had her anxieties of mind continually on her . . .

[1] Macaulay seems to refer to a similar satire (III, 1418 [xi]).

God knows what she suffered inwardly and to a high degree." '[1]

Other contemporaries also bear witness to the Queen's regard for her father. Burnet tells us that he noticed in Mary 'a great tenderness' for her father's person—that is, a fear lest he should be wounded or killed—and that his escape safe and sound in the battle of the Boyne made her joy over that victory complete. King William cautioned the Duke of Leeds to say nothing before the Queen 'that looked like disrespect to her father', for that she never forgave anybody. The Marquis of Halifax, he said, 'had lost all manner of credit with her, for some unseasonable jests he had made upon the subject.' The Earl of Nottingham, who was much in the Queen's confidence, went so far as to assert that if Mary had survived her husband she would certainly have done her utmost to restore James to his throne, though under restrictions.[2] One may doubt the truth of Nottingham's prediction, but the fact that it could be made is significant. Mary's Memoirs reveal the tenderness for her father's person of which Burnet speaks, and they also show how difficult James made it for that feeling to survive.

When William set out for Ireland in 1690 Mary was greatly perturbed, not only on her husband's account, but also on her father's. First for the sake of William:

> The concern for his dear person who was so ill in health when he went from hence, the toil and fatigue he was like to endure, the ill air of the country he was going [to], his humour when I knew he would expose himself to all dangers, then again the cruell thought that my husband and my father would fight in person against each other, and if either should have perished in the action, how terrible it

[1] Memoirs, i. 264-5, 298.

[2] Own Time, ii. 47, 55, 134 n.

must have been to me: these were the cruel thoughts I had upon his going, which none can judge of, that have not felt the like.

The same fears beset her in 1692 when James projected landing in England with a French army.

This was the only thing I dreaded to thinck my father and husband might once more meet in the field; and the fears that my father might fall by our arms, or either of them fall where t'other was present, was to me the dreadfullest prospect in the world.[1]

The encounter Mary had feared did not happen, because the victory of La Hogue put an end to the intended invasion, but four months later the discovery of the plot of Grandval, an agent employed by the French government to assassinate William, reduced her to the deepest dejection, and destroyed any affection she had left for her father.

The 10th of August I received Grandvals tryall, in which I saw that which must afflict me while I live, that he who I dare no more name father was consenting to the barbarous murder of my husband. T'is impossible for me to express what I then felt. I was ashamed to loock any body in the face. I fancied I should be pointed at as the daughter of one who was capable of such things, and the people would believe I might by nature have as ill inclinations. I lamented his sin and his shame; I feard it might lessen my husbands kindness to me. It made such impressions upon me that I was uncapable of comfort. As for the printing of the tryal, I could not tell what I should do. The Lords all thought it necessary. I saw it was so, I knew it would be printed beyond sea, but I thought it was a hard thing on one hand for me to publish my own shame, and it might loock as ill on the other to conceal the mercys of God in saving my husband. So I kept the paper by me till the French one

[1] Doebner, pp. 29, 48.

came over printed, of which blame was laid upon Ld. Nottingham, who was not in fault; and I had the trouble of seeing it come out, and the fears of displeasing my husband. But he was so kind as not to take it ill of me or not to love me less for that my great and endless misfortune.[1]

There is no reason why Mary should have greatly repented her conduct to her father, granting her facts. He had endeavoured to overthrow a true religion in order to set up a false one, had palmed off a spurious heir upon the nation in order to defraud her of her rights, and had concerted the murder of her husband. To lose his throne was not too severe a penalty: the awkward thing was that she had taken it.

Nevertheless, Mary came to regard her quarrel with her sister Anne as a judgement on her for her treatment of her father. Macaulay treats their quarrel at considerable length, and allowing for a certain prejudice against Anne, his account is in the main correct.[2] But the authorities at his disposal were rather insufficient. Burnet deals somewhat briefly with the subject. He mentions it unwillingly, 'because it cannot be told without some reflections on the memory of the queen whom I always honoured, beyond all the persons I had ever known.' He thinks that after the breach in 1692 the Queen showed too much resentment. 'The matter went so far that the Queen ordered, that no public honours should be shewed the Princess besides many other lesser matters, which I unwillingly reflect on, because I was much troubled to see the Queen carry such a matter so far.'

Burnet tells us that the alienation of the two sisters began in the winter of 1689. The Princess 'thought herself too much neglected by the King', particularly because she was

[1] Ibid. pp. 54-5.

[2] IV, 1816-20 (xv); V, 2124-30 (xviii).

given no settled income. Consequently, 'thinking she was to be kept in a necessitous dependance on the court,' she instigated her friends to make a motion in Parliament that a suitable income should be granted her. The Queen resented her appealing to Parliament 'before she had tried, in a private way, what the King intended to assign her'.[1] The story she tells in her Memoirs confirms Burnet's narrative.

I had a very sensible affliction also at this time, which was to see how my sister was making parties to get a revenue setled, and said nothing of it to me. The King did not thinck fit I should say any thing of it to her, and indeed she avoided carefully ever since I came from Hamptoncourt all occasions of being alone with me. This bussiness went on till there were great heats in the House of Commons about it, at last in a committee it was carried against her; upon which the King the next morning sent her a message by the Ld. Shrewsbury to desire that she would put an end to all this, and that he would for this year give her 50,000 p. and when his own revenue was setled would take care that sum should be setled upon her, and being sensible she must be in debts, he offerd to pay her debts besides. This the Ld. Shrewsbury first proposed to the Lord Marlborough, who beggd he would not own he found him, his wife would by no means hear of it, but was like a mad woman and said the Princess would retire if her friends would not assist her; and when he spoke to my sister her self, the answer was, she had met with so litle encouragment from the King, that she could expect no kindness from him, and therefore would stick to her friends. When I heard this I thought it no longer time to be silent, but upon her coming to me next night I spoke to her. She could tell me no one thing in which the King had not been kind to her, and would not own her self in the wrong for not speacking to either of us, so that I found as I told her she had shewd as much want of kindness to me as respect to the King and I

[1] Own Time, ii. 90-1.

both. Upon this we parted ill friends, and she will make no advance to me not having once been at Kinsington since ; so I came hither the day before Christmas Eve, and t'is now the last day of the old year. But the King thought it an ungenerous thing to fall out with a woman, and therefore went to her and told her so, upon which she said, he should find by her behaviour, she would never give him cause. But neither upon this did she say anything to me.[1]

Anne obtained from Parliament a grant of £50,000 a year, but she was not content, and the alienation of the sisters continued. Mary attributed this to Lady Marlborough. 'Had there been none else concerned, I should not have scrupeld speacking to her [Anne] of it ; but I saw plainly she was so absolutly governd by Lady Marlborough that it was to no purpose.' Mary suggests a new reason for the continuance of the breach—that the High Church party, dissatisfied with the ecclesiastical policy of the King and Queen, endeavoured to foment it for party reasons, regarding Anne as holding sounder Church principles than Mary. 'And she herself affected to find fault with every thing [that] was done, especially to laugh at afternoon sermons, and doing in litle things contrary to what I did.'[2]

There is a third reason, of which Macaulay says much and Burnet scarcely a line : the intrigues of the Earl of Marlborough with the agents of James II. The Earl was in communication with one of them in 1691.[3] Princess Anne, a mere tool in the hands of Marlborough and his wife, was induced in December 1691 to write 'a most penitential and dutyfull letter' to her father.[4] How far Marlborough

[1] Doebner, pp. 17-18. [2] Ibid. p. 24.

[3] Macaulay, V, 2117-24 (xviii) ; Life of James the Second, ii. 446-9.

[4] Life of James, ii. 477 ; Original Papers Containing the Secret History of Great Britain [1660-1714], ed. James Macpherson (2 vols. ; 1775), i. 241; Klopp, vi. 26.

meant to carry the negotiation is uncertain. William discovered that he was plotting and on January 10, 1692, dismissed him from all his offices. Anne was very naturally required by Mary to dismiss Lady Marlborough as well, and the Princess, declining to part with her favourite, left Whitehall and took up her residence at Sion House.

Mary gives an account of Anne's refusing to dismiss Lady Marlborough :

> When Lord Marlborough was put out, and she was told in all the gentle and kind wais that could be thought on, that she must part with his lady, she retired to Sion and shewed great passion and kindness for her, and so much indifference and coldness to me that it really went to my heart. But when I saw no kindness could worck upon her, but afterwards when she had had time to consider, and that I did what I could towards a reconciliation without effect, it made me change quite and grow (at least endeavour to grow) as indifferent as she. But in all this I see the hand of God, and look on our disagreeing as a punishment upon us for the irregularity by us committed upon the Revolution. My husband did his duty and the nation did theirs, and we were to suffer it, and rejoice that it pleased God to do what he did. But as to owr persons it is not as it ought to be, tho' it was unavoidable, and no doubt that it is a just judgment of God, but I trust the Church and nation shall not suffer, but that we in owr private concerns and persons may bear the punishment as in this we do.[1]

Mary is Macaulay's heroine, and although there is no reason to suppose that he exaggerates her virtues and charms, he seems to represent her too much as an early-Victorian rather than as a seventeenth-century lady. It is tempting to imagine that he saw in her the ideal submissive and admiring spouse he would have married if

[1] Doebner, pp. 45-6.

Providence had been kind to him. However, it is safer to be content with the assumption that Mary, partially at any rate, accepted the standard of morality of her own generation than to attribute to her an almost superhuman patience and devotion. In his Advice to a Daughter, Halifax enunciates the rule :

> You are to consider, you live in a time which hath rendered some kind of frailties so habitual that they lay claim to large grains of allowance. . . . Remember, that next to the danger of committing the fault yourself, the greatest is that of seeing it in your husband. Do not seem to look or hear that way ; if he is a man of sense he will reclaim himself ; the folly of it is of itself sufficient to cure him. If he is not so, he will be provoked, but not reformed. . . . Be assured that in these cases your discretion and silence will be the most prevailing reproof.

Many examples might be cited to show that Halifax correctly interpreted the views then prevalent : Henrietta Maria's partiality for Henry Jermyn, even when he had seduced one of her maids of honour, may be explained on the ground that she thought it sufficient to be chaste herself and did not exact chastity from her friends ; Charles II's retention of his wife's love in spite of his many sins ; William III's anger at his friend Zulestein for marrying Jane Wroth after he had betrayed her ; Mary's acceptance of her husband's lapses as an unavoidable evil. After all, she had the first, if not the sole, place in his affections.

There is abundant proof that William was really very fond of Mary and esteemed her highly. For weeks after her death his grief incapacitated him for all business. He commemorated the day of her death with mournful solemnity : he wore on his breast a lock of her hair for his remaining days.

CHAPTER XIV

MACAULAY'S CHARACTER OF WILLIAM III

In forming his estimate of William's character, Macaulay naturally relied most on Burnet among contemporary writers. The Bishop justly claims[1] that he had excellent opportunities of studying William through personal intercourse, and his first impressions may be compared with his final judgement. In addition to the many anecdotes about William which are scattered through his pages, Burnet gives three descriptions of considerable length. The first was written in 1686-1687, the other two after William's death.[2] The earliest character of William, when only Prince of Orange, is as follows :

> The Prince has shewed by his conduct and action that notwithstanding all the defects of his education, and his total want of literature, nature is capable of producing great matters, even when she is not at all assisted by art. He has a great application to affairs, and turns them much in his thoughts, and indeed perhaps too much ; for his slowness in coming to a resolution is much complained of ; but if he is slow in taking up a resolution he is as firm in adhering to it. He has a vast memory, and a true judgement. . . . He is the closest man in the world, so that it is not possible so much as to guess at his intentions, till he

[1] 'I had occasion to know him well, having observed him very carefully in a course of sixteen years : I had a large measure of his favour, and a free access to him all the while, though not at all times to the same degree : the freedom that I used with him was not always acceptable.' Own Time, ii. 306. For William's opinion of Burnet, see Foxcroft, Halifax, ii. 222, 229, 232.

[2] Supplement, pp. 190-3 ; Own Time, i. 689-90, ii. 304-6.

declares them: he is extremely calm both in council and actions, and hears very gently things that are said to him, even when he is not pleased with them; but he has the haughtiness of a great mind not to forget too soon injuries done him, but he has never been observed to affect revenges, only he does not easily return to confidences with those that have offended him. His courage is indeed greater than it ought to be, and though it was very fit for one that had the ambition of arriving at the reputation of his ancestors to hazard his person sometimes, that so it might appear that he was a soldier as well as a general, yet his great carelessness of all personal danger both in time of peace and war has been censured as excessive. . . . He has a true notion of government and liberty, and does not think that subjects were made to be slaves; but after the laws and foundations of government are overturned by those who ought to maintain them, he thinks the people may assert their freedom. He is a close manager of his affairs, and though he spends much in building, yet he is not thought so free-hearted and generous as a great prince ought to be. His martial inclinations will naturally carry him, when he comes to the crown of England, to bear down the greatness of France; and if he but hits the nature of the English nation right at first he will be able to give laws to all Europe. . . . But if the Prince does not in many things change his way, he will hardly gain the hearts of the nation; his coldness will look like contempt, and that the English cannot bear; and they are too impatient to digest that slowness that is almost become natural to him in the most inconsiderable things; and his silent way will pass for superciliousness.[1]

This prophecy may be contrasted with Burnet's estimate of William after he was dead:

His designs were always great and good: but it was thought he trusted too much to that, and that he did not descend enough to the humours of his people, to make him-

[1] Supplement, pp. 190-3.

self and his notions more acceptable to them: this, in a government that has so much of freedom in it as ours, was more necessary than he was inclined to believe: his reservedness grew on him, so that it disgusted most of those who served him. . . . He did not like contradiction, nor to have his actions censured: but he loved to employ and favour those who had the arts of complacence, yet he did not love flatterers. . . . He loved the Dutch, and was much beloved among them; but the ill returns he met from the English nation, their jealousies of him, and their perverseness towards him, had too much soured his mind, and had in a great measure alienated him from them, which he did not take care enough to conceal, though he saw the ill effects this had upon his business. . . . He was so apt to think that his ministers might grow insolent, if they should find that they had much credit with him, that he seemed to have made it a maxim, to let them often feel how little power they had, even in small matters. . . . I considered him as a person raised up by God to resist the power of France, and the progress of tyranny and persecution: the series of the five Princes of Orange, that was now ended in him, was the noblest succession of heroes that we find in any history. . . . After all the abatements that may be allowed for his errors and faults, he ought still to be reckoned among the greatest princes that our history, or indeed that any other, can afford.[1]

Apart from Burnet, Macaulay drew many 'touches' from every kind of contemporary memoir. But he rightly attached the greatest importance to the letters of William which were then at his disposal, and relied very largely on William's correspondence with Bentinck and Heinsius. William's letters to Bentinck are in the possession of Bentinck's descendant, the Duke of Portland. Transcripts of them, made for Sir James Mackintosh, were used by Macaulay and are now in the British Musuem.[2] Extracts are

[1] Own Time, ii. 304-6. [2] Add. MS. 34,514.

given in Macaulay's notes, but the letters have only recently been published as a whole.[1] For William's letters to Heinsius, Macaulay used transcripts, likewise in Mackintosh's collection, which were not copies of the Dutch originals but translations of them into French.[2] Some portions of the correspondence were in print when Macaulay wrote:

(a) Volume ii of the Earl of Hardwicke's Miscellaneous State Papers, published in 1778, contains English translations of letters, filling about 60 pages, about the Partition Treaties.

(b) Others of the same period, also in English, were printed by Paul Grimblot in 1848, in a work called Letters of William III and Louis XIV and of Their Ministers (1697-1701).[3]

(c) Quotations and fragments of others were to be found in the volumes of a Dutch historian, Sirtema de Grovestins, of which the last edition was published in 1868.[4]

Thus Macaulay used, perforce, either translations of William's letters or short extracts, for in no case were the original letters completely printed. Since he wrote, the letters have been printed in full in three volumes which comprise the Third Series of the Archives de la Maison d'Orange-Nassau.[5]

As Heinsius did not become Grand Pensionary till the middle of 1689 these letters do not throw any light on the expedition to England and the Revolution settlement. On

[1] See above, p. 77. A few appear in S. A. Strong's Catalogue of Letters and Other Historical Documents Exhibited . . . at Welbeck (1903). A useful work is William Bentinck and William III, by Marion E. Grew (1924)

[2] Cf. Macaulay, III, 1373, n. 2 (xi).

[3] Macaulay occasionally quotes Grimblot. VI, 2711, 2716 (xxii).

[4] Cf. Macaulay, III, 1373 (xi).

[5] Ed. Krämer. Ranke prints some of these letters in volume vi of his History.

the other hand there were published in 1873-1880 two volumes of letters from William [1] to his friend the Prince of Waldeck, edited by P. L. Müller, which do elucidate both.

These private letters illustrate William's character and temper at the most critical moment of his career, and their frankness and sincerity inspire confidence in every expression of opinion or feeling they contain. Waldeck was in command of the forces left to defend Holland against a possible attack from the French (who did not declare war against the Dutch till November 16-26) and to assist in the defence of western Germany.

The first letters, written in the autumn of 1688, deal with the preparations to be made against the French attack on Germany. Then comes one of October 26 announcing the Prince's intention to embark the next day. On November 2 follows another, announcing that the fleet has been scattered and driven back by a storm, but that it will put to sea as soon as possible—'the greatest loss is the time and the horses, of which quite two hundred have been killed or wounded.' The next letter, written on November 16 from Exeter, proves that William was not discouraged by the slowness of his adherents in England to join him, as Macaulay suggests.[2]

The state of things here is in accordance with representations made to me before my departure from Holland, so that I can hope, with God's blessing, to succeed in this great undertaking. The beginning is favourable. . . . It is unfortunate that we have been obliged by the wind to land here in the west, where we are so much out of the way of correspondence with Holland that we are quite out of the

[1] Wilhelm III von Oranien und Georg Friedrich von Waldeck (1873, 1880).

[2] III, 1144 (ix).

world,[1] knowing nothing but what happens in the neighbourhood. I hope in two days to be able to advance and then we shall know in a short time whether we shall be forced to fight to decide the business. . . . Some reports say that the King and his army will not dare to go far from London, from which we are fifty leagues away and consequently a long march.[2]

William writes from Hungerford in a still more cheerful mood on December 9:

Would that your affairs were in as good a state as ours appear to be. And I hope with God's help that this country will in a short time assist ours, for the people seem very bent on it.

William's next letter is dated St. James's, December 18-28—that is, it was written on the day when James left London for the last time, and William entered it. He regrets that on account of the season he can send Waldeck no cavalry, but thinks that in a short time he will be able to spare him five or six regiments of infantry. What prevents him of course is the unsettled state of the English government: he could cut the knot and make a settlement but will not do so.

If my disposition were not so scrupulous as it is, I should not be so embarrassed, and could finish the matter soon; I have more trouble than you can imagine. I hope that the good God will guide me as He has done up till now.

In every letter Waldeck continued to press for troops, and in reply William had to explain the political and con-

[1] This proves that William meant to land on the east coast. Surprisingly, Macaulay does not discuss the question where William intended to disembark, but it may be inferred from III, 1122 (ix), that he believed, erroneously, that the landing on the southwest coast was the result of design, not of an adverse wind. A parallel is afforded in 1651. S. R. Gardiner, Commonwealth and Protectorate (1903), i. 94, 105-6.

[2] Müller, ii. 118.

stitutional conditions which kept him from settling the question as quickly as Waldeck expected.

I am quite convinced that you need troops, and I do not doubt that in a short time I can send you some, both from the forces of this country and from those I brought with me. I would send you all of them, but so long as things are in their present state, I am sure that if you were here on the spot and knew as much as I know you would not advise me to send them. Yesterday the Lords met and resolved to ask me to take over the government of the kingdom until a Convention can meet, which is almost the same thing as a Parliament, being composed of the same people, and which they have asked me to convoke for January 22, O.S.

Tomorrow I shall have a great quantity of gentlemen who were formerly members of the Lower House and of aldermen [*deputes*] of this town, who apparently will make the same request before I may give any answer to the Lords who have lately been with me. I am passive in all this matter, without speaking to anyone whatsoever, although I have been extremely tormented. And if I had wished to give the least encouragement, I am persuaded they would have declared me king, which I do not want, not having come hither for that. What they will do when the Convention meets I do not know, but I fear that they mean to force me to accept what I do not ask for, although I foresee that the world will judge otherwise. If I accept the government, I can send you immediately the help which in case of war England is obliged to give to Holland, which I believe amounts to 6,000 men, and I can prepare everything to make a considerable diversion next spring, when the Convention or a Parliament will have given money.[1]

Four days later William announces that, being now provisionally in charge of the government, he is able to send

[1] Müller, ii. 125-6.

the 6,000 auxiliaries the treaties [1] between England and Holland provided.

On February 13 the Convention offered the crown to William and Mary and they accepted it. Next day William announced his acceptance of the crown to Waldeck in the following terms:

I wished not to delay in informing you that after the petition which Parliament has made to ask me to be their King, I have accepted and we have just been proclaimed. I assure you it is no light burden, and I considered it thoroughly, but could not exempt myself.

Later he added:

I imagine that you know me well enough to believe that the lustre of a crown does not dazzle me. If it had not been absolutely necessary I should not have accepted it —as those who have been here can witness—and unless I was willing to lose everything I could not have acted otherwise.[2]

Doubtless these utterances represent the real facts of the case. The paramount consideration with William was that the resources of England could not be utilised in the struggle for European independence unless he became king. Neither as regent nor as prince consort would he have possessed adequate power to guide the course of public affairs in England. Even as king he had immense difficulties to combat. He was at first hopeful that his task would be easier than he originally thought. He was able to send a number of regiments [3] back to Holland and to promise more, but events moved very slowly in England

[1] These were the treaty of Mar. 1678, and three earlier ones, renewed on Aug 7-17, 1685.

[2] Müller, ii. 137, 139.

[3] See above, p. 155.

and the landing of James in Ireland disturbed the task of organisation.

Matters here in Parliament are satisfactory enough, and I do not doubt that I shall have reason to be satisfied with them, but their manner and form of government do not allow things to proceed as quickly as is necessary at this conjuncture. It is certain that King James has left Brest or will do so the first favourable wind for Ireland. He has only officers and money with him. This business will give me more occupation here than I could have wished at this conjuncture, and above all if he has planned to cross into Scotland, as I have reason to believe. I work as hard as I can to put everything in order, but as my reign is very new and affairs in great disorder everywhere, I have no little difficulty, and my health is not of the best and the climate here makes my cough much worse, which makes me very feeble.[1]

Again and again he has to complain 'that the affairs here in Parliament do not proceed as quickly as the urgency requires, which gives me no little annoyance not to be able to remedy.' Waldeck had to contend with difficulties of a similar kind in the Netherlands. 'I am persuaded that you and I have on our hands the most troublesome affairs in all Europe,' wrote William. 'I pity you with all my heart for all the torments and vexations which you have. I assure you that I have as many here. It is only the good cause which can console us and give us the necessary patience.' In another latter he announced Mackay's defeat at Killiecrankie: it was uncertain yet whether that general was killed or taken.[2] A French squadron which it was hoped to intercept had got safe to Brest and for three weeks there had been no news of the English fleet.

[1] William to Waldeck, *ca.* Mar. 5-15, 1689. Müller, ii. 143.

[2] This sentence casts doubt upon the story told by Macaulay (IV, 1636 [xiii]) of the reception in London of the news of Killiecrankie.

It is impossible to have more chagrin than I have at all the difficulties you meet with everywhere and at my present incapacity to make things a little easier for you. I see that they are annoyed in Holland and fear unhappy results, which we must work as hard as we can to prevent, and, for the rest, leave the issue to Divine Providence and not be too annoyed. It is a lesson I need as much as you do. The difficulties here are incredible. God knows whether they are insurmountable.[1]

Both of them must stick to their task till the end. Waldeck must not dream of resigning.

You know that it is an impossibility without the greatest prejudice in the world not only to the state but to the public good. I acknowledge that your employment is very difficult, and often gives you just causes of annoyance, and if this were not a duty due to God I should long ago have had the same thought which you have, although I am not your age, for assuredly I have too heavy a burden, my shoulders are not strong enough to support it, and without the miraculous assistance from above I well foresee that I shall succumb. The good God can give you the strength necessary to support your burden, as you have done so well up till now. And for the love of His cause I beg you no longer to entertain this thought of retiring, but to think now of the next campaign in order that this winter we can get everything ready and take such measures that we shall have reason to hope that the coming year will be happier for us than this.[2]

William's difficulties were far greater than those of Waldeck. Waldeck had the task of facing stronger forces with a weaker and more heterogeneous army. William's task was not alone to wage a foreign war, but also to reorganise the government of England, subdue a rebellion in Scotland, and reconquer Ireland. But his greatest difficulties arose

[1] Müller, ii. 143, 156, 158, 168,

[2] Ibid. 177-8,

from the failure of the English people to understand him, and his failure to understand them. As little did he understand the English Constitution—a Constitution which at the moment was in a somewhat chaotic condition : he had to work an imperfect and defective machine.

The conversations of William with Halifax, which are recorded in Miss Foxcroft's Life of Halifax,[1] and which run from December 1688 to about May 1690, throw the clearest light on the opinions of William during the first year of his reign, and explain his difficulties. It is obvious that William neither before nor after his accession made much effort to seek popularity. He did not think it part of the business of a statesman or a ruler to please people. He told Halifax that 'he would never put it in his head to think people would be satisfyed with anything. Hee would do what was right, and have [? leave] it there.' Halifax thought this sincere but foolish. 'I told him that was not enough for a king, and especially here. The world is a beast that must bee cozened before it bee tamed.' Another time William said 'hee would think no more of doing things popular, but doing what was right.' On this Halifax remarks that, 'till mankind is more reasonable, that may bee a dangerous maxime for a prince.' It was the more dangerous because William always understood Europe much better than England. According to Halifax, he hardly understood the English Constitution and consequently did not know how to work it.[2] 'He had a wrong notion of the Privy Councell: thought the government was to reside there.' Consequently he was too anxious to limit the numbers of the Privy Council, and did not include in it as many members as he should have done. 'Double the number would have

[1] ii. 200-52. These conversations were unknown to Macaulay.

[2] Cf. Burnet, i. 691.

done no hurt, and would have ingaged men of quality,' comments Halifax.[1] This was in February 1689, when William began his reign. The number of the Council was then fixed at thirty.[2]

Before the end of the year the King had come to understand the convenience of a limited council or committee. In September he discussed with Halifax who should be 'of the Cabinet' or 'in the Cabinet', meaning thereby a committee of the Privy Council or 'Cabinet Council'. It is evident that this body was intended to be 'a Committee of Foreign Affairs' such as Charles II had habitually maintained. The difficulty, William recognised, was that the various members of this Cabinet Council, representing a mixture of parties, had no confidence in each other. In January 1690 he 'agreed the necessity of a Cabinet Councill, but said hee did not know of men, who would speak freely before one another.'

Halifax noted many indications which seemed to show that William did not sufficiently esteem the British peerage, and did not fully appreciate the political importance of the House of Lords.[3] In March 1689 William said he would raise regiments, but would not give the command of them to peers. 'Hee hath taken those away which the Lords had first raised,' records Halifax, who could not but own that 'the humour and character of a peer of England do not agree very well with the discipline to which a colonell must be subject.'[4]

Failing to understand the political importance of the Lords, William did not at first accept advice to raise exist-

[1] Halifax, ii. 210, 211, 219, 204.

[2] No doubt William was inspired by the same theories which prompted Temple's scheme for remodelling the Privy Council in 1679.

[3] Cf. Macaulay, V, 2265, 2274 (xix).

[4] Halifax, ii. 205-6.

ing peers to a higher degree as a way of strengthening the King's party in the Upper House without adding to the number of the peerage. Later in his reign William adopted this expedient: in 1694 for instance he made Bedford, Devonshire, Carmarthen, Clare, and Shrewsbury dukes. Halifax further observes that 'by the want hee hath of the Commons and by his not coming to the House of Lords where hee might see, how necessary they are to the support of his crown; hee doth not think them of much moment.' Halifax pressed him to attend the debates of the House of Lords now and then, as Charles II had done. Halifax says William 'agreed to come sometimes to the House to keep up his clayme to it; but since hath shewed such an aversion to it, that hee is no more to be mooved in it.' When Halifax urged him again he said 'with some anger, that hee had no time for it.'[1] Later in the reign, however, he followed Halifax's advice, and was occasionally present at debates.[2]

William appreciated better the importance of the Lower House, but had no love for it. He said to Halifax in March 1689 that 'the Commons used him like a dog', and this probably reflects his wrath at their long delays and quarrels over the grant of a revenue.[3] Halifax says 'their course usage boyled so upon his stomack, that hee could not hinder himselfe from breaking out sometimes, against them.' In July 1689, after a few months' experience, he wanted to

[1] Ibid. pp. 207, 218, 244.

[2] Burnet, ii. 44 n.; Macaulay, IV, 1826 (xv), and V, 2268, 2418 (xix, xx). In his interesting volume entitled The House of Lords in the Reign of William III (1913), A. S. Turberville states that William 'made thirty elevations to the peerage' (p. 7). The number should be twenty-seven, the names of Strafford, Craven, and Willoughby de Broke being wrongly included. Of these new creations six were in favour of the eldest sons of peers, who all succeeded to their fathers' peerages. Promotions were fairly numerous, as Mr. Turberville shows (pp. 10-11).

[3] Cf. Macaulay, IV, 1816 (xv).

prorogue Parliament, and when Halifax gave advice against it William said 'hee was so weary of them, hee could not bear them ; there must be a recesse.' [1]

The evolution of William's political opinions is not difficult to trace. He did not share either the passions of the Whigs or their political theories, though circumstances obliged him to depend upon them when his reign began. The Whig view of the royal function seemed absurd to him. He told Halifax that 'a king of England who will governe by law as hee must do, if hee hath conscience, is the worst figure in Christendome. Hee hath power to destroy the nation and not to protect it.' He started with a prejudice against the extreme Whigs before he came to the throne. On December 30, 1688, he told Halifax that 'the commonwealth party was the strongest in England', which Halifax thought a perfectly erroneous view instilled into William by members of that party for their own ends. Anyhow, William said bluntly 'hee did not come over to establish a commonwealth.' After he became king he thought the extreme Whigs no better than republicans. In July 1689 he asserted that he had discovered plainly that their design was to establish a commonwealth. As indications of this design he pointed out the reluctance of the Whigs in the Convention to grant him an adequate and independent revenue. He thought they were always trying to lop the rights or the revenue of the Crown. 'The persuading him to give away the chimney money was with a designe for a commonwealth.' [2] The Habeas Corpus Act was a very inconvenient piece of legislation. He thought the Declaration of Rights went a little too far, and 'Said it was to be considered, whether all the articles in the Declaration, were to

[1] Halifax, ii. 207.

[2] Cf. Macaulay, III, 1346 (xi) ; Burnet, ii. 13.

be confirmed in the bill of succession. Hee had no mind to confirme them, but the condition of his affayres overruled his inclinations in it.' He held the attempt to revive the Triennial Act untimely, and fought throughout against any bill of the kind.[1]

Quite apart from all this, William had personal objections to the leaders of the extreme Whigs in the Convention. He declared 'young Mr. Hampbden was mad', and that he would send him to Spain as ambassador to be rid of him. As for Jack Howe, he 'had said that, for which, if hee was not king, hee must either fight, with him or cudgell him.'[2] He had no better opinion of the Lords who were the Whig leaders in the Upper House. Of Mordaunt, Earl of Monmouth, William observed that 'the more one knew him, the more objection one had to him,' and of the Duke of Bolton, that he was mad, though he 'had great influence upon the House of Commons'.[3]

William had an equally low opinion of the Tory leaders, with one or two exceptions. His wife's two uncles, Clarendon and Rochester, he briefly described as a couple of knaves. Nottingham he termed 'an honest man', but he seemed to have doubts about Danby. 'For Lord Nottingham hee dealt plainly with him, but for Lord Danby, hee knew not what to make of him.' Halifax notes that William 'ever shewed an inclination to Lord Godolphin', and thought him 'a very honest man'.[4]

This confidence in Godolphin and Nottingham the King retained throughout his reign. Nottingham continued to be Secretary of State until December 1693, and William parted with him much against his will. He had to do it to

[1] Halifax, ii. 221, 203, 205, 217, 244.

[2] Macaulay, III, 1336 (xi).

[3] Halifax, ii. 204, 229, 245, 226.

[4] Ibid. pp. 202, 206, 205, 242.

conciliate the Whigs. 'Himself', says Mary, 'thought his case so bad that he was forced to part with Lord Nottingham, to please a party who he cannot trust.'[1] Shrewsbury, Nottingham's colleague as Secretary of State, was one of the few Whigs the King trusted, but he resigned in 1690. William was much annoyed thereby, and still more dissatisfied with the reason for the resignation—that the King was engaged in measures in which Shrewsbury could not concur. The King said that Lord Shrewsbury 'did not consider how kind he had been to him', adding 'that he had a very good understanding, but he was young and new in his place.'[2]

Even more annoying to William was the resignation of Halifax. Their conversations show that William had great confidence in Halifax, and Halifax great admiration for him. Yet one feels that Halifax's admiration was tempered by criticism. All the time he seems to be studying William as a sort of abstract problem, endeavouring to estimate the character of the new sovereign from all the indications his talks afford, instead of giving his mind to the political questions they were discussing. William was more practical, and here, as Macaulay suggests,[3] may have been a cause of difference between king and minister. However, in February 1690 when the Marquis gave up the seals, the King told him 'hee did not know where to place them in so good hands', and that he would not take them unless Halifax promised 'to come into imployment againe when it was for his service'. 'I said', reports Halifax, 'I would, if my health would give mee leave; Tush replyeth hee, you have health enough.'[4] This utterance too is characteristic. William's view was that so long as a man was alive he had

[1] Doebner, p. 61.
[2] Halifax, ii. 250-1; Burnet, ii. 45.
[3] IV, 1760-2 (xv).
[4] Halifax, ii. 248-9.

health enough for great affairs—discomforts and difficulties did not count. He must go on to the end for the sake of the cause.

By the close of 1689, as Macaulay points out,[1] William was thoroughly disgusted with the Whigs on account of their factiousness and their desire to limit the power of the Crown and the executive. He was gradually making up his mind to a change of system. If it was impossible to create a middle party consisting of the sensible and moderate elements of both parties, he would make the experiment of trusting the Tories.

This is clearly revealed in the conversations with Halifax. William 'ever told me he was a Trimmer'. His natural inclination therefore was to endeavour to combine the moderate men of both parties. In August he concluded 'there was nothing to bee done, but to form a party between the 2 extreames.' In January 1690 he said that 'hee would continue to be a Trimmer, but upon discourse of the next meeting of a Parliament, hee said that though hee should seem to declare for one party more than for another, if his kindnesse was not answered, hee could take the others by the hand.' Halifax answered that the experiment was doubtful and dangerous. So in February 1690 William began to court the Tories. 'He said hee wished, hee could trimme a little longer, but things pressed so, hee could not.' In January he felt that 'it was dangerous to trust the High Tories', but as Halifax adds in a note, 'that inclination changed since.'[2] By dissolving the Convention Parliament in February 1690 William broke with the Whigs and threw himself upon the support of the Tories, or rather the moderate men of both parties. It was hazardous but it seemed the only resource.

[1] IV, 1791-2 (xv). [2] Halifax, ii. 229, 244, 247, 243.

Macaulay tells a story at great length and with much dramatic effect, that William was so disgusted with the quarrels of English parties that he seriously thought of abdicating :

The King, argued Macaulay, was weary of his crown. He had tried to stand neutral amid party conflicts, with the result that he was unpopular with both Whigs and Tories. His efforts to still political strife during a national crisis had completely failed. Schomberg's campaign in Ireland had accomplished little, and the malpractices that had helped to decimate his army were as rife as ever. The administration was thoroughly disorganised, and the people angry and disappointed that a foreign king had not immediately mended the machinery of government. Most of the ministers were more intent upon attacking each other than in assisting William. Yet if he ventured to employ a Dutchman whom he could trust both factions united in protesting. Therefore William, feeling that he could no longer render effective service to the great cause to which his whole soul was devoted, determined to return to Holland. He would leave Mary, an Englishwoman with feminine grace and tact, to try her hand at composing the disputes that distracted the State and the Church.

Holland, under his government, and England, under hers, might act cordially together against the common enemy.

He secretly ordered preparations to be made for his voyage. Having done this, he called together a few of his chief counsellors, and told them his purpose. A squadron, he said, was ready to carry him to his country. He had done with them. He hoped that the Queen would be more successful. The ministers were thunderstruck. For once all quarrels were suspended. The Tory Caermarthen on one side, the Whig Shrewsbury on the other, expostulated and implored with a pathetic vehemence rare in the conferences of statesmen. Many tears were shed. At length the King was induced to give up, at least for the present, his design of abdicating the government. But he announced another design which he was fully determined not to give up. Since he was still to remain at the head of the English administration, he would go himself to Ireland. He would try whether the whole royal authority, strenuously exerted on the spot where the fate of the empire was to be decided, would suffice to prevent peculation and to maintain discipline.

That he had seriously meditated a retreat to Holland long continued to be a secret, not only to the multitude, but even to the Queen.[1]

Macaulay was plainly relying upon Burnet, whose story is as follows:

He was once very near a desperate resolution; he thought he could not trust the Tories, and he resolved he would not trust the Whigs: so he fancied the Tories would be true to the Queen, and confide in her, though they would not in him. He therefore resolved to go over to Holland, and leave the government in the Queen's hands: so he called the Marquis of Caermarthen, with the Earl of Shrewsbury, and some few more, and told them, he had a convoy ready, and was resolved to leave all in the Queen's hands; since he could not see how he could extricate himself out of the difficulties into which the animosities of parties had brought him: they pressed him vehemently to lay aside all such desperate resolutions, and to comply with the present necessity. Much passion appeared among them: the debate was so warm, that many tears were shed: in conclusion, the King resolved to change his first design, into another better resolution, of going over in person, to put an end to the war in Ireland; this was told me some time after by the Earl of Shrewsbury: but the Queen knew nothing of it,

[1] IV, 1789-90 (xv).

till she had it from me; so reserved was the King to her, even in a matter that concerned her so nearly.[1]

The Bishop wrote this in 1705. In his original account, written in 1691, which is simpler and shorter, Burnet mentioned neither Shrewsbury nor Caermarthen, and omitted the tears. He touched up the bald original story just as Macaulay expands the narrative of the bishop. Though there is the statement that William meant 'to go over to Holland, and leave the government in the Queen's hands', that is not quite the same thing as a 'design of abdicating the government'.

The only other authority referred to by Macaulay is Lord Lonsdale, then Sir John Lowther.[2] Lowther tells us in rather general terms that, shortly after the Revolution, there was a great revival of factions and party spirit. Men who had invited the King to undertake the government began to oppose it. In Parliament 'the buried names of Whig and Tory were revived'. At court there were factions: in council no agreement. 'There was no council but only for form, and things were left to manage themselves.'

'The King, as I was well assured, either really weary or disdaining the nation for these reasons, or willing either to try their temper or reconcile their differences, called some of the principal of them together and proposed going back into Holland, and either leaving them to provide for their own security or the Queen here, with whom they would perhaps be better pleased as nearer related to the Crown.' What followed the proposal or when it was made Lowther does not say. But he intimates that it took place shortly be-

[1] Own Time, ii. 39-40.

[2] His narrative is printed in the English Historical Review, xxx. 90-7.

fore he was made Commissioner of the Treasury (March 18, 1690). Burnet too seems to place it about the end of 1689 or the beginning of 1690.

In itself the story is improbable. William was not the man to abandon a task he had undertaken, because he met with more difficulties than he expected. Still less was he the man to shift to weaker shoulders a responsibility which he found too heavy. Least of all was he likely to forget that his abdication would mean the detachment of England from the European league against Louis XIV. Abdication was not in keeping with William's character or possible in William's position.

But though the story may be absurd, the question how it came to be invented and circulated and credited is worthy of examination. Was there anything in William's words or actions which could be so misconstrued that it might give rise to the story? Certainly there was. William came to England for two objects: to restore the religious and civil liberties of England, and to utilise England for the defence of the liberties of Europe. His English ministers hardly realised the place which the second object filled in his mind. The discovery that he was thinking as much of Europe as of England, or perhaps more of Europe than of England, came as a shock to them. This can be traced in Halifax's conversations. He found the King eager for war with France, 'a good while before the warre was declared,' and observes that 'his eagernesse that way never ceased; it may bee a question, whether that thought was not the greatest inducement to his undertaking.' Another day the King said 'hee had thought as much as hee could think and that there must bee a warre with France'. The war was declared against France on May 4-14, 1689, and in the same month William spoke to Halifax about a landing in France.

'Hee hath such a mind to France, that it would incline one to think, hee tooke England onely in his way,' noted Halifax.[1] This plan was frustrated by the landing of James in Ireland. 'This business of Ireland is a violent misfortune for us,' William wrote to Waldeck on March 29. 'There is a kingdom to conquer which will give me no small difficulty, and be a terrible misfortune for the Allies,' he said in a second letter.[2] It forced him to send to Ireland the regiments he had raised in England or hired from Denmark to make a descent upon the French coast, according to the plan of campaign he had discussed with Schomberg.[3]

William struggled hard against this necessity. More than once he said to Halifax that to effect a landing in France would be the best way to save Ireland. More than once he said that the war must be carried into France, till Halifax told him 'it must not bee talked of before hand.'[4] For a time William hoped that Schomberg in one pitched battle would rout James, and recover Ireland before 1689 was over. 'The King said, if the war was dispatch'd this year in Ireland as he hop'd it would be this winter, there was nothing to be [done] but making a descent in France to give a diversion or else the Confederates would make peace, even Holland itself.' William owned that he wished to conduct the expedition in person. No doubt he meant to leave Mary, assisted by a council, to govern England in his absence, as she did in 1690 when he was in Ireland. On June 24, 1689, Halifax notes: 'The King said, if hee left us, the Queen would governe us better. I told him, hee could not do that, now that hee was King, Hee said, yes: that would not

[1] Halifax, ii. 210, 212, 218, 219, 220.

[2] Müller, ii. 152, 157.

[3] Ibid. pp. 149, 158; Klopp, iv. 345, 400, 465, 524.

[4] Halifax, ii. 218, 220, 235.

hinder. I asked him whether it was not because hee had a mind to command the army against France; hee said nothing, but did not deny it.' [1]

Here is plainly shown what William meant when he spoke about leaving the government to the Queen. The words referred, not to an intended abdication, but to a temporary absence from England for military purposes.

William's hope that Ireland would be conquered in one campaign was speedily destroyed. Schomberg landed on August 13, and encamped at Dundalk about a month later. On September 21 James and the Irish offered battle, but Schomberg would not fight. Throughout the winter of 1689-1690 the English army remained stationary in the camp at Dundalk, suffering great hardships and great losses, which were mainly due to the badness of the military organisation.

William had come to the conclusion that he himself was the person 'most proper for the service', and would therefore undertake the subjugation of Ireland. On December 3, Hoffman, the Austrian agent, wrote to Vienna: 'At the conclusion of this letter I was assured by a good hand, that the King had resolved to go in person to Ireland in February, and to prosecute the war there through his presence, which the situation requires.' He went on to say that, since it was an open unfortified country, William hoped to bring the war to an end in a single battle.[2] A month later the secret was out. In Luttrell's Brief Historical Relation, which is a summary of the information given in the newspapers and newsletters of the day, it is said, under January 8: 'The King has declared his final resolutions to goe to Ireland.' [3]

[1] Ibid. pp. 228, 222.

[2] Klopp, v. 64-5, 339.

[3] Luttrell, ii. 3.

The news startled the Whigs. Some of their leaders sent letters of protest to the King, and they meant to promote an address in the Commons against his proposed journey to Ireland.[1] He had no intention of yielding to this clamour. On January 10-20, he wrote to Portland: 'I find that people begin to be very anxious about my journey to Ireland, particularly the Whigs, who fear to lose me too soon before they have done with me all they wish; for as for their friendship you know what that is worth in this country.'[2]

William discussed the question with Halifax. He told him (January 6) 'he must go into Ireland, and that nothing would stirre here, except hee had ill successe there.' The fact that Parliament disapproved was of little weight with William, though 'he was apprehensive they would make addresses against it.'[3] He frustrated parliamentary opposition by a prorogation. The position on the Continent gave him more anxiety. He realised that the Allies would dislike his going into Ireland. He was badly needed in Holland, where the magistrates of Amsterdam had raised difficulties which he had sent Portland to settle but could have better settled himself. A congress of the allied powers was about to meet at The Hague, and William's presence might be vital to the outcome. 'I tremble about the voyage of Your Majesty to Ireland,' wrote Waldeck; 'for many reasons a journey here for a fortnight would do the public more good than a voyage thither.'[4]

William was eager to go to Holland but knew it was impossible. If it were possible without wishing to abandon everything here he would embark tomorrow, he wrote to

[1] Klopp, v. 88.

[2] Correspondentie, ed. Japikse, i. 69-70; Macaulay, IV, 1791 (xv).

[3] Halifax, ii. 244-5.

[4] Müller, ii. 207.

Portland.[1] To Waldeck, who urged that to act on the defensive in Ireland, and to carry out the projected descent on France, was the best strategic combination,[2] William explained that his present plan was the only feasible one.

> The constitution of this kingdom and of the people is such that it is an absolute necessity that I govern myself at present according to their humour, and that I attempt to put an end to this business, before I can dream of another. . . . I assure you that if I was not entirely convinced that unless I go to Ireland nothing beneficial will be done there, I should never have taken such a resolution. I recognise all its inconveniences and difficulties, which are not few. I hope by the grace of God to surmount them, and that He will assist me with His all-powerful hand as he has done up till now, in order that by finishing this business happily and promptly I can be more useful to all the Allies and act more vigorously against the common enemy.[3]

It has been necessary to go into detail in order to show exactly what the facts are which refute Burnet's story and how they could be so perverted as to make the story seem plausible. There are two facts which could be misunderstood or perverted so as to create the impression embodied in the legend. In the first place, about the beginning of December 1689 William created a great deal of excitement in political circles when he changed his plans and decided to go to Ireland in person as soon as possible. But the plan he abandoned was not one to return permanently to Holland, but to leave England in order to take command of a proposed expedition to France. In the second place, the words which William used in speaking about the proposed arrangement for the government of England during his

[1] Undated. Ranke, iv. 581.
[2] Müller, ii. 206.
[3] Ibid. p. 210.

temporary absence might, if they were misrepresented or detached from their context, give rise to the impression that he intended to leave England permanently.

Burnet, who did not know William's real plans, misconstrued his words in this way. But Burnet does not go nearly so far as Macaulay. All Burnet says is that William 'resolved to go over to Holland, and leave the government in the Queen's hands.' He does not say whether William meant to go to Holland temporarily or permanently, though the latter might not unnaturally be inferred from the way in which the story is introduced and related.

But Macaulay goes further than his authority and describes William as announcing 'his design of abdicating the government'. If he had known that for nearly a year William had been seriously meditating an expedition to France he would probably have estimated Burnet's story at its true value. But he did not know either the conversations between William and Halifax or the letters from William to Waldeck, or the references to the scheme that are contained in the diplomatic correspondence referred to by Klopp. All these have come to light since Macaulay wrote.

No doubt William, like other great men who had to struggle against extreme difficulties and bitter disappointments in the pursuit of public ends, sometimes found his burden almost too heavy to be borne and talked of his desire for a private life and the charms of retirement—as Cromwell did. But a man who is conscious that a great cause depends upon him bears his burden to the end, whatever expressions of weariness may escape him. There is a character of William, sent by the ambassador of Savoy to his master in 1690, which refers to some of these expressions, but the ambassador very wisely refrains from taking them seriously.

As your Royal Highness ought to have a close connection with the King of England, it seems right that you should know him thoroughly. For this reason I am going to make his portrait as much like him as possible. He is forty two years old, of medium height, very thin, always troubled by a violent inflammation of the lungs, and constitutionally so feeble that his life seems to hang by a thread, but as he refrains from every kind of excess and avoids everything at variance with his temperament, he looks after the little health he has so well that he resists the fatigues of war and the chase, which are his two ruling passions. He is naturally melancholy, loving silence and retirement. His genius is vast and prompts him to large designs. His firmness and patience are proof against the greatest obstacles which never deter him, but his procrastination and irresolution stop him on the smoothest roads.[1] This fault, which is the only one he can be reproached with, is capable of ruining his affairs, for although he works unceasingly, negotiating and writing day and night, he never finishes anything in time, and this makes his ministers grumble and complain that they have to speak to him a hundred times about the same thing without receiving a definite reply. When I try to plumb the causes of this irresolution I find the three principal to be: the first his birth in a country where men are naturally sluggish in making up their minds; the second the feeling that he has gained much in the past by not hurrying, and the third an eagerness to do everything himself, because he distrusts the fidelity or the capacity of his ministers. Hence spring all kinds of confusion. Men are not recruited, the troops destined for the Low Countries are not transported, the fleet is not ready, and many necessaries are lacking for the descent (on France) which is talked about. To this procrastination is attributed the squandering of his financial resources. . . . At any rate King William, all things considered, does not fall short of a great prince, and his authority is so well established that

[1] Cf. Burnet, ii. 89, and above, p. 334, for William's slowness in transacting business.

so far as human affairs can be gauged it cannot be overthrown. The nation is generally content and the people love him because he has no mistresses nor favourites, because he does not spare himself nor sacrifice anything to his pleasures. He does not, however, appear to be satisfied. The little success gained up till now disgusts him, and he is embarrassed by the weight of affairs he is charged with from all quarters, and he cannot get rid of them quickly enough. At the end of the last campaign he said to one of his friends, from whom I learnt it, that he was tired of the figure he made in the world, and that he was often tempted to leave the world in order to retire to one of his German estates and lead a private life there. This friend, who by his great age, his experience and services, had acquired much credit with him (William) loudly upbraided him for having thoughts, unworthy of a great man, destructive of his reputation and his friends if they were known.[1]

It is certain, however, that there was one moment when William did seriously consider the question of abdicating. That was in December 1698, when Parliament after the treaty of Ryswick determined to reduce the army to a number William rightly deemed insufficient for the security of England. The evidence for this is contained in a letter from Somers to Lord Shrewsbury, dated December 29, 1698.

His resolution is, when the next Wednesday's business is over, to come to the Parliament, and tell them, that he came over to rescue the nation from the ruin impending over them, in which he succeeded, and had brought them to the end of a dangerous war, without any great misfortune; that now they had peace, and might provide for their own safety; that he saw they were entertaining distrusts and jealousies of him, so as not to do what was necessary for

[1] Report of M. de la Tour, envoy of the Duke of Savoy, to his master (1692). Krämer, Archives de la Maison d'Orange-Nassau, 3d Ser., vol. i, pp. xxviii-xxxi.

themselves; that he was, therefore, determined to leave England, but, before he went, would consent to any law they should offer, for appointing commissioners of both Houses, to administer the government, and, then they would not be jealous of themselves.

When he first mentioned this to me, I treated the notion as the most extravagant and absurd, that ever was entertained, and begged him to speak of it to nobody, for his own honour. He heard me patiently talk against it, for two hours, but concluded at last, as of a notion he still retained.[1]

The speech William intended to make is extant.[2] Macaulay states that 'The King's strong understanding had mastered, as it seldom failed, after a struggle, to master, his rebellious temper. He had made up his mind to fulfil his great mission to the end.'[3]

William's letters to Heinsius show precisely how long this resolution to retire lasted. He referred to it first in a letter of December 20, 1698, and lastly in a letter of January 6. By January 13, he had given it up and could speak of the state of public affairs.

I am sorry to tell you that things here go worse than anyone could have imagined and on all sides I see nothing in prospect but confusion. If France has spent its money here for the purpose, it might have saved it. I assure you nothing is so superfluous. For men here are generally so blind and so ill disposed that they need no payment to make them give away their own safety.[4]

This bitter letter was written when William was cruelly mortified by the decision of the Commons to send his

[1] William Coxe, Shrewsbury Correspondence (1821), pp. 572-3.

[2] Ibid. p. 574; Original Letters, ed. Henry Ellis, 2d Ser., iv (1827), 216-7. A facsimile of it is reproduced in Macaulay, VI, 2867-9 (xxiv).

[3] VI, 2879 (xxiv).

[4] Klopp, viii. 273-8.

favourite Dutch Guards back to Holland. The unwise reduction of the standing army to 7,000 Englishmen[1] coincided with the annulment of the first Partition Treaty by the death of the Electoral Prince of Bavaria, and William had good cause to complain of the blindness of Parliament. During 1699-1700 the attention of politicians was focussed on the grants of land forfeited in Ireland. The report of the commission, states Macaulay, 'brought the nation nearer than it has ever since been to the verge of another revolution.'[2] At the same time the public was absorbed by accounts of the disasters which attended the Scottish expedition to Darien and the piracy of Captain Kidd. The effect of these unfortunate events, and of the passions they roused, is not exaggerated by Macaulay. At Madrid the ministers thought that William might be insulted with impunity: 'He could hardly be said to have an army. He could take no step which would require an outlay of money without the sanction of the House of Commons; and it seemed to be the chief study of the House of Commons to cross him and to humble him.'[3]

To some extent William had himself to thank for this perversity of Parliament, for he deliberately kept his own ministers in ignorance of his diplomacy. A French memorandum on the affairs of England, written in 1698, says of him: 'The Secretaries of State whom he has had, if we except the Duke of Shrewsbury, have been only a hired kind of clerks, who had only the despatch of the current affairs in the offices, and no share whatever in his secrets, which are in the hands of his Dutch favourites.'[4]

It does not appear that the confidence in Shrewsbury amounted to very much. In a letter of January 8, 1695,

[1] VI, 2906 (xxiv).
[2] Grimblot, i. 235-6, n.; ii. 191.
[3] Cf. above, p. 145.
[4] VI, 2890 (xxiv).

Shrewsbury explains that, as for the peace recently offered to the Allies at Maestricht by Louis XIV, he was 'as much unacquainted with [it] as any gentleman that lives in the country, having never heard otherwise of it than as they may do in news letters.' [1]

Perhaps the most striking examples of William's reluctance to admit his English ministers to any share in foreign policy occur in connection with the Partition Treaties. The first was virtually concluded before William wrote to Somers, bidding him communicate it under a pledge of secrecy to Vernon and such others as he considered necessary.[2] There was no suggestion of consulting the Privy Council or the Cabinet, and the Whig leaders acquiesced in this secret diplomacy. When the first Partition Treaty was nullified by the death of the Electoral Prince of Bavaria, and it became necessary to arrange a second, Englishmen were similarly excluded from the negotiations, although on this occasion William did communicate the treaty itself to the Council 'in great secrecy'.[3] This treaty was also useless because just before Charles II of Spain died he made a will in favour of the Duke of Anjou, and Louis accepted the Spanish crown for his grandson.

William was now in a most difficult position. In England, he told Heinsius,

> it was no sooner said that the King of Spain's will was in favour of the Duke of Anjou, than it was the general opinion that it was better for England that France should accept the will than fulfil the treaty of partition. . . . I am perfectly persuaded, that if this will be executed, England and the republic are in the utmost danger of being totally

[1] The Lexington Papers, ed. H. M. Sutton (1851), p. 40.

[2] Aug. 15-25, 1698. Grimblot, ii. 119-22.

[3] Feb. 6-16, 1700. Ibid. p. 397.

lost or ruined. . . . It is the utmost mortification to me in this important affair, that I cannot act with the vigour which is requisite, and set a good example; but the republic must do it, and I will engage people here, by a prudent conduct, by degrees, and without perceiving it.[1]

It is certain that William never exerted greater skill nor exercised more forbearance than in 1700-1701. He wisely decided to appeal to Parliament for its advice and support instead of ignoring it. On February 6, 1701, in his speech on opening Parliament, he desired that earnest consideration might be immediately given to the alteration in foreign affairs occasioned by the death of the King of Spain. 'I make no doubt', he continued, 'but your resolutions thereupon will be such, as shall be most conducing to the interest and safety of England, the preservation of the Protestant religion in general, and the peace of all Europe.' He did not mention the increase of the army, for this might have alienated members, but urged the augmentation of the navy, 'which is the great bulwark of the English nation.'[2] A little later he declared his pleasure that the Commons welcomed his communicating the state of negotiations he had entered into pursuant to their addresses, and expressed his conviction that nothing could so effectually contribute to the happiness of England and the peace of Europe as the concurrence of Parliament in his negotiations and a good understanding between him and his people.[3]

The result of the respect William had shown was that the Speaker of the same House of Commons that had violently attacked the Partition Treaties and tried to impeach Portland, Somers, and other Whigs for their share in them, declared that they had given greater supplies than were

[1] Ibid. pp. 477-8. [2] Parliamentary History, v. 1233.
[3] Ibid. p. 1238.

ever previously granted in times of peace to enable William to support his Allies and to 'procure either a lasting peace, or to preserve the liberties of Europe by a necessary war'.[1] The defiant policy of Louis XIV forced England into 'a necessary war'. On the night of February 5-6, 1701, French troops occupied the fortresses in the Netherlands which were garrisoned by the Dutch in accordance with the treaty of Ryswick. The demand that the English and Dutch should be guaranteed the same commercial rights in Spain they had enjoyed under the late king was refused. All compensation was denied to the Emperor. Finally, on the death of James II, his son was recognised at the French court as king of England.

The insolence of Louis provoked a storm of indignation in England. 'All over the kingdom,' says Macaulay, 'corporations, grand juries, meetings of magistrates, meetings of freeholders, were passing resolutions breathing affection to William, and defiance to Lewis.'[2] William dissolved Parliament and obtained a majority eager for war. In his speech on December 31, he summed up the aggressions of France.

By the French King's placing his grandson on the throne of Spain he is in a condition to oppress the rest of Europe, unless speedy and effectual measures be taken. Under this pretence, he is become the real master of the whole Spanish monarchy . . . and by that means has surrounded his neighbours in such a manner, that tho' the name of peace may be said to continue, yet they are put to the expence and inconveniencies of a war. This must affect England, in the nearest and most sensible manner, in respect to our trade, which will soon become precarious in all the valuable branches of it; in respect to our peace and safety at home, which we cannot hope should long continue; and in re-

[1] June 24, 1701. Ibid. p. 1322. [2] VI, 2991-2 (xxv).

spect to that part which England ought to take in the preservation of the liberty of Europe. . . . Let there be no other distinction heard of among us for the future, but of those who are for the Protestant religion and the present establishment, and of those who mean a Popish prince and a French government. . . . If you do in good earnest desire to see England hold the balance of Europe, and to be indeed at the head of the Protestant interest, it will appear by your right improving the present opportunity.[1]

William died before the declaration of war against France, but he lived long enough to lay the foundations of the alliance that brought low the lofty pride of France. He himself realised that success was about to crown the efforts of a lifetime, and grieved that he was not permitted to witness the triumphant conclusion of the long duel with Louis. 'He had very lately said to one of those whom he most loved: "You know that I never feared death; there have been times when I should have wished it; but, now that this great new prospect is opening before me, I do wish to stay here a little longer."'[2]

[1] VI, 2995 (xxv). [2] VI, 3004 (xxv).

INDEX

INDEX

INDEX